On the Western Front
with the Rainbow Division

On the Western Front with the Rainbow Division

A World War I Diary

By Vernon E. Kniptash

Edited by E. Bruce Geelhoed

Foreword by William R. Kniptash

University of Oklahoma Press : Norman

Also by E. Bruce Geelhoed

Charles E. Wilson and Controversy at the Pentagon, 1953 to 1957 (Detroit, Mich., 1979)
(with Millicent Anne Gates) *The Dragon and the Snake: An American Account of the Turmoil in China, 1976–1977* (Philadelphia, 1986)
(with the assistance of James F. Hobbs) *Margaret Thatcher: In Victory and Downfall, 1987 and 1990* (New York, 1992)
(with Anthony O. Edmonds) *Ball State University: An Interpretive History* (Bloomington, Ind., 2001)
(with Anthony O. Edmonds) *Eisenhower, Macmillan, and Allied Unity, 1957–1961* (New York, 2003)
(ed. with Anthony O. Edmonds and the assistance of Michael Davison) *The Macmillan-Eisenhower Correspondence, 1957–1969* (New York, 2005)

This book is published with the generous assistance of the McCasland Foundation, Duncan, Oklahoma.

Library of Congress Cataloging-in-Publication Data

Kniptash, Vernon E., 1897–1987.
  On the western front with the Rainbow Division : a World War I diary / by Vernon E. Kniptash ; edited by E. Bruce Geelhoed ; foreword by William R. Kniptash.
    p. cm.
  Includes bibliographical references and index.
  ISBN 978-0-8061-4032-2 (hardcover : alk. paper) 1. Kniptash, Vernon E., 1897–1987—Diaries. 2. World War, 1914–1918—Personal narratives, American. 3. Germany—History—Allied occupation, 1918–1930. 4. United States. Army. Field Artillery, 150th. 5. United States. Army. Infantry Division, 42nd. 6. Soldiers—United States—Diaries. I. Geelhoed, E. Bruce, 1948– II. Title.
  D570.9.K63 2009
  940.4'1273092—dc22
  [B]

                                                                        2008046520

1 2 3 4 5 6 7 8 9 10

Contents

Illustrations

Figures

Maps

Foreword

SHORTLY AFTER THE UNITED STATES DECLARED WAR ON
Germany in April 1917, Vernon Kniptash, who graduated in 1914
from Manual High School in Indianapolis, decided to enlist in the
United States Army. He joined the First Indiana Field Artillery, a
National Guard unit that was eventually activated as the 150th Field
Artillery of the 42nd Infantry Division, the famed Rainbow Divi-
sion. Kniptash served as radio operator with the Headquarters
Company of the 150th Field Artillery.

Throughout the war, Kniptash kept a running commentary on
the action in which the 42nd participated across France, leading up
to the Armistice in November 1918. He witnessed and participated
in the war on the ground and observed it in the air. He was then
called on to remain in the Army of Occupation in Germany until
his unit was shipped home in April 1919.

This diary exhibits the writer's ability to describe the physical and
mental strains of war and yet add humor to his work. During his
service in France, Belgium, Luxembourg, and Germany, in addition to keeping the diary, Kniptash collected numerous items of
historical importance. These included photos of many battle areas
and both German and American soldiers, a German flag, various
German propaganda broadsheets, transcribed messages from the
wireless transmissions of many British and French sources, and
several playbills from musical performances for the American and
Allied troops during the occupation. The readers of the diary will
be engrossed with its contents—the day-by-day descriptions of the
progress on the front line, the loss of troops due to battle and sickness, the steady progress made by the Rainbow Division in the face

of fierce opposition, sea travel to the United States. And through all these situations the prized artifacts that came to make up the Kniptash collection were gathered, and remained intact, with few exceptions.

In their later years, Vernon and his wife, Margaret, moved from their home to Marquette Manor, a retirement home in Indianapolis. In the process of moving, all of their extra furnishings were put in storage at the manor. At this time, Vernon's son, William Kniptash, and his wife, Betty, had no knowledge of the diary and the collection of artifacts from the war. After the deaths of Vernon and Margaret, all of these possessions were moved to the home of Bill and Betty Kniptash, and it was there that the World War I articles were found in a large box with books and other personal items. It is still difficult to imagine how all of these belongings were transported home to Indiana under such conditions as long months of battle and weather that brought snow, ice, rain, mud, sickness, and so forth, but somehow they all survived in good condition.

In 2002 the Kniptash home in the Indianapolis suburb of Fishers was struck by lightning, destroyed, and had to be completely rebuilt. Despite this destruction, Vernon's war trophies, especially his remarkable diary, were not damaged and survived in good condition.

William R. Kniptash

Acknowledgments

I WISH TO THANK A NUMBER OF PEOPLE WHO PROVIDED
support and assistance in editing Vernon Kniptash's World War I
diary. First, William R. Kniptash, the son of Vernon Kniptash,
patiently explained the contents of his father's diary and encour-
aged me to edit it for reading by people who were interested both
in World War I and in military history. Bill also spent many hours
explaining important details about his father's life and the experiences of the Kniptash family in Indianapolis over the past century.
Betty Kniptash, Bill's gracious wife, offered valuable insights into
the character and personality of her father-in-law. The Kniptashes
also dug deep into their treasure trove of photographs, newspaper
clippings, items of German propaganda, and other materials that
Vernon brought back from France with him in 1919. Many of these
artifacts are included as illustrations in this volume. Thanks also to
William C. Ervin, a military history enthusiast, who first introduced
me to the Kniptash diary and provided valuable encouragement as
the editing process unfolded.

I owe gratitude to members of the Department of History faculty
and staff of the Center for Middletown Studies at Ball State University who spent a considerable amount of time on this project. Graduate assistant Michael C. Sears proved to be an excellent researcher
and gained valuable experience working with the Kniptash diary as
well as other extraordinary, original historical material. Michael
Hradesky, staff cartographer in the Department of Geography,
expertly prepared the maps that are used in the book. Laura
Shuherk Pittman worked on the project as a student assistant and
helped in the transcription of the diary as well as the preparation of

various drafts of the manuscript, cheerfully and without complaint. Also, Julie Gibboney, Laura's successor, joined the project in its later stages and likewise was a fine contributor to the final product. Michelle Christopher and Joshua Burress provided valuable technical assistance, especially in the preparation of illustrations. I am especially indebted to Kelly Conger Sheridan, whose expertise contributed to preparation of the final copy of the manuscript. Marsha Andrews and Michelle Gage provided additional assistance. Carolyn Goffman and Jeni Sumawati, two of my graduate assistants in the Center for Middletown Studies, were generous with their help on the Kniptash diary, too. Dr. David Ulbrich, a faculty member in the History Department at Ohio University and a specialist in military history, read the manuscript and made useful suggestions. Dr. Christopher S. Thompson, associate professor of history at Ball State University and a specialist in the history of France, graciously helped translate Vernon Kniptash's copy of the November 11, 1918, French communiqué (figure 14 in the book) that announced the Armistice. I also wish to thank John B. Straw, director of the Archives and Special Collections at Ball State, and the members of his staff for their assistance.

A special note of gratitude belongs to Dr. Gregory J. W. Urwin, professor of history and associate director of the Center for the Study of Force and Diplomacy at Temple University. An accomplished military historian, Professor Urwin graciously reviewed the manuscript and made numerous helpful suggestions for its improvement. Also, Richard Baker of the United States Army's Institute of Military History at Carlisle Barracks, Pennsylvania, generously provided copies of World War I surveys submitted by three veterans of the 150th Field Artillery unit, which proved very useful. Ray Boomhower and Paula Corpuz of the Indiana Historical Society also deserve my gratitude for permitting use of material from the Kniptash diary that appeared previously in my article "Rainbow Soldier: Vernon Kniptash and World War I," *Traces of Indiana and Midwestern History* (May 2006), and in Robert Ferrell's edition *A Soldier in World War I: The Diary of Elmer Sherwood* (2004).

I also wish to thank the archivists at the Indiana State Library, the Indiana War Memorial Commission, and the Marion County Library in Indianapolis for their help in locating valuable material about the 42nd Division that supplemented the observations made by Vernon Kniptash. My thanks to Tim Frank, who was instrumental in locating materials about the 150th Field Artillery in the National Archives at College Park, Maryland. Thomas Bryan generously shared information about his grandfather Norman Bryan, who was also a member of the 150th Field Artillery and served in World War I with the Rainbow Division. He also provided a poster from his family's files that is used as an illustration in this book. All photos in the book, unless otherwise noted, are from the Kniptash family files and are reproduced courtesy of the Kniptash family.

Finally, I want to thank Deborah Geelhoed, my loving wife of thirty-seven years, and our two sons, Marc and Steven, for their support and encouragement. A book project such as this has a tendency to involve family members to a greater degree than the author originally anticipates, and I always value my family's patience, assistance, interest, and especially their good humor.

E. Bruce Geelhoed

On the Western Front
with the Rainbow Division

Introduction

ON APRIL 25, 1917, A TWENTY-YEAR-OLD INDIANAPOLIS architectural draftsman named Vernon Kniptash enlisted in the First Indiana Field Artillery regiment, a National Guard unit that was soon to be activated for service in World War I. The grandson of German immigrants, Kniptash volunteered for military service out of a patriotic desire to serve his country at a momentous time in its history. Just three weeks earlier on April 6, 1917, Congress had officially declared war on Germany, thereby placing the United States of America into the conflict on the side of Great Britain, France, and Russia.[1] Realizing that military service would soon be expected of most American young men, Kniptash decided to enlist and, as he later wrote, "to volunteer and not hang around Mumsey's skirts and let 'em come and get me."[2]

Starting with the date of his enlistment, Vernon Kniptash began the compilation of a diary that became the record of his service in

1. Citing the threat to American security caused by Germany's declaration of unrestricted submarine warfare against American shipping early in 1917, President Woodrow Wilson asked Congress for a declaration of war on April 2, 1917. The Senate voted 82–6 in favor of Wilson's request on April 4. The House of Representatives followed suit on April 6 by a vote of 373–50. See Farwell, *Over There*, 33, 35; Ferrell, *Wilson and World War I*, 1–3; Gilbert, *First World War*, 318; Keegan, *First World War*, 351–52.

2. Initial entry, April 1918, Diary of Vernon Kniptash, 1917–1919, found in Vernon Kniptash ms., Ball State University, Archives and Special Collections. A copy of the manuscript may be found in the Manuscripts Division of the Indiana State Library. Kniptash's career in World War I is also summarized briefly in my essay "Rainbow Soldier: Vernon Kniptash and World War I," *Traces of Indiana and Midwestern History* (May 2006): 16–25.

3

World War I. Kniptash maintained his diary for the next two years until he received his honorable discharge from the U.S. Army at Camp Taylor in Louisville, Kentucky, on May 9, 1919. Over this two-year period, Kniptash recounted in two red cloth-covered volumes the multifaceted experience of being a soldier in World War I. The first volume of diary entries covers the period from his enlistment in April 1917 to December 5, 1918; the second book covers the period from December 6, 1918, through his discharge in May 1919.

In his entries Kniptash writes of the surge of enthusiasm that accompanied his enlistment. He tells movingly of the horrors, and occasionally the humor, of military combat on the western front and its effects on ordinary soldiers. He describes the daily routine and drudgery of military life and the discomfort of living a thoroughly regimented existence. He draws unforgettable individual profiles of his fellow soldiers, both American and French, and the officers who commanded them. He details the reaction of the soldiers to the Armistice in November 1918, and the subsequent occupation of Germany in the winter and spring of 1919. When finally transcribed and compiled, Vernon Kniptash's diary ran to over 150 typescript pages of vivid, almost daily recollections of a member of the American Expeditionary Forces (AEF).

Any reader of the Kniptash diary will be impressed with the poignancy of the entries. The diary presents a drama replete with contrasts. In March 1917 Vernon Kniptash was living a comfortable, relatively carefree life in Indianapolis. He held a steady job as a draftsman with the local architectural firm of Vonnegut and Bohn. Kniptash resided at his family's home on Orange Street in a predominantly German American community south and east of downtown Indianapolis. The family consisted of his parents, Wilhelm and Ollie Kniptash, and his younger brother, Robert. Vernon Kniptash was seriously courting Maude Wolfe, a young Indianapolis woman, and though not engaged, the couple had entertained thoughts of marriage.

Just one year later, however, the pleasant, comfortable, and relaxed existence that Vernon Kniptash had enjoyed was completely shattered. In March 1918 Kniptash, along with hundreds of thousands of other American soldiers, found himself on the western front in France, engaged in a furious effort to turn back the first of several major German offensives. For the next eight months, Kniptash participated in what was likely the most violent period ever encountered in human warfare to that point in history. Between July and November 1918, Kniptash was part of the massive Allied counteroffensive that ultimately forced Germany to seek an end to the war, which became effective on November 11, 1918. After the Armistice, Kniptash participated in the brief Allied occupation of Germany until he was notified of his departure to America in April 1919. Kniptash returned to Indiana in May 1919 and resumed life in much the same fashion that he had left it two years previously. The Kniptash diary recounts this remarkable story of one man's transition from peacetime to warfare and back again.

To understand and appreciate the value and importance of Vernon Kniptash's diary, as well as the people and events he describes, one must first learn about Kniptash's family, the unit in which he served during World War I, and the military circumstances that existed at the time of the U.S. entry into the war in April 1917. This background enlarges the scope of the portrayal of World War I as set out in the diary.

The Kniptash family traced its origins in America to its immigration in 1881. The family that emigrated from the small German village of Eucherath, near Cologne, consisted of the husband and patriarch, Jakob Knipptasche (as the name was then spelled), fifty-one years of age; his wife, Elisabeth, forty-two; and their seven children: Louise, fifteen; Katherine, thirteen; Wilhelm, eleven; Henrich, nine; Agnes, seven; Jodocus, four; and Joseph, two. The family's primary reason for leaving Germany has remained somewhat unclear, although objections to the Prussian control of the German state and to the arbitrary nature of Kaiser Wilhelm I's regime may have played a role.

The Knipptasche family were adherents of Roman Catholicism, and Jakob Knipptasche occasionally found himself at odds with the hierarchy of the local Catholic church. It would be incorrect to say, however, that the Knipptasches left Germany primarily for religious reasons. Even in the United States, Jakob Knipptasche often differed with the practices of his local Catholic church, and as a result, the Knipptasche family began transferring its membership to

Protestant congregations, and most have remained Protestants to the present day.

Upon arriving in America, the Knipptasches set out for their destination of Terre Haute, Indiana. The reasons for the selection of Terre Haute are unclear, although large numbers of German immigrants chose to settle in Indiana during the late nineteenth century. No one in the family spoke English, and their experience of their new country began inauspiciously when the entire family got off the train at the wrong location. Disembarking in the small community of Seelyville, fifteen miles east of Terre Haute, Jakob and Elisabeth and the seven children then had to carry their luggage the remaining distance to Terre Haute on foot.

Once in Indiana, the Knipptasche family name underwent some changes. In their new hometown of Terre Haute, they changed the spelling to *Kniptasch*, dropping the second *p* in the middle of the name and the *e* at the end. The family later altered the spelling to its present form, *Kniptash*, dropping the *c* from the last syllable.

After a modest grade school education, Wilhelm Kniptash, Jakob and Elisabeth's third child and oldest son, began working as a laborer with the firm of Havens and Geddes, a wholesale dry goods merchant in Terre Haute. In the early 1890s, Wilhelm married a young woman named Ollie Cottom, also from Terre Haute. Around the same time, a fire destroyed the main building of Havens and Geddes, and the company's management decided to relocate the business to Indianapolis. Wilhelm and Ollie Kniptash moved with their children—Vernon, born on December 6, 1896; and Robert, born in 1901—to a German American neighborhood on Orange Street in southeast Indianapolis. Wilhelm resumed his work with Haven and Geddes, eventually rising to the position of chief purchasing clerk. Ollie Kniptash remained a homemaker; Vernon and Robert began and completed their public school education.

For the Kniptash family, life revolved around work, the local Catholic church, and the south side athletic club, the *Turngemeinde*, or as it was commonly known, the South Side Turners. The South Side Turners emphasized physical training and the preservation of German culture.[3] Both Wilhelm and Vernon Kniptash became

---

3. For a brief discussion of the *Turngemeinde*, see Bodenhamer and Barrows, *Encyclopedia of Indianapolis*, 41, 46, 1344–45. The great rival in Indianapolis of the

expert tennis players and represented the Turners in numerous athletic contests, not only against club rivals in Indianapolis but also at other locations across the country in events sponsored by turnvereins.

As a student at Manual High School in Indianapolis between 1910 and 1914, Vernon Kniptash displayed special talents in mathematics and art. His skill in math so impressed his teacher, Arda Knox, that she found him a part-time job with the architectural firm of Vonnegut and Bohn. Known locally as "V + B," the firm of Vonnegut and Bohn was one of the city's prominent architectural design firms, and Kniptash worked as a part-time draftsman during his final years in high school. After his graduation in 1914 from Manual High School, he accepted a full-time position with V + B. Kniptash's employment at V + B was interrupted in 1917 when he enlisted in the First Indiana Regiment for service in World War I.

In addition to knowing something about the background of the Kniptash family and particularly Vernon's early life, one must understand the importance of the U.S. Army unit to which he belonged during World War I, in order to appreciate the significance of the Kniptash diary. The military unit in which Vernon Kniptash eventually served was the 42nd Division (National Guard), the celebrated Rainbow Division, which consisted of an integration of twenty-six state National Guard units from across the United States and the District of Columbia. The creation of the Rainbow Division occurred during the summer of 1917 in response to pressure arising from state legislatures and state commanders of the National Guard for more-active roles for their units. Newton Baker, the secretary of war, supported the concept advanced by Major Douglas MacArthur of the Army General Staff that utilization of National Guard units would enable the United States to raise a fighting force more rapidly than by reliance on the Regular Army, composed of draftees and enlistees. Unlike other

---

South Side Turners was the Athenaeum, another German American turnverein located several blocks north of the *Turngemeinde* building. Each turnverein built "turnhalles" that combined social, cultural, recreational, and athletic facilities. Bill Kniptash, Vernon's son, remembers the main hall of the South Side Turners as a combination "gymnasium, dance hall, and beer garden." William R. Kniptash, in discussion with the editor, September 1997.

U.S. military forces at the time, the National Guard units were already organized and many had seen active duty in the recent border clashes with Mexico in 1916.[4]

Baker and MacArthur also undertook the ambitious scheme of forming an entire division of these state National Guard units rather than assigning them to Regular Army commands. As Baker and MacArthur explained the composition of the division: "It will stretch over the whole country like a rainbow"[5]—hence, the 42nd Division became the Rainbow Division.

In September 1917 several individual National Guard units began arriving at Camp Alvord I. Mills in Mineola, New York, for their basic training in preparation for eventual overseas deployment. Secretary of War Baker named General William A. Mann, a West Pointer who had seen action in the Spanish-American War, the Philippines, and the Mexican border operations, as the 42nd Division's first commander. Then Baker promoted MacArthur to the rank of colonel and named him the Rainbow Division's chief of staff.[6] Since the objective of forming the Rainbow was such a romantic, idealized concept, Baker hoped that the individual units of the "composite National Guard division" would coalesce in a spirit of patriotism and national purpose.

Such was not the outcome. State and sectional rivalries prevailed, and numerous altercations broke out between the units, both during training and during off-duty hours. As historian James J. Cooke has written: "A special antagonism developed between the New York and Alabama units, and the soldiers from the two units

4. A number of accounts have been written about the exploits of the Rainbow Division in the Great War; see esp. Cooke, *Rainbow Division*. Older studies include Reilly, *Americans All*; Tompkins, *Story of the Rainbow Division*; and American Battle Monuments Commission, *42nd Division*. For a complete study of the American military effort in World War I, see Eisenhower, *Yanks*. Eisenhower provides a good description of the formation of the AEF and the role of the Regular Army, the National Guard, and the National Army, comprised of draftees; see 23–24.

5. Quoted in Cooke, *Rainbow Division*, 4; see also Coffman, *War to End All Wars*, 149–50; James, *Years of MacArthur*, 1:135, 140–42; Manchester, *American Caesar*, 79; Persico, *Eleventh Month*, 161–62. An effort to include an African American unit in the 42nd Division was unsuccessful; see Slotkin, *Lost Battalions*, 70.

6. Cooke, *Rainbow Division*, 5; James, *Years of MacArthur*, 1:135; Manchester, *American Caesar*, 79.

repeatedly clashed in fist fights and brawls. In one particularly nasty fight, military police were summoned to separate the combatants but not before one Alabama soldier died."[7]

Notwithstanding such difficulties, the Rainbow Division eventually became organized into a fighting force. The principal units of the 42nd Division were the 83rd Infantry Brigade, the 84th Infantry Brigade, and the 67th Field Artillery Brigade. The 67th Field Artillery Brigade was commanded by Brigadier General Charles P. Summerall and consisted of the 149th Field Artillery Regiment (formerly the 1st Illinois Field Artillery), commanded by Colonel Henry J. Reilly; the 150th Field Artillery Regiment (formerly the 1st Indiana Field Artillery), commanded by Colonel Robert H. Tyndall; the 151st Field Artillery Regiment (formerly the 1st Minnesota Field Artillery), commanded by Colonel George E. Leach; and the 117th Trench Mortar Regiment (formerly the 3rd and 4th Companies, Maryland Coast Artillery), commanded by Captain Robert J. Gill.[8] Kniptash belonged to the 150th Field Artillery Regiment, which by the end of its training at Camp Mills consisted of three battalions. When the 150th Field Artillery departed for France in October 1917, its commander was Colonel Tyndall; Major Guy A. Wainwright commanded the 1st Battalion; Major Solon J. Carter commanded the 2nd Battalion; and Major Marlin A. Prather commanded the 3rd Battalion.[9] Such was the military universe inhabited by Vernon Kniptash when he left for Europe.

During World War I, the 42nd Division distinguished itself as one of the premier fighting units in the American Expeditionary Forces as well as the most outstanding National Guard division. The Rainbow's combat record placed it among the top five divisions of the AEF in terms of time spent on the front lines, combat performance, casualties incurred, and objectives achieved.[10]

7. Cooke, *Rainbow Division*, 15.

8. Tompkins, *Story of the Rainbow Division*, 240, 247; Coffman, *War to End All Wars*, 149–50.

9. For information about Tyndall, see the Robert H. Tyndall Collection, Indiana Historical Society, Indianapolis (hereafter cited as RHTC); and for Tyndall, Wainwright, Carter, and Prather, see Tompkins, *Story of the Rainbow Division*, 237.

10. Cooke, *Rainbow Division*, 239.

For its part, the 150th Field Artillery earned a reputation as a worthy contributor to the American effort. The regiment, which went into action in February 1918, participated in virtually every American action from that point until the Armistice in November. As Major General Charles T. Menoher, the commanding officer of the 42nd Division in France, said near the end of the conflict: "Indiana may well be proud of the One Hundred and Fiftieth Field Artillery and of its commander, Colonel Robert Tyndall. I hope the Indiana people have an appreciation of what the Tyndall regiment did in the war. . . . It made a name for itself and its record is one of which the state and, indeed, the nation may well be proud."[11]

The entry of the United States into the war came at a critical moment for the British and French. As historian Martin Gilbert has written, World War I had ceased to be a conflict "of rapid victories" by the end of 1914.[12] After four months of deadly, brutal combat, the opposing forces of Germany, on the one hand, and France and Great Britain, on the other, had dug themselves into roughly matching networks of trenches spanning from the North Sea on the coast of Belgium south to the Franco-Swiss border. The war of attrition lasted well into early 1917. Every so often, one side or the other attempted an extensive and well-prepared offensive only to be repulsed (at great human sacrifice) by the opponent's shells, machine-gun fire, and poison gas. For the most part, war on the western front "focused on raids into the enemy trenches, spasmodic bombardments, and occasional small-scale attacks."[13] For the combatants, the conflict was characterized by skirmishes, shellfire, and gas alarms. By the end of 1916, the Central powers—Germany, Austria-Hungary, Bulgaria, and the Ottoman Empire—held the upper hand.

Between 1914 and 1917, Woodrow Wilson's administration attempted to steer a course of neutrality between the combatants. By late 1915, however, U.S. policy had begun tilting toward the British and French, especially when it came to providing loans, foodstuffs, and weapons. Such behavior infuriated the Germans,

---

11. *Indianapolis Star,* January 13, 1919 (clipping in Kniptash family files).
12. Gilbert, *First World War,* 78; see also Keegan, *First World War,* 176–80.
13. Gilbert, *First World War,* 173. See also Farwell, *Over There,* 17.

and in October 1915 Kaiser Wilhelm II pointedly informed James W. Gerard, the U.S. ambassador to Germany, that his government strongly objected to America's presumed favoritism directed toward his enemies. "America had better look out after this war," the Kaiser told Gerard. "I shall stand for no nonsense from America after the war."[14]

American sympathies for the Allied side and the prevailing opinion in the United States opposing German militarism (and even the possibility of a German victory) were insufficient to create a popular groundswell for U.S. entry into the conflict from its outset through early 1917. Early that year, however, two events quickly transpired that mobilized American opinion in favor of intervention. First, on January 31, 1917, the German government announced its intention to resume unrestricted submarine warfare against shipping bound for Britain. The Germans clearly intended to stop the flow of American food and weapons to the British and to counteract the highly effective Allied blockade of German ports. In response, Wilson suspended diplomatic relations with Germany on February 3.

Second, on March 1, the U.S. government revealed that the German foreign minister, Alfred von Zimmermann, had been plotting with the government of Mexico to engage the United States in war, should America declare war on Germany. This scheme, revealed in an intercepted telegram dated in mid-January, called for the extension of German financial support to Mexico, which, in the event of a German victory in Europe, would result in the promised return of Texas, New Mexico, and Arizona to Mexico.[15] The telegram raised the specter of meddling by Mexico on the United States' southwestern border and a serious threat to the nation's continental security. Relations between the United States and Germany worsened in March once the full implications of the now-famous Zimmermann telegram became known. In early April the United States formally declared war.

14. Quoted in Gilbert, *First World War*, 205.

15. See Gregory, *Origins of American Intervention*, and Tuchman, *Zimmermann Telegram*, for a discussion of the roles played by Germany's resumption of unrestricted submarine warfare and the Zimmermann telegram in the U.S. entry into World War I. See also Fleming, *Illusion of Victory*, 2, 27.

Once the United States chose to enter the conflict, its action meant new hope for the British and French, who were war-weary to the point of exhaustion. As historian Robert H. Ferrell has written, when America joined the fighting in 1917, "the Allies stood in dire peril of failure—of losing the war."[16] Locked in a stalemate against the numerically and technologically superior German forces, neither the British nor the French possessed the strength to mount a sustained offensive against the enemy. On the respective home fronts in Britain and France, morale had slipped to dangerous levels. The troops on the western front could hardly have been cheered by the prospect of more fighting, either. Vincent Weeks, a British soldier, described his situation as one fraught "with mud and slime and vermin, with patrols in no-man's-land, with nightly ration parties, working parties, and burying parties with continual casualties from shell, bomb, mine, and sniper, with sudden bombardments and raids and minor attacks, with hours of cold and wet, boredom and minor discomfort, punctuated by minutes of deadly peril."[17] Such was the type of existence that awaited Vernon Kniptash and his fellow Americans when they arrived in France in November 1917.

Vernon Kniptash began writing his diary at the time of his enlistment in April 1917. Perhaps he sensed that he was about to embark on a historic experience and wanted to maintain a permanent record of it. There are no indications at any other point in his life, whether before or after his experience in World War I, that Kniptash kept a diary.

As mentioned earlier, the Kniptash diary contains two years' worth of an American soldier's recollections, from April 1917 to May 1919. It contains no divisions according to topic or theme. The entries are simply a chronological account of Kniptash's experiences, written on-the-spot (or shortly thereafter).

Kniptash's writings are genuine expressions of this unprecedented period in his life as a young American soldier and of the broader historical context of the war. Kniptash wrote clearly, succinctly, thoughtfully, and at times humorously. His diary reveals

---

16. Ferrell, *Wilson and World War I*, 13–14.
17. Weeks, quoted in Gilbert, *First World War*, 122.

him to be a candid, even shrewd, observer of people (both officers and ordinary soldiers) and their motivations. He told the story straight, without flowery language or artificial melodrama, in the vocabulary and idiom of his day.

For purposes of readability, I have taken the liberty of dividing the diary into five sections, covering distinct time periods during which certain events occurred unique to each period. The first section includes the entries from April 1917 to February 1918, the period during which the 150th Field Artillery was organized, trained, dispatched to France, and received training in the use of French artillery at a base called Camp Coëtquidan.

The second section covers the period February 20 to July 21, 1918, during which the Rainbow Division was dispatched to the Lorraine front and assisted in the vital effort to stem a series of German offensives, the fifth occurring in mid-July. During this time, the Rainbows (Kniptash included) encountered their first taste of combat and the horrors accompanying it.

The third section covers the period July 21 to November 11, 1918. Kniptash's entries in this section cover the Allied counteroffensive that began in July and culminated with the announcement of the Armistice. This section recounts the successful Allied operations at Château-Thierry, Saint-Mihiel, and most importantly, in the Meuse-Argonne offensive that led up to the Armistice and, eventually, to the cessation of hostilities.

The fourth section, covering the period from November 12, 1918, to April 2, 1919, contains Kniptash's recollections of the reassignment of the Rainbow Division to become part of the Army of Occupation that remained in Germany through the winter and spring months of 1919. Here, Kniptash recounts the 42nd Division's "March to the Rhine," from France through Belgium and Luxembourg into Germany, where it remained until the late spring. Kniptash contrasts the wartime experiences of the AEF soldier with those of peacetime and explores the unique experience of being part of a U.S. occupying force while eagerly anticipating his return to the United States.

The final section of the diary covers the two months of April and May 1919. During this time, Kniptash recounts the experiences of being notified about his return home, the voyage back to America, the welcoming parades and processionals as the 150th rode via train from New York to Indianapolis, and his subsequent honorable discharge from the army to rejoin his family.

Vernon Kniptash was, of course, not the only member of the 150th Field Artillery, or of the Rainbow Division, to keep and maintain a written account of World War I. For examples, both Elmer Frank ("Pete") Straub and Elmer Sherwood, two other members of the 150th, published accounts of their wartime experiences. Colonel Robert Tyndall, the commanding officer of the 150th Field Artillery, also kept a diary, but it has remained unpublished.[18] In some respects, Straub's and Sherwood's accounts, but not Tyndall's diary, whose entries tend to be quite brief, have some advantages of perspective over Kniptash's account. Straub and Sherwood each were assigned to individual battery units and were closer to actual physical combat than was Kniptash, who spent most of his time with the Headquarters Company. Their accounts are thus more detailed in terms of battlefield conditions and situations than that of Kniptash.

In fairness to Kniptash, however, his position with the Headquarters Company provided him a wider scope to view the events of the war. From mid-1918 until the signing of the Armistice, Kniptash read the daily accounts of the battle situation not only in the French and American sectors but also in the British sector. Because of this broader perspective, Kniptash was often able to speculate, in his diary entries, as to what future activity was in line for his unit, instead of merely commenting on events as they transpired. For that reason, his vantage point was better informed than those of his fellow Hoosier diarists.

Furthermore, Kniptash is the only diarist who provides a comprehensive account of the experience of an Indiana soldier from the time of enlistment through the callup and training period, the

18. See Straub, *Sergeant's Diary*; Sherwood, *Diary of a Rainbow Veteran* and *Rainbow Hoosier*. Historian Robert H. Ferrell has edited a revision of Sherwood's diary titled *A Soldier in World War I: The Diary of Elmer Sherwood*. In this study, Ferrell's revised edition is cited as *Diary of Elmer Sherwood*. See also Ferrell's account of another Hoosier diarist in World War I, Kenneth Gearhart Baker, in "'Oatmeal and Coffee,'" 31–76. Tyndall's diary may be found in "Diary, 1918–1919," Folder 12, RHTC.

transatlantic voyage, the experiences of combat, the occupation, and the eventual return voyage to the United States. Straub covers most of these topics, except for the important occupation period, when he was reassigned to work in Britain. Sherwood writes extensively about the wartime experiences of the 150th Field Artillery regiment but little about the occupation period, although a recent revision of Sherwood diary by historian Robert Ferrell includes a more complete account of the early months of 1919. For his part, Colonel Tyndall was seriously ill in February and March 1919, during the occupation period, and thus was unable to comment in his diary about much that happened in the field at that time.

The Kniptash diary is replicated in much the same fashion as Kniptash wrote it. In the process of editing, I kept many of the abbreviations ("Indpls" for Indianapolis, or "Bn." for "Battalion," to cite two examples) that Kniptash used. The reader will notice a dash (—) between sentences in numerous entries. These dashes were used by Kniptash most likely as an indicator of an entry that was made at a different time of day from an earlier entry (for the same date). Kniptash was sometimes inconsistent when recording the date. Occasionally he spelled out the entire date: month, day, and year. More often, he abbreviated some or all of the date (e.g., leaving off the year). These aspects of Kniptash's diary have been preserved to retain the element of authenticity.

Kniptash frequently refers in his diary to fellow soldiers, personal acquaintances, and other individuals by either their first or last names, as well as some military jargon. By examining other corroborative accounts, such as service records of individual soldiers, the mention of members of the 150th Field Artillery listed in various newspaper sources, and a wartime poster (see the appendix), I have sought to give as complete an identity as possible to the people mentioned by Kniptash. For some persons, however, a full identity was impossible to discover, and thus their names appear only as Kniptash recorded them.

Likewise, some military jargon used by Kniptash does not lend itself to a clear description. Finally, the reader will notice numerous places throughout the text where a break is indicated with an "x" followed by a dashed line followed by another "x" on the same line. This unusual marking, which appears frequently throughout the diary, was made using a pencil with a red lead, whereas Kniptash wrote the entries with a normal lead pencil. No ready explanation exists for these markings, but I suspect that Kniptash made them once he had returned home and was rereading the diary, perhaps to note the place where he had left off. Since they appear quite prominently throughout the diary, I have included the markings in the final text.

As a primary source, the Kniptash diary represents a unique account, that of an untrained novice American soldier encountering a totally new experience of violent warfare. The diary captures the emotion of the conflict and reveals the personality and character of its author. As such, it represents a contribution to the ever-growing historiography of first-person accounts from soldiers who served in the Great War.[19] If World War I has become "The War We Forgot," as Tony Dokoupil argued in a recent issue of *Newsweek*, the existence of these first-person accounts provides a lasting body of literature that preserves the memory of America's participation in this global conflict.[20]

19. These first-person accounts take various forms, such as personal memoirs, diaries, and editions of letters sent by soldiers in France to their families and loved ones in the United States. Historian Robert Ferrell, who has been especially active since 2001 in editing and publishing such accounts, has edited the diaries of Hugh S. Thompson, of the 168th Infantry Regiment, 42nd Division (see Thompson, *Trench Knives and Mustard Gas*); William H. Wright, commander of the 89th Division (see Wright, *Meuse-Argonne Diary*); and Horace L. Baker, of the 128th Infantry, 32nd Division (see Baker, *Argonne Days*); as well as revising the Elmer Sherwood diary. In addition, three other accounts are also valuable reading: those of George Browne, of the 117th Engineer Regiment, 42nd Division (see Browne, *American Soldier*); Warren R. Jackson, of the 1st Battalion, 6th Marines (see Clark, *His Time in Hell*); and Harry H. Spring, of the 37th Engineer Regiment (see Spring, *Engineer's Diary*).

20. Tony Dokoupil, "The War We Forgot," *Newsweek*, February 18, 2008, 50.

CHAPTER 1

From Indianapolis to the Western Front,
April 26, 1917–February 19, 1918

> The boat is slipping away and the Statue of Liberty is getting fainter
> and fainter. It sure makes a fellow feel funny under these conditions.
> How many of us will get to see that statue when this war ends?
>   Vernon Kniptash to his diary, October 18, 1917

THE FIRST SECTION OF VERNON KNIPTASH'S DIARY
covers the period from his enlistment in April 1917 until his departure for the western front in October and his subsequent artillery
training at Camp Coêtquidan in France. The narrative includes a
recounting of his summer's training at Fort Benjamin Harrison in
Indianapolis and the move to Camp Alvord L. Mills in Mineola,
New York, where the 42nd (Rainbow) Division was assembled.
Kniptash and his fellow soldiers spent the months of September
and October engaged in intense military preparation, a life that
the new enlistee found difficult. Even so, Kniptash's introduction
to military life had its compensations, primarily because the close
proximity of Camp Mills to New York made frequent visits to the
city possible. Even at the young age of twenty, Kniptash had learned
to enjoy musical and theatrical entertainment. Visits to New York
enabled him to attend some of the famous shows that were playing
to packed houses on Broadway.

Late in October, the 42nd Division received notification of its
departure for Europe. On October 18 Kniptash and six thousand
other members of the Rainbow Division boarded the USS *President
Lincoln*, formerly a German passenger ship that had been seized by
the U.S. government as a wartime measure and then converted into
a troop transport, and began the fourteen-day voyage to France.

Although the transatlantic crossing was a chaotic and disorganized affair, Kniptash's diary entries do not convey an intolerable level of frustration and discomfort.

Once Kniptash landed in France, the artillery units of the 67th Brigade marched from the seaport town of St. Nazaire to the primary training camp for artillery units in France, Camp Coêtquidan. For the next three months, the 67th Field Artillery Brigade trained at Camp Coêtquidan while the infantry units of the 42nd Division trained at other camps in France. During this period, Kniptash learned of his transfer to the Headquarters Company of the Regiment and his departure from Battery A. While initially disappointed to leave his friends in Battery A, Kniptash quickly discovered that work at the Headquarters Company was always interesting and would give him a glimpse into aspects of the war previously unknown. By mid-February, the Rainbow Division was ready to be ordered into action near the front.

The first American troops had arrived in France in May 1917, when Kniptash was still living in Indianapolis and not yet been called to active service. On the western front, the French army was on the verge of collapse; indeed, mutinies had broken out in numerous units.[1] Shortly after General John J. Pershing, the commander of the American Expeditionary Force, arrived in France in the spring of 1917, a colleague warned him: "There is a limit to what flesh and blood and endurance can stand. The French have just about reached that limit."[2] Pershing set about organizing and training the U.S. troops in France, but both he and Secretary of War Newton Baker steadfastly refused to commit these soldiers to action until they were convinced that the men had attained the necessary readiness. In the summer of 1917, Pershing expressed the view that the necessary training of American forces might take "10 or 12 months" before the troops were ready for action against the Germans.[3]

The desperate condition of the British and the French forces on the battlefield, however, required that U.S. troops be committed

1. Gilbert, *First World War*, 333–34.
2. Ibid., 340–41; see also Farwell, *Over There*, 19, 20, 168.
3. Gilbert, *First World War*, 342, 350, 359–60.

much earlier than Pershing anticipated. By the end of October 1917, American troops had taken up positions in the quiet sector near the town of Luneville, attached to French troops who occupied that sector of the front line. By mid-January 1918, the American 1st Division (known as the Big Red One, Pershing's favorite) moved into the line near Ancerville along the Saint-Mihiel sector.[4]

By this point, American troops were involved in the fighting, though not in the quantity demanded by the British and French. The Rainbow Division encountered its first taste of combat within a matter of weeks after the 1st Division began its combat action. In his diary entries, Kniptash made no mention of the uncharacteristically cold winter of 1917–18, despite the fact that the troops found themselves ill-prepared for the harsh weather conditions. As historian Thomas E. Fleming wrote, "Still in summer uniforms, the men shivered in unheated barns and attics as the temperature sank to seven below zero."[5]

In telling the story of his first nine months as an American soldier, Kniptash conveys a variety of emotions. His moods regularly shift from exhilaration to anticipation to apprehension and even to astonishment. His accounts also reveal the thoughts and feelings of a young man facing an uncertain future who optimistically expects that his courage and training will be sufficient for the task ahead. Kniptash concurred with the sentiments later expressed by fellow Hoosier Elmer Sherwood, who considered the 42nd Division a representative group of "Americans, the greatest soldiers on earth, on the way to win the great World War."[6]

4. Ibid., 359–60, 368, 372, 397.
5. Fleming, *Illusion of Victory*, 184.
6. Sherwood, *Rainbow Hoosier*, 186. The records for the 150th Field Artillery Regiment may be found in Record Group 120, Records of the American Expeditionary Forces (World War I), Organization Records, 42nd Division, 150th Field Art'y Regt., Box 38, 39. This collection is referred to hereafter as 120/AEF/42/FA and box.

PREFACE. I had been reading the papers and magazines and had watched the battle line sway back and forth. It took me some time to grasp the bigness of the thing; the number of men involved; the cost of it all. Dad and I had long talks and arguments concerning the right and wrong and as to which side was fighting for the right. Both agreed that the Allied powers were fighting back a long prepared, machine-like Army. Dad told me the kind of life the German people lead, how they have nothing to say as to who their leaders should be; how they are taught from childhood to reverence the Kaiser, how, to say a single word against him would mean a heavy penalty to the offender, and finally how the Prussian Govt. was supreme and the whole country abided by what they said and did. Then I read about some of the atrocities the Germans were pulling off, including the rape of Belgium and other horrible deeds.[7] These were done to frighten the French and English into submission. France and England were slowly cracking under the strain, I believe, and another six months would see the end with Germany on the long end. Then I read about the Lusitania disaster and I read the chain of events that finally led up to our break with Germany.[8] After a long talk with Dad and Mumsey, I decided to get into the mess at my first opportunity.

7. Historians have written extensively on the sympathy of German Americans to the German cause in World War I, prior to U.S. involvement in the conflict. See, for example, Farwell, *Over There*, 60, and Fleming, *Illusion of Victory*, 60–62. Although they were a German American family, the Kniptashes did not hold pro-German sentiments. The German occupation of Belgium and parts of France brought stories of remarkable brutality before the world. By October 1914 the Germans had systematically destroyed many Belgian towns and had taken numerous Belgian hostages and executed those considered saboteurs of German communication lines. In France, German troops who were forced to retreat after the Battle of the Marne in August 1914 burned houses and businesses in the towns they evacuated. See Gilbert, *First World War*, 52, 88; Keegan, *First World War*, 82.

8. Like most Americans, Kniptash followed the course of the war and was convinced that Germany had the upper hand by the end of 1916. Likewise, he was shocked by the sinking of the British transatlantic liner, the *Lusitania*, by a German submarine in May 1915, which resulted in almost 1,200 deaths, including 128 Americans. German atrocities committed against civilian populations in Belgium during the early months of the war also shocked Americans' sensibilities. See Farwell, *Over There*, 23; Gilbert, *First World War*, 52, 88, 156–58.

On April 6, 1917 the U.S. declared war on Germany. Count Von Bernstoff was called back to Germany and the U.S. entered into the game immediately.[9] There was talk of draft, volunteer, etc. and everything was more or less a muddle in my head. Having no dependents I believed the best thing I could do would be to volunteer and not hang around Mumsey's skirts and let 'em come and get me. I firmly believed that every full blooded American ought to offer his services right off the bat and not wait till the Govt. gave him a number and dragged him into the thing. So I kept my eyes open waiting for some opening. I wanted to get in the artillery branch of service, but didn't know the proceedings. Finally a friend of mine, Bill Keller, joined Battery A and came home telling the boys all about its prowess and reputation.[10] I made up my mind to join the battery and Bill took me up. I passed the medical exam okay.

April 26, <u>1917</u>   I joined Battery A. Lieutenant [Daniel I.] Glossbrenner swore me in.[11] I held up my right hand and by so doing, put myself under Uncle Sam's care for six years. From April 26th till June 25 we practiced at the Armory on Northwestern Ave. three times a week. I bought myself a uniform and had a hard time getting accustomed to it. The people were only lukewarm and patriotism didn't run very high. It didn't bother me because

9. Kniptash's reference is to Count Johann von Bernsdorff (not *Bernstoff*), the German ambassador to the United States, who informed the American government in late January 1917 that Germany intended to resume its unrestricted submarine warfare against shipping bound for Great Britain. Relations between Germany and the United States deteriorated for the next six weeks until the Wilson administration suspended diplomatic relations. See Farwell, *Over There*, 32; Ferrell, *Wilson and World War I*, 11; Gregory, *Origins of American Intervention*, 120; and Tuchman, *Zimmermann Telegram*, 190–94. Ambassador von Bernsdorff has been described by historian John Eisenhower as a "dapper little man [who] was a superb envoy"; *Yanks*, 5. The German ambassador had been engaged in a delicate diplomatic effort aimed at postponing American entry into the war by encouraging President Woodrow Wilson to continue his efforts to find a diplomatic solution to the conflict.

10. Bill Keller was a friend of Vernon Kniptash's from high school.

11. See Daniel Glossbrenner, Roll No. 8, "Forkert, Edward M.—Gray, Harry A. M.," Indiana State Archives, Commission on Public Records, Adjutant General, WWI Service Records, 401-B-4, 1990161; this collection is hereafter cited as WWI SR.

I knew I was in the right and was doing the bigger thing by offering my services. I'll admit that I thought the whole thing as much an adventure as I thought it my duty. Service overseas sounded good to me. I read the war stories and descriptions and had a fair idea of what a soldier had to put up with. I made up my mind that I would put up with the worst of conditions uncomplainingly.

June 25, 1917   We were told to report to our Armory. They sent out telephone calls and messages to round the fellows up. I happened to be down at Charlie Wacker's cottage fishing. I was enjoying the first two days of a two-week vacation. Charlie came down in his bus and told me that I was to report. Ott Janert hauled me back in his bus. It was my first sacrifice. I was cheated out of my vacation, and, although I hated it, nobody knew it, but myself. When I got to the Armory, they told me to report at the [Indiana state] fairgrounds the next morning. From June 25 to July 1 we camped at this place and learned the elementary principles of a soldier's life.

July 1, 1917   We moved to Fort [Benjamin] Harrison. Major Bush took charge of the Regiment, which consisted of three Indiana and three Ohio batteries. He was a hard man and was especially hard on the Indiana boys. He had very few friends in the fellows under his command. We drilled and learned the handling of our 3" guns. I had a hard time breaking into Army routine. I was never used to discipline; I was never used to being told when I could eat and when I could sleep and when I could rest. I was never used to having everything done by the count, but I tried hard to get accustomed to it. I made up my mind to be a good soldier and I knew that a good soldier had to learn discipline above all other things. We stayed in this place until July 25, 1917.

July 25, 1917   We moved to another location in the reservation. Struck tents and the move was made without a hitch. We settled down to routine once more and were all waiting for the time when Colonel Robert A. Tyndal will come out and take charge.[12]

12. Colonel Robert H. Tyndall (not *Tyndal* or *Tyndel* as Kniptash spells the name) was an experienced artillery officer who previously saw military action in the Spanish-American War and in the Mexican border conflict. After the war, Tyndall became a successful banker and businessman in Indianapolis and served as

Aug. 5, 1917   Today all Indiana Guard was called out. Some of them went to Hattiesburg, but most of them came out to the Fort. Colonel Tyndal came out and took charge. We now have a supply company, a headquarters company, and batteries A, B, C, D, E, and F. This constituted our regiment.[13]

Aug. 15, 1917   Found out today that we changed from 3" to 6" guns. Our Regiment will be a 6" Howitzer Regiment.

Aug. 20   The papers talk like our Regiment will see immediate service in France. The boys are all elated to think that they are going to be among the first to see service. It speaks well for an organization. We're packing and shipping our bulky material and we move sometime soon.

Aug. 31, 1917   Things are looking more as if we were going to move shortly. Nothing left now but some necessary equipment and the tents.

Sept. 1, 1917   I was asked to get on the B.C. [Battery Commander] detail.[14] I feel quite honored and am going to make a try for it. It's deep stuff, but I know that if I apply myself, I can make it.

Sept. 2, 1917   Rested all day. Tomorrow is Labor Day and I understand we get another rest. Sounds too good to be true.

Sept. 3, 1917   Labor Day and we sure labored. Drilled all morning and paraded all afternoon. There's no rest in the Army. A new flag was presented to the Regt. and A Battery was made Color Guard. Quite an honor.

Sept. 4, 1917   Am deep in the mysteries of B. C. work. Can't see my way clearly yet, but have learned the Semaphore Code.

---

mayor of the city between 1943 and 1947. See Bodenhamer and Barrows, *Encyclopedia of Indianapolis*, 1346; RHTC; Sherwood, *Rainbow Hoosier*, 40; Ferrell, *Diary of Elmer Sherwood*, 13.

13. The reference here is to Camp Shelby in Hattiesburg, Mississippi. Within the 150th, Batteries A and E were formed with soldiers from Indianapolis; Batteries B and D with soldiers from Fort Wayne; Battery C with soldiers from Lafayette; and Battery F with soldiers from Bloomington. For rosters of these units, see "Rosters of 150th Field Artillery and Base Hospital 32," *Indianapolis Star*, May 7, 1919, 16.

14. "B. C." was an abbreviation for Battery Commander's detail. See Straub, *Sergeant's Diary*, 346–47, for an extensive listing of the vocabulary used by members of the 150th Field Artillery.

Sept. 5, 1917   Payday today. The horses left the Fort, the shipment to follow.

Sept. 6, 1917   Captain Prather told us that we move tomorrow and so I went home and bid 'em good-bye this evening. Mom smiled and tried hard to be brave, but I knew it was hurting her. Lord, but how I felt for her. I'll never forget that last minute as long as I live. I can at least say that my mother didn't whine and carry on when I kissed her good-bye. Dad walked uptown with me to get me a half dozen bags for the boys in my tent to pack their clothes in. He took me up to Illinois and Washington Street and waited with me for the car that was to take me up to see Maude. We talked about little things and about Mumsey's brave good-bye. Lordy but we were proud of her. My car finally came up. Pap and I shook hands and his last words were, "Well, son, give 'em Hell and hurry home. Good-bye." Typically Dad for you and I loved him for it. Went up to see Maude, and although she cried, she said good-bye very bravely. The two of us went up to bid Fred and Dot Munroe good-bye and I made a prophesy [sic] that I would see their baby again before he got to be another year older. I wonder how I'll miss it. I returned to the fort rather happy because I dreaded the parting with the folks.

Sept. 7, 1917   Mumsey's birthday today and we leave. Well, we finally got away. Got on the train in a downpour of rain feeling wet and miserable. Later, my clothes have dried and I feel myself again. Pretty good transportation for a soldier, sleepers and everything. We left the Fort at 3:30 P.M.

Sept. 8, 1917   We passed thru Buffalo this morning. Am train tired, but happy. The people in the different town[s] have been treating us royal.

Sept. 9, 1917   Well, we finally arrived. Mineola, they call it, it's a 45 minute ride from New York. I had to pitch tents in the dark; did a bum job of it, too.[15]

Sept. 10, 1917   We went all over our tents. Got 'em lined up after three trials. The idea of the whole thing is to make a Model

15. This entry gives Kniptash's first description of Camp Alvord L. Mills, located in Mineola, New York. Kniptash refers to Camp Mills by name only on occasion. For a description of the training regimen at Camp Mills, see Cooke, *Rainbow Division*, 8; James, *Years of MacArthur*, 1:140–44.

Camp of the whole Division. We skimmed off all the grass and, as a result, have dirty black dust to contend with. We have to furl our tents every morning and lay out our clothes for inspection. We're having intensive training and it's some intense. When we come back from drill—hot, dirty, and half-mad—we find our clothes covered with a layer of fine black dust. It's very discouraging. I thought we were soldiering at Ft. Harrison, but I see it was a vacation alongside of this. The boys are just about ready to call [it] quits.

Sept. 17, 1917   We started graveling today. Going to cover this dust so that we can live like white men again. We drill all day and gravel after mess. We sleep whenever we get a chance. Intensive training, Hell, it's exhaustive training. Things are looking better now, though.

Sept. 24, 1917   Well, everything is graveled and we all feel better. I'm getting my mail from home with clocklike regularity and it helps to drive away any homesickness that I may get. Went to New York tonight. It was one of my ambitions to see this town and I was delighted with the sights. Took in a show.

Sept. 30, 1917   Mustered for pay today. Am about broke so they can't pay me any too soon.

Oct. 5, 1917   No pay yet. Am flat broke. Too much New York. Been using my 24 hour passes to good advantage.

Oct. 12   Well, pay day finally arrived, but not until I had wired home for money. I had to send the wire C.O.D. Never was so flat broke before in my life. Things look like we leave this place shortly. Well, I'm getting tired of Camp Mills and am longing for foreign service.

Oct. 15, 1917   Looks more and more as if we pull out of here shortly. They are censoring the mail now.

Oct. 16, 1917   The Capt. told us to prepare to move any minute now. We packed our ditty bags and they are on the way. We carry about 100 pounds on our backs. The tents stay here. We emptied all the straw on our cots and sent the ticks away with our ditty bags.[16] I wouldn't be surprised if we leave tonight. I just saw the

16. "Ticks" was army slang for the straw-filled mattresses used by the troops.

Minnesota Regt. leaving. We leave at night. Well, we're all ready, waiting for the word.

x--x

Oct. 17   I've made the B.C. Detail and am proud of it. Found out today that we get out of all regular fatigue, no more Kitchen Police and other hard labor. However, we have to study while the other boys are having a good time, so the two counter-balance. I've been talking in big terms today. I signed a $10,000 Life Insurance Policy and taken out a $10 a month allotment. Haven't got a thing to show for it, but I trust Uncle Sam absolutely. We were told that no matches, candy, or flashlights will be taken along. Our cots were shipped today. We sleep on the ground tonight. I've got a big hunch we leave about 3:00 o'clock tomorrow morning.

Oct. 18, 1917   Well, my hunch worked. At 3 bells this morning the whistle blew. We made our packs, policed tents and camps, had breakfast, at 5:30 A.M. we were on our way to Garden City. Reached Long Island City at 11:30 A.M. and were ferried across to Hoboken, New Jersey. Boarded the "President Lincoln" at 12 o'clock. She's a big boat and she's going to carry 6,000 soldiers this trip. Battery A sleeps on the third deck (C3), and it's terribly close down here, no ventilation. They say that when the boat gets to moving things change for the better, though. The "Fatherland" lies alongside of us and she makes this ship look like a rowboat. The "President Grant" lies on the other side. The "Fatherland" doesn't cross this time, the "Grant" will be part of the convoy.[17] It's night now and I can see the New York skyline

17. The *President Lincoln* was a German transatlantic liner seized by the government after the declaration of war on Germany. Formerly a ship in the famous Hamburg-America line, it carried six thousand soldiers on the voyage that Kniptash experienced. See Sherwood, *Rainbow Hoosier*, 24–25; and Ferrell, *Diary of Elmer Sherwood*, 8–11. The Indiana regiment was justifiably proud to sail to Europe on a ship named after President Lincoln. Such was not the case with the Alabama regiment of the 42nd Division that sailed to France aboard the *President Grant*. See Cooke, *Rainbow Division*, 19, Farwell, *Over There*, 97. On the entire convoy, fifty-six thousand troops left America for France. See Straub, *Sergeant's Diary*, 26. Kniptash also mentions another ship, the *Fatherland* (*Vaterland* in German), which was also seized by the U.S. government as a wartime measure and then renamed the *Leviathan*. See Farwell, *Over There*, 81. Coincidentally, the *Leviathan* was the ship that carried Kniptash on his return voyage to the United States in April 1919, after the conclusion of the war.

from the upper deck. Every window ablaze and a million windows, the most wonderful sight I've seen since I left home. The boat is slipping away and the Statue of Liberty is getting fainter and fainter. It sure makes a fellow feel funny under these conditions. How many of us will get to see that statue when this war ends? The boys were unusually silent, and all were thinking of the same thought, I guess. All is blackness now and the states are "somewhere out there." I've been blue at times, but never as blue as I am right now.

Oct. 19, 1917   Slept like a top last night. Went up on deck and couldn't see land anywhere. We are going due east. There are 7 transports, a battleship, and several destroyers. Things are not very well organized on this boat and there is much confusion. Feeding the soldiers is the big problem. We had to wait until 10 o'clock for breakfast. The grub is good when we do get it, but we don't get it at regular hours. The boys are beginning to get seasick and I feel sort of tipsy myself. The sights are very comical. We are making about 18 knots and that means 14 days of this misery. Oh, Lord.

Oct. 20, 1917   Second day at sea and some rough sea. 7 out of 10 fellows are terribly sick. I'm one of the few that's not. So far everything that I've eaten has stayed with me. I'm knocking wood when I say this because we still get two weeks more of it. I saw some funny sights today. I saw one fellow go to the mess room, get his mess, come out on deck to eat it, look at it, and get pale behind the gills, take his mess hurriedly to the garbage can, and in a still more hasty manner make a beeline for the rail. When he snapped all that was possible, he put on a sheepish grin and reckoned as how he didn't enjoy either meal very much. I honestly believed him, but wished he had turned his grub over to me, rather than the garbage pail. A sailor told me the secret of seasickness the day we boarded. He said a man with an empty stomach was more subject to it than a man with a full stomach. I heeded his advice and filled up immediately and consequently I'm enjoying the trip. Most of the boys are longing for a "sub" to hit us and put us out of our misery. They're weaker than cats and groan something awful. It's pitiful, but laughable. We've been having lifeboat drill everyday and every soldier knows just what to do in case we are torpedoed. I honestly believe there will be no confusion. There's plenty of boats and rafts and a fellow wouldn't be in the water 20 minutes before the other boats would pick him up. Submarines are the least of my worries. The sea is quiet again and the boat moves without a sound. I'm dead tired and it's time for sleep.[18]

Oct. 21, 1917   Today is Sunday, and by the way, the first Sunday I ever spent at sea. I'm none the worse for it, though, because I'm feeling fine and certainly enjoyed the chicken dinner we had today. We also had fruitcake, sweet potatoes, coffee, corn, and bread and butter. Some meal. There are very few cases of seasickness today, and I think that from now on the boys will be O.K., once more. I thought sure I'd get sick, but I didn't, and they all say that if a fellow doesn't get sick the first four days, he won't get sick at all. I guess I'm sitting pretty for the rest of the trip. It's terribly hot when we sleep, and a sailor told me that was because we had entered the Gulf Stream. I'm sitting here on the upper deck now and it's perfect summer weather. The boys all say we are going to have target practice. One fellow said he read the Semaphore signal which told the "President Grant" to drop targets.

Oct. 22, 1917   The weather is so warm that it's almost unbearable. I was on guard tonight and I enjoyed every minute of it. On land during my second shift I usually have to pinch myself to keep awake, but tonight I was wide awake and enjoyed salty breezes and [the] big moon to the limit. Early in the evening four old sailors formed a quartette and sang silhouetted against that big yellow moon. It was just like a stage setting. I'm seeing the things I used to read about in books and it's all like a dream to me. I'm always afraid someone will come along and wake me.

Oct. 23, 1917   All the boys are on their feet again and not one case of seasickness, everybody happy. Had target practice today and

18. Kniptash mentions the concern aboard the *President Lincoln* about a submarine attack, but he does not mention any sightings of German submarines on the voyage. The *President Lincoln* was sunk by a German submarine on a return voyage to America, four months after it ferried the 42nd Division to France. See Ferrell, *Wilson and World War I*, 41–42. Kniptash's diary entry for October 20, 1917, has been published in Ferrell, *Diary of Elmer Sherwood*, 170n9.

made some good hits. One red-headed sailor boy hit a moving target 10 out of 12 shots. That's quite some good shooting. We cheered and rooted for the redhead and he was King for awhile. It's getting colder again. We must be getting out of the Gulf Stream. The colder weather is making it more comfortable in the sleeping quarters, however.

Oct. 24, 1917   Getting colder and colder. The ship is sailing north by east now.

Oct. 25, 1917   Everything is tightening up now. We're in the danger zone. I understand that we land this coming Sunday. Every possible precaution is being taken. The men all know just what to do when the alarm sounds. There will be no confusion. I was told that a submarine can follow the wake of a boat so our boat is changing its course every twenty minutes. This causes it to take a zigzag course and has the tendency to keep a "sub" a-guessing. It's getting colder all the time. Overcoats are being worn by the men.

Oct. 26   Sighted a sailboat today. Must be nearing land because there are no more waves. It swells. Looks like the water we had at Hoboken.

Oct. 27   The Captain [Sidney S. Miller] gave us orders to sleep in our clothes tonight.[19] That means everything but blouse and gun. All these articles want to be where a fellow can reach them and put them on without the loss of a second. The Capt. said to expect a call at any time now. It means we are right in the center of the war zone and all the chance in the world of taking a nice cold bath before morning.

Oct. 28, 1917   The second Sunday on board and still going fine. I'm a sea-going soldier but I'm getting rather tired of water. Lord, but isn't the ocean full of it? Today, for dinner, we had chicken, fruitcake, bread, butter, lima beans, potatoes, and coffee. Another excellent meal. I'm sure longing for a sight of land, now, and every day I got to hand it to Mr. Columbus for being some brave man.

Oct. 29   Monday and still no land. Some rough sea today. Am on guard tonight.

19. See also Straub, *Sergeant's Diary*, 16, for information about Captain Miller. See also Sidney S. Miller, Roll No. 19, "Mead, Fonny—Mize, James," WWI SR.

Oct. 30, 1917   This morning at 6:00 when I was relieved I hustled
up on deck in time to see five French destroyers steam up,
exchange greetings with our convoy, and proceed to lead us to
our destination. Our big battleship and destroyers sent us a message of good luck, then turned around and made a beeline for
America. Their job was finished. These French destroyers are all
painted up stripes and dots of every color. It was my [first]
glimpse at camouflage, the art the French are noted for. When
the destroyers are close up it appears as if one could distinguish
them at any distance because of the violent color but this same
color makes them almost invisible at 1000 yards.

We must be near land now because I saw a couple of very small
sailboats and I'm sure they wouldn't venture very far from land.
Everybody seems to think we see land tonight or tomorrow
morning. The Captain assembled the battery and gave the boys
a heart-to-heart talk. He said that all indications seemed to be
that we reach port tomorrow. He talked about the women in this
town and the chances the men were taking in case they had sex-
ual intercourse. He said that the women that hung around the
camps were all diseased and that the soldiers in case they should
contract the disease could not receive the proper medical attention and stood a good chance of ruining their lives.[20] He talked
about the liquor question. There is no law in France that keeps
wine etc. from the soldier and he put every man on his honor to
use common sense in his drinking. Since I'm a total abstainer, I
don't think much about the drinking question and I'm certainly

20. In spite of warnings from their officers, troops in the Rainbow Division generally contracted venereal disease at a rate higher than other units. Once the
troops landed, and even as they moved from camp to camp and town to town, the
presence of French prostitutes was constantly visible. The Americans quickly
learned that the trade was divided into those women who associated with established houses of prostitution and others, known as "lone wolves," who worked
independently. The Rainbow soldiers appear to have preferred the affections of
the latter group. See Cooke, *Rainbow Division*, 67; Farwell, *Over There*, 143–47; Freidel, *Over There*, 44. The problem of sexually transmitted diseases affected all Allied
armies in the field. The British army had twenty-three thousand men in the hospital, on any given day, suffering from venereal disease. The French army reported
more than a million cases of syphilis and gonorrhea. See Fleming, *Illusion of Victory*, 216–17.

going to keep away from the women. I promised myself that I'd return to the States in just the good condition I left them. I've got a mother and a girl back there that I think too much about to run wild over here. I think the training Mumsey gave me will make me walk the straight and narrow over here.

Oct. 31, 1917   Land!! Good old black hills on each side; little fishing smacks here and there waving welcome to us. Clear day at first and now a mist has fallen so thick that one cannot see land or water. But the boys saw it when the weather conditions were good and that was enough to start 'em off. They yelled and cheered like madmen. It made me feel just the same way. It was getting monotonous to wake up every morning and see nothing but big waves. Good old land and we'll probably be walking on it tomorrow. I think we are speeding up a river this morning. — Later — Well, we finally bumped and are at rest in home port. We just finished passing thru a series of locks. We're here safe and sound. I have no idea where we are and care less. It's a pretty good thing to happen on Halloween night.[21]

Nov. 1, 1917   The name of this port town is St. Nazaire. It is one of the rottenest towns in France. Full of lewd women and infested with German spies. They've even caught German spies masquerading in U.S. uniform. Well, they'll never learn anything from me. I understand our camp is just three miles from here. We will probably leave this boat tomorrow and hike to it.

Nov. 2   Still here and "snow" has is that we stay on this boat till Monday.[22] They are unloading boats on each side of us, working

21. Kniptash appeared to have weathered the long journey to France aboard the *President Lincoln* better than most other Indiana soldiers. Pete Straub described the voyage as "most miserable. Sanitary conditions were very, very bad." *Sergeant's Diary*, 13. Similarly, Elmer Sherwood wrote that the *Lincoln* had been converted into a transport with the aim of accommodating as many soldiers as possible, and with little consideration for comfort; *Rainbow Hoosier*, 24.

22. "Snow" was Kniptash's most frequently used term of army argot. A difficult term to define, it attempts to convey a combination of sound news, gossip, rumor, speculation, and hearsay into one coherent meaning. The term was used to describe meaningful information obtained from commanding officers about future actions affecting ordinary soldiers. For a brief, albeit insufficient, definition, see Straub, *Sergeant's Diary*, 347. Since army "snow" often turned out to be false, erroneous, or misleading, we can presume that the origin of the phrase

day and night. It has rained every day since we've been here but today the sun came up bright and shows up a seaport town of France in the best light. The sailors are washing down the sides of the boat in preparation for the trip back; the different bands are playing snappy airs; the fellows are moving restlessly about trying to find something to kill time; little rowboats full of dirty French kids come up to the ship and sell chocolate to the soldiers; the signal flags of the big ships are all fluttering, drying in the warm breeze. The weather is soft and balmy, wonderful weather for November. The real significance of the Stars and Stripes never hit me till I saw her floating over the U.S. Consul's house at the far end of the harbor. It sure made a fellow proud of it floating there 3000 miles from the land it represents. Everybody's happy and longing for the time when we walk on land again. About 25 German prisoners, under a couple of French guards, are working on the deck below! They laugh and joke with one another and look sleek and fat, so I guess they are taken care of fairly well. A big French dirigible floated overhead and headed north. Must be patrolling the coast. The troops are leaving the boat but Lord only knows when our turn comes.

Nov. 3, 1917   The ship that was holding us up pulled out last night and ours moved in immediately. We worked all night loading cargo. This morning we took our first hike and the surrounding countryside was just like fairyland to me. The houses are quaint, simple little dwellings, typically French. Not a frame house anywhere. All brick and stone. Little wine gardens scattered here and there; quaint old French men and women, all wrinkles and fat; all sorts and descriptions of soldiers. Everything just as I had

------

"snow job" may have derived from this term. For a useful listing of army colloquialisms from World War I, see Farwell, *Over There*, Appendix A, 301–305; the term "snow" is not included on Farwell's list, however. In St. Nazaire, the Americans found a town largely depleted of able-bodied men. Philip Fitzsimons, a member of the Headquarters Company of the 150th Field Artillery, recalled that "people were slow [and] tired. Only old [and] crippled men [were] available." See Philip Fitzsimons, Military Survey, World War I, June 3, 1983, U.S. Army Military History Institute, Carlisle Barracks, Pennsylvania, 5.

read about it in books. We are going to take another hike this afternoon. We will live on the ship until further notice. I'm the happiest kid in the world. The people treat us wonderfully. This morning the Frenchies threw flowers at us and yelled in their strange tongue. It is all too wonderful for words.

Nov. 4, 1917   Another Sunday and a busy one at that. The battery was given a three hour pass and I never had a better time in my life. We bought French pastries and, in fact, everything that we had been craving for the past two wks. These people can't understand us and we can't understand them. We just point to what we want; hold out a handful of change, let them take all their conscience will permit 'em to, and bid 'em adieu. I'm learning fast, though. I had some of my money changed into francs and ½ francs, and buying a French/English dictionary, went around hunting trouble. I got what I wanted but I usually ended up breathless when I did. Of all the calisthenics and turning the pages of that book! I laughed more in those three hours than I ever did before in my life. This afternoon I helped unload the boat and tonight I'm on wharf guard. There's about 49 of us left behind. The rest of the boys are on the way to camp. We follow tomorrow.

Nov. 5, 1917   We're at camp now. I did my hitch of guard duty and then joined the rest of the bty. late this evening. Too dark and can't tell much about the camp but I do know that it's 2½ miles from St. Nazaire and that we sleep on the ground floor tonight.

Nov. 6, 1917   Woke up this morn and viewed one of the prettiest sunrises I've ever seen. It was gaudy in its splendor. An artist could have sold a picture of that sunrise for a million dollars. The camp is on a hill that commands a beautiful view on all sides. The cantonments are knock down affairs and have dusty floors. I wasn't here last night when they gave out straw for the ticks so I had to sleep on the hard ground. I was so tired, though, I could have slept standing up.

Nov. 7, 1917   This camp must be a resting place for soldiers. We haven't drilled an hour so far. It has rained every day and things are miserable. This morning the sun came up bright as a dollar and five minutes later it was raining like Billy be damned and has continued so ever since. Sure is funny weather.

<u>Nov. 8</u>   Went on an 8 mile hike this morning. The scenery was the best so far. We've been taking two hikes a day, averaging about 7 miles each hike. The grind of the hike isn't noticed by the men because there's so much to see. — We are going to leave this place within the next two days. The Col. gave us a talk today and he said from now on the fun ceases and the hard work and sacrifice commence. He said we got a man-sized job ahead of us and we were going to handle it as men should. Well, the boys are sure ready for anything that comes.

Nov. 9   Raining again this morning and everything looks miserable.

Nov. 12   On guard last night and for once it didn't rain. This morn we had hot biscuits for breakfast and I ate four of 'em before I tossed 'em. Lordy, but they were good after days and days of hardtack and canned willy.[23] Several of our batteries have left for another camp but I don't know when we follow up.

Nov. 15   Still here and no pay yet. The boys all figure we leave tomorrow. Have been working pretty hard for the last two days on an Engineering detail. It's to be a big reservoir to supply water to the Camp. Common pick-and-shovel labor and 9½ hours a day. Am dead tired at the end of the day. No mail yet. Haven't heard from home since we left Camp Mills and getting hungry for letters. Understand it's all waiting for us at our next camp.

<u>Nov. 16</u>   Payday and I am now the doubtful possessor of a pocketful of French money. Got a one hundred franc note that would make a beautiful picture if it only had a frame around it; however, the French people use it for money so I guess it's O.K. The weather is foggy, damp, and cold. We move from here soon, and they say the new camp is a peach.

23. Hardtack and canned willy (sometimes called corned willie) were the ration staples for the ordinary soldier. Hardtack was a biscuitlike food and canned willy was corned beef. Soldiers hated the taste of both items. For that reason, one reads frequently of Kniptash saving his money to purchase meals at the YMCA, the Salvation Army, from local French civilians who offered food for sale, or in French cafés in towns near where the troops were stationed. See Cooke, *Rainbow Division*, 29; Farwell, *Over There*, 302.

Nov. 17   Left this evening for St. Nazaire to help load material. We leave for our next camp at 4:00 o'clock Sunday morning. I'm dead tired as I've been working like a fool all day.

Nov. 18   Well we finally got entrained at 5:30 Sunday morn. Slept on a concrete floor last night and will admit that I didn't sleep very comfy. Am very tired right now. Am writing this while the train moves at a terrific speed of 8 miles an hour, slowest service I ever saw. — We arrived at Guer at 5 o'clock P.M. after 12 hours of traveling. We make 100 miles in 12 hours. The speed almost took our breath away. Guer is directly north of St. Nazaire and near Brest. Our training camp is just 3½ miles from here and we hike it. — Later — Finally reached our camp and it's a peach, iron beds with mattresses and pillows, stoves and everything, comes as near being home as anything I've hit yet.

Nov. 19   Monday in our new camp, she's sure a daisy.[24] I can hear the different batteries of the 51st Brig. (26th Div.) at target practice on a range a mile away. Our horses and guns are here waiting for us. This 26th Div. is the 2nd Div. to come across. They came right after the 1st Div., who are at the front now. That makes us the third Division to land in France and we're among the first 100,000 Americans over here. We're going to put in 6 weeks of the hardest kind of training morning till night and no time for play. Well, I'm sure feeling the best and it don't worry me much.

Nov. 20   I find that this is a French camp, too. Then there must be a whole Regiment of German prisoners. I'm trying out for a wireless detail and if I make good I'll be a wireless operator. It's all Greek to me now. Having learned the code helps me considerably, but I've got to learn speed. This will come with practice. Then there is numerous abbreviations to learn. These are used

---

24. This entry records Kniptash's arrival at Camp Coêtquidan, the camp that housed the artillery school for French and then American soldiers. By the standards of World War I, Camp Coêtquidan was a comfortable site for obtaining artillery training. See Sherwood, *Rainbow Hoosier*, 35; Cooke, *Rainbow Division*, 32–35; Ferrell, *Diary of Elmer Sherwood*, 11–16. At this location, Kniptash and his fellow Hoosiers learned to fire the French 75 mm howitzers, the weapon that "was the artisan of the [French] victory in the [Battle of] the Marne," in the words of historian Hew Strachan; see *First World War*, 55. See also Farwell, *Over There*, 44.

to signal aeroplanes. The work is very interesting and I'm tickled to think I was one of the four B.C. men to be chosen. I received 18 letters today, just bubbling over with joy. Sat right down and spent three hours answering 'em.[25]

Nov. 21   Our hours are from 7:30 A.M. till 4:30 P.M. with an hour for dinner. The time flies fast, though, thanks to the novelty of the work.

Nov. 23   Everything the same and working hard. Was talking to a Sergeant of the 1st Division who had been sent back as an instructor. He didn't get to see much of the front, but he said what he did see wasn't so bad. They were stationed near Luneville. He said there must be 400,000 Americans over here by this time, and I claim that number [is] quite large for this early in the game. Tomorrow is inspection and I wash my clothes and am slicked up for it. Pete Straub was left behind at St. Nazaire at a hospital. He had something the matter with his eye and it caused him to have a continual headache. They were going to operate on him. Sure hope he pulls through.[26] Several of the boys are sick here. Two have measles. As for me, I never felt better in my life.

Nov. 24   Inspection passed and everything lovely. It was the first inspection in this camp and the first one under our new Major. Major Wainwright left for officer school and Major Carter took his place. He is now in charge of our battalion. This afternoon I went to my first military funeral. In fact, it's the first funeral of any kind I ever attended and I hope I'm never present at another. Some boy from Battery D died of pneumonia and his burial was the solemnest affair imaginable. His grave is in a big

25. Kniptash initially followed the British spelling "aeroplanes." Also, like all the American troops, Kniptash coveted news from home and especially letters from his family. As Elmer Sherwood wrote: "The baser things in life assumed practically no place in a soldier's thought, while the real fundamental facts attained their correct place. Country, loved ones, friends, and home received almost all his thoughts. Nothing was so valuable, yes priceless, as a letter from home." *Rainbow Hoosier*, 129.

26. Straub recounts his surgery, his difficult hospitalization, and his recuperation in *Sergeant's Diary*, 15. Actually, the surgery was performed on Straub's sinus area rather than his eye.

pine forest. The whole Indiana Regt. (150th) and all the officers, including Brig. Gen. [Charles] Sommerall were present.[27] The body, at rest in a rough pine coffin, was hauled from the hospital to the grave on a caisson and the casket was draped with an American flag. The caisson had the march followed by the officers, the band, and the rest of the regiment. The band played a slow, melancholy funeral march. When the grave was reached, the regiment formed a semi-circle around it. The chaplain delivered the prayer, 8 men fired their rifles three times over the grave, and then the bugler blowed taps. We'll frankly say that it brought that mean little lump to my throat. His best pals acted as pallbearers and I sure felt sorry for them. They were about ready to break down, but didn't want to appear weak before all of us and the boys sure sympathized with them. That boy got a much better funeral than some of us are going to get, up at the front they don't take the time, they dig you a hole, and kick you in, and there you are. Passes for 36 hours were given to 10% of the battery to go to Rennes. I was one that had to stay. It's a town of some 100,000 people. Bet the bunch have some time.

Nov. 25   Sunday and a drizzly, muddy, dreary one too. Sat around studying and playing the uke. Had the Blues bad. Heard of a new pastry shop that just opened. Hustled down and found that the baker was a man who had baked for 10 years in Chicago. He came back when war broke out, got wounded, and is now making his living selling good old American pies and cakes. I just finished an apple pie that made me think [of] home and mother. From now on, I'm his regular customer. Found out just what our program calls for here. There will be 6 weeks of intensive training, then 4 weeks of maneuvering in which the batteries, Regiment, and Brigade tackle some of the problems they can expect to run into at the front. Then at the end of the 10 weeks we

27. The reference here is to Brigadier General Charles P. Summerall, the first commanding officer of the 67th Field Artillery Brigade (not *Sommerall*, as Kniptash spells the name). The soldier who died from pneumonia on November 23, 1917, was Leslie C. Kayser of Fort Wayne. See "Rosters of 150th," *Indianapolis Star*, May 7, 1919, 16. See Cooke, *Rainbow Division*, 21.

entrain and go to some quiet sector where there's not much doing, but where our targets will be something worth shooting at and where the boys will get used to shell-fire, etc. No doubt we will have casualties up there, but it will harden the boys up to war re: things to come. The boys are into the heart of things and all are longing for the time when we get to see some war. Chances are we'll get our belly full before it's all over, but we'll take a chance on that.

Nov. 27   Went to a French movie tonight and I knew less when I came out than when I went in. Every time some deep acting took place and I waited for the explanation to flash on the screen, it came down in French and, of course, made things clear as mud. Every time the hero received a letter, it was flashed to show the audience what he was reading and most of the audience, being Americans, nobody had any idea what was troubling the hero. Very good show for the fix it was in, but it sure was in a Hell of a fix.

Nov. 28   No wireless class this afternoon and I put in the time studying and fooling with the range-finder. Tomorrow has been declared a legal holiday for all the soldiers and we are going to have some Thanksgiving. There's 130 lbs. of turkey for one thing. The cooks and kitchen police will work all night tonight, then I understand mail will be given out, so there's little more a fellow could ask for.

Nov. 29, 1917   Well, the big day came and has gone. It left me with a very full stomach. The menu: turkey, cranberry sauce, mashed potatoes, gravy, dressing, biscuits, butter, peas, ½ a big apple pie, and a cup of cocoa, some dinner! Then this evening we had sweet cider and doughnuts. Only one blot on the whole day and that was there was no mayo, however, outside of that one gloom ingredient, the general mixture was a big joy day. The band gave a big concert in the afternoon and the boys danced with one another and raised Hell in general. I say God bless the pilgrims.

Nov. 30   Mustered for pay today, no mail yet, so muster don't interest me much. I want letters not money. It's been two weeks since the last batch. I get to go to Rennes tomorrow and Sunday. Perry Lesh, Pete Clift, and myself are going to make up one party and if there's any good time to be had in that town, we'll sure have it.[28]

Dec. 2   Well, we went to Rennes and I sure crammed a week's fun in there in those 24 hours. I saw every soldier from the Allied powers now. Everyone from British tommies down to Hindus or some country that claims black men as citizens. There were Russians, French, English, Italians, Algerians, Chinese, and Americans.[29] We had a picnic mingling with them and trying to talk to them. Our band gave a concert at the station square and everybody went wild about it. I saw a bunch of men, too, who work in munition factories. Poor devils, made me sick to look at them. When they take their jobs they are told they have only a year to live. These men were a dirty orange color. Their clothes had this orange dust on them.[30] We slept at the Hotel Centrale quite a hotel, feather beds and everything.

Early Sunday morning I asked the maid in my very best French to bring us water so that we could wash and she rushed away singing "Toute de suite" over her shoulder.[31] She returned with a bottle of cider. That was pretty close! I guess my French must be pretty bad. It is 20 miles from Camp Coetquidan to Rennes. It took the train 2½ hours to get here and 3 to get back. I had to stand up all the way back. Rather tired when we hit camp, but bucked up a 100% when I found four packages and 15 letters waiting for me. Three of the packages were from V + B and believe me they will sure hear from me tomorrow. I've had a lot of real light friends, but V + B runs second to none of them. The other package was from Mumsey. God bless her. I'd give half my

28. Perry Lesh and Charles "Pete" Clift were also from Indianapolis and became friends of Vernon Kniptash's during the war.

29. Most likely, the Chinese to whom Kniptash refers were from Indochina, brought by the French to serve as vehicle drivers during the war. See Cooke, *Rainbow Division*, 123; Farwell, *Over There*, 167, 227; Fleming, *Illusion of Victory*, 230.

30. On this occasion, Kniptash encountered one of the grim realities of the war. Most likely, these men who worked in munitions plants had developed poisoning from the explosive TNT. Sometimes the poisoning caused the skin to discolor into a yellowish shade. See Gilbert, *First World War*, 345.

31. The French *toute de suite* is translated as "right away" or "at once." Americans pronounced the term "toot sweet," and it became a common expression used by the soldiers.

life to talk to her for one minute. I never knew what a wonderful mother she was till I got over here. There is one thing about these packages I don't understand. Every one of them enclosed a card wishing me a Merry Xmas. They should've arrived around the 25$^{\underline{th}}$ instead of the second. It looks to me now as if I won't have a very Merry Xmas. However, I've opened them now and enjoyed 'em like a kid does over a new toy so I won't crab. Some of the stuff came just when I needed it the most, especially the tobacco. K. Vonnegut must read my mind.[32]

He seems to know just when I'm running low and his packages always arrive when needed the most.

Dec. 3   Battery A had target practice today. It was the first time they fired their new guns and everybody was tickled with the results. My ears are still ringing from the roar.

Dec. 6   My birthday today, 21 years old. I threw a supper for Sgt. [Wilbur] Morgan and [Gipson] "Gip" Hastings and Perry Lesh. Had quite a feed. Found out today that this portion of France is the backwoods and resembles our Kentucky at home. This accounts for some of the sights I've seen. I couldn't believe France could be as backward as this part of it is. People here are too slow to catch a cold.

Dec. 7   Still working hard. Study radio in the morning and go on to the range in the afternoon. Never knew a fellow had to know so much science in order to fight a modern war. Several of the boys are in the hospital with measles, colds, and pneumonia. Pete Straub hasn't come back from St. Nazaire yet.

December 7–12   Nothing much new. Same old grind. The officers are becoming very efficient at firing their problems. Capt. Miller handles everything in his usual thorough manner. He's a wonderful soldier. I hate to see a vacancy occur because he'll be a Major sure as it does. He knows the Army game too well to be a Captain. All the French people I talk to seem to think that the

32. Kurt Vonnegut, Sr., was one of the senior partners in the architectural firm of Vonnegut and Bohn. Vonnegut, Sr., was the son of Bernard Vonnegut, cofounder with Arthur Bohn of the firm in 1888. Otto Mueller joined the firm as a partner in 1920. The firm then became known as Vonnegut, Bohn, and Mueller. Vonnegut, Sr., was also the father of the famous fiction writer, Kurt Vonnegut, Jr. See Bodenhamer and Barrows, *Encyclopedia of Indianapolis*, 1388–99.

war will be over next spring. I hope they're right, but I think a year from next spring will hit it closer. I'm anxious to find out how I'll act under shell fire! I know I'll be scared, but there's no dishonor in that. If you stick to your post, no matter how scared you are, that's the thing that counts. We'll see.

Dec. 14   Mail day today and it brought me 21 letters. There's more to come tomorrow. News from folks back home puts the new life in a fellow.

Dec. 21   The boys are receiving packages daily, and I haven't had any since those four on the 2nd. Mine must be marked Xmas and will be handed out next Tuesday. Just as long as they're over here and not down in Davy Jones' locker. I should fret. We are getting our heads together for the Xmas entertainment. The kitchen is all decked up in evergreen, holly, and mistletoe. Sure makes a beautiful kitchen. — Later — Another big joy carnival. I just received 14 letters and two packages. One of the packages was a big box of candy from Maude and a carton of Camels from Uncle Docus was the other.[33] Then the letters told me that both Mumsey and Maude had received four of my letters apiece. That made me happy. I was beginning to worry because I sure sent 'em a bunch. Pete Straub came back at last and is looking fine. He spent the biggest part of his time trying to get transportation to this camp. Was sure glad to see him.

Dec. 25, 1917   Well, the big day has come. Last night, Xmas eve, the boys put on a big show and I never saw a home talent affair pulled off so nicely. There wasn't a hitch in the whole program. Music, boxing, and singing. Every act a hummer. The boys were then given their Xmas boxes and all left for their cots with a good taste in their mouths. I sure was one happy kid. — Xmas day — slight drizzle, but everybody happy. The captain asked Bill Hall and I to put on our little sketch at the HQ's show this afternoon.[34] I made up a rather poor parody dealing with our soldier

33. "Uncle Docus" was Kniptash's uncle Jodocus Kniptash, a younger brother of Wilhelm Kniptash. Jodocus was seven years younger than Wilhelm and was the third son and sixth child in the family. He lived his entire life in Terre Haute.

34. Kniptash and Bill Hall eventually formed a string sextet and organized a musical show called "The Hoosier Follies." Kniptash and Hall made their "premier performance" on Christmas Day, 1917. Kniptash also refers to a "Xmas box,"

life from Ft. Harrison up till now and it seemed to have pleased him. He asked me to sing it again. The Xmas boxes I got just about knocked me silly, everything I wanted and needed and plenty of candy, nuts, etc. The gang at V + B sent me a box full of sweets and cigarettes. They're sure the kind of friends a fellow likes to have. Mumsey and Maude sent me heaps. God bless 'em both. Lordy, but I'm happy. Had a scrumptious dinner, duck, dressing, mashed potatoes, gravy, biscuits, jam, pickles, slaw, doughnuts, peach pie, cake, figs, and coffee. Then they passed out chocolate, cigarettes and cigars. I'm so full I'm in misery. Later the 150th lined up and marched pell mell through the camp raising Hell. Had a picnic. A wonderful Christmas and I'm the one happy boy.

Dec. 31   The last night of 1917 and quiet everywhere. At 12:00 the band got up and played syncopated airs, but outside of that, there was no excitement. So ends 1917. Wonder if I'll live to see 1918 leave us.

Jan. 1, 1918   The very first day was a holiday and all the boys are sitting around the stove swapping lies. I was asked to sing my parody at B battery's show tonight. I may go over.

Jan. 6, 1918   School ended yesterday and that means we have to stand guard once more. Haven't walked the dog since we broke camp at St. Nazaire. Couldn't stand guard and go to school, too.

Jan. 7, 1918   The 1st Div. had several men taken prisoners by the Bosche.[35] Our Intelligence Department sends down the report that a party of Bosche led them out in full view of our men and cut their throats. Said their reason was because they considered the American soldier and people an inferior race and it was the best way to get rid of them. It made my blood boil. Damn dirty

---

probably of candy, sent to the troops by the Rainbow Cheer Association of Indiana. See Sherwood, *Rainbow Hoosier*, 42; Ferrell, *Diary of Elmer Sherwood*, 15.

35. Once again, Kniptash chose his own form of spelling, this time for the word *Boche*, the derisive term applied by the French to the Germans. Kniptash spells the term "Bosche" throughout his diary. Originally a loose translation of a French word meaning "rascal," according to Farwell it first appeared in an article in the British newspaper *Daily Express*, on September 30, 1914; see Farwell, *Over There*, 301.

dogs. Hope the folks back home hear the details. Maybe it will stir things up a bit.[36]

Jan. 16, 1918   Another issue of mail today. Got a package containing candy and cakes from Mumsey and it had a card enclosed wishing me happy birthday returns. Arrived a little late as a birthday present, but it was disposed of just as heartily as it would've been on December 6, 1917. I got a wonderful letter from her too and a peach of a one from Maude. The mud around here just about takes all the joy out of life. We have no boots and when we go to the stables and slop around in mud, it's up to our knees. It's enough to take the heart out of any man. We're sure doing some real soldiering now. The "snow" is that we will be issued hip boots tomorrow. Lord, I hope it's so.[37]

Jan. 17, 1918   Received some more letters today and 2 cartons of Camels from Fred and Dot Munroe. We were issued hip boots today, so Hurrah!

Jan. 23, 1918   Today is the first day I've been off my feet since we landed. Diarrhea, and I got it bad, first time in my life I've ever had it and it's got me down. This is the tenth day and today I had to stay in and dope. I'm beginning to believe I've played in hard luck in regards to my job in the Army. They are not going to use the battery men as wireless operators, just the HQ's boys are going to get the job. It's pretty discouraging after working 6 weeks getting all the dope and not get a chance to use it. I'll be way behind the rest of the boys. I don't know enough about telephone work to hold a job there. Things look pretty Blue now, but I hope something will be done. We're having our hikes and

36. In his account of his service in World War I, George C. Marshall also told of an incident where an American soldier had his throat cut by the Germans; see *Memoirs*, 47.

37. In addition to the dangers of combat, the great environmental enemy in World War I was mud. Mud afflicted soldiers everywhere, not only in the trenches and in the camps but also in their numerous marches from place to place. As one soldier wrote: "Mud is where men sink—and what is worse—where their souls sink. Mud hides the stripes of rank, there are only poor suffering beasts. Hell is not fire, that would be the ultimate in suffering. Hell is mud." Quoted in Gilbert, *First World War*, 313. Compounding the problems for the Americans was the lack of footwear (either shoes or boots) capable of keeping feet dry in the wet conditions of France. See Cooke, *Rainbow Division*, 42; Farwell, *Over There*, 112.

maneuvers now as per schedule and it won't be long now till we'll be leaving for the front. The French officers who are instructing our officers in the handling of their guns say that our Brigade is firing as good as any artillery at the front so that looks like a move before the last of February.

Jan. 26, 1918   Minnesota Regt. had bad luck yesterday. A gun cpl. and #1 one man were killed when their gun blew up. The corporal told a "hope" lieutenant that the gun was in no condition to fire but the "hope" ordered him to fire. Again, the cpl. said the gun was defective, but the lieut. wouldn't listen. The cpl. had to obey orders and those orders caused his and his pal's death. The "hope" is under arrest.[38] We're due to leave camp any day now. We practiced loading our 6" guns on flat cars and have got it down pat. New "snow" is that we go to the Swiss border for our first time up. The boys are "rarin" to go.

Jan. 30, 1918   We've been going on long rides the last few days, start early in the morning and come back late at night. I'm stiff, sore, and tired and smell like a horse. Yesterday, we covered 25 miles. Quite a few miles for a fellow who hasn't ridden a horse since the Ft. Harrison war. This cantonment has been quarantined for diptheria [sic]. Bill Brunning developed a case of it and we all get a "shot" between the shoulder blades as a precaution.[39] That, along with a throat swab twice a day, makes me hope for an early lift of the quarantine. Five of the boys are in the Hospital with the mumps. Don't know what will come next.

Feb. 3   Am sitting in the Y.M.C.A. with Perry Lesh. Thinking over the different events of last week gives me the Blues. Four wireless men from A Battery are to be transferred to H.Q. Co. That means I have to leave A Battery and all the friends I made, why, it's just like leaving home again. The H.Q. Co. is a rattling good

38. Kniptash's use of the term "hope" is unclear, although it might relate to the German word *haupt*, meaning "chief" or "head." Letter, Charles S. Moody, Jr. (volunteer researcher, U.S. Army Military History Institute), to the editor, September 24, 2008.

39. Brunning was a sick man for some time. His case of diphtheria gave him a fever of 104°F and sent him to the hospital. Soldiers who had bunked near him were quarantined and not allowed to eat with the rest of the unit. Like Kniptash, Brunning was from Indianapolis. See Straub, *Sergeant's Diary*, 29 (Brunning's name was occasionally spelled *Bruning*).

organization, but there's only one A Battery. Understand Captain Miller and Colonel Tyndal went round and round about the transfer and Colonel Tyndal told Captain Miller that whenever the H.Q. Co. needs men they get 'em whether or no. He threatened to confine Captain Miller to quarters if he said another word. Made me feel good to know that the Capt. stood up for us. Well, so the old war runs and no more will be said.[40]

Feb. 6, 1918   We've been working with the H.Q. Co. and living with A Battery, fairly well satisfied. The boys have been issued gas masks, both English and French. They're devilish looking things, but the gas is worse.

Feb. 10   Last Friday we went thru a hut filled with chlorine gas. I haven't been issued an English mask yet and had to use my French. Had a hard time breathing at first, but soon got used to it. Moved my belongings over to HQ Co. Ate my last meal with Battery A at dinner today. Had pie and trimmings. I sure hated to leave the bunch. I had a friend in every man there. However, there's a good bunch here too so I know I'll get along O.K.

Feb. 11   Had another funeral today. Sergeant Richie of D Battery.[41] He was killed accidentally by a stray bullet.

Feb. 13   Our ditty bags left yest[erday] for billets. We move shortly, but just how soon I don't know. Am having a picnic with the H.Q. Bunch. Every night we get around the stove and raise Hell. A fine bunch and I'm at home already. They're all like A Battery, want to get to the front so they can get close to Fritzie.[42]

Feb. 19, 1918   Tomorrow morn at 2 bells we move. That is, Regt'l detail does and I'm included. Don't know whether we go straight to the front or billets or a little of both, hope we go to the front. They say we have a 3 day ride ahead of us. Boxcars will be used for Pullmans. I'm making my pack now.

---

40. Along with three others, Prescott Hill, Edward Mooney, and Major P. Harrison, Kniptash was transferred to the 150th Headquarters Company as a wireless operator; see Straub, *Sergeant's Diary*, 35.

41. The reference is to Sgt. Kent Stephenson Ritchie, from Indianapolis, who was shot accidentally on February 9, 1918. Ritchie was buried at Camp Coêtquidan. See Sherwood, *Rainbow Hoosier*, 193.

42. "Fritzie" was one of the many names used by American troops to refer to the German enemy; see Farwell, *Over There*, 303.

CHAPTER 2

Stemming the German Offensives, February 20–July 20, 1918

Oh, I've been wounded in this fight;
Shot at sunrise; gassed at night.
Outside of that I feel allright,
And I ain't got weary yet.

From Sherwood, *Diary of a Rainbow Veteran*

ON FEBRUARY 20, 1918, VERNON KNIPTASH AND THE 150th Field Artillery departed Camp Coêtquidan with the rest of the 67th Brigade and headed for the Luneville sector of the western front. Around the same time, the other regiments of the 42nd Division left their training camps and began the move to Luneville. Their purpose for moving was the provision of support for the French army units that were holding that sector of the front.

By this time, General Pershing had placed Major General Charles T. Menoher, an artillery officer and former West Point classmate, in charge of the Rainbow Division. Menoher succeeded Major General William T. Mann, who was returned to the United States.[1]

The 42nd Division became involved in actual combat soon after arriving at Luneville, although its actions were limited to reconnaissance and some minor skirmishing.[2] Elsewhere, however, preparations for a major intensification of the war were occurring.

Epigraph. From a popular song of the AEF; see Sherwood, *Diary of a Rainbow Veteran*, 18.

1. Menoher's leadership of the Rainbow Division has been widely applauded. Historian John Eisenhower credits Menoher with maintaining the morale of the Rainbows at a time when pessimism "infected" other units of the AEF; see *Yanks*, 86–87.

2. Gilbert, *First World War*, 400; James, *Years of MacArthur*, 1:154–56.

On March 3, 1918, Germany and Russia signed the Treaty of Brest-Litovsk, by which Russia ceded vast territories in Eastern Europe to Germany as the price for withdrawing from the war. The elimination of their enemy on the eastern front enabled the Germans to begin the process of moving vast quantities of troops and equipment westward in the expectation that a major offensive could defeat the French and British before the impact of the U.S. contribution was fully felt.

The Germans began the first in a series of several major offensives on the western front on March 21. In a devastating display of artillery bombardment, air raids, and offensive troop movement, the Germans pushed back the British and French from their entrenched positions along the entire western front. But while their offensive succeeded in driving the Allied forces southward, the Germans suffered enormous casualties in the process, a circumstance that would be repeated numerous times over the course of the next five months.

Regardless, the situation for the British and French forces grew increasingly desperate as the German drive unfolded in March and April. British prime minister David Lloyd George and French premier Georges Clemençeau appealed to General Pershing and then to President Wilson to send American troops into the lines (under British and French command) to bolster the exhausted Tommies and *poilus*.[3] Pershing initially resisted the pressure, preferring instead to concentrate on building up an American army capable of mounting a sustained offensive in the spring of 1919. Lloyd George and Clemençeau believed that such postponement of American participation might well result in a German victory. On April 2 Pershing agreed to send some contingents of American troops into the British and French lines, although the great majority of American forces remained out of action.[4]

---

3. British troops in World War I were known as "Tommies," probably after the character Tommy (Atkins) in the eponymous poem by Rudyard Kipling. French soldiers were known as *poilus*, or "hairy ones," since their long assignments in the trenches on the western front gave them few opportunities for shaving or haircuts. See Fleming, *Illusion of Victory*, 123–24; Farwell, *Over There*, 303, 305. For a more complete listing of terms used by soldiers in World War I, see Dickson, *War Slang*.

4. Gilbert, *First World War*, 408–14; Keegan, *First World War*, 372–73.

The German advance continued throughout April. In near desperation, Lloyd George and Clemençeau appealed to Pershing for more troops. "It is maddening to think that though the men are there, the issue may be endangered because of the shortsightedness of one General [i.e., Pershing] and the failure of his government to order him to carry out their undertaking," Lloyd George lamented on May 2.[5] In response, Pershing gave the order to move increasing quantities of men and matériel into the battered Allied lines.

Americans were soon making their way into the effort to stop the German advance. Though untested in battle, the presence of fresh American troops moving toward the front raised the morale of the Allied forces as nothing had previously. As Vera Brittain, a British nurse serving in a field hospital in France, wrote:

They were swinging rapidly toward Camiers and, though the sight of soldiers marching was now too familiar to arouse curiosity, an unusual quality of bold vigour in their stride caused me to stare at them with puzzled interest. They looked larger than ordinary men; their tall, straight figures were in vivid contrast to the undersized armies of pale recruits to which we were grown accustomed. At first, I thought their spruce, clean uniforms were those of officers, yet obviously they could not be officers for there were too many of them; they seemed, as it were, Tommies in heaven. Had yet another regiment been conjured up out of our depleted Dominions? I wondered, watching them move with such rhythm, such dignity, such serene consciousness of self-respect. But I knew the colonial troops so well, and these were different; they were assured where the Australians were aggressive, self-possessed where the New Zealanders were turbulent. Then [I] heard an excited cry from a group of nurses behind [me], "Look! Look! Here are the Americans!"[6]

Throughout May and June, American troops continued their move into the Allied sectors. Then, in mid-July, the Germans tried

5. Quoted in Gilbert, *First World War*, 421; see also Freidel, *Over There*, 97.
6. Quoted in Gilbert, *First World War*, 414.

again to break the Allied lines and force a capitulation. In a three-day barrage of shell, shot, and fire, between July 15 and 17, the Germans pounded all along the front, sustaining horrendous casualties. The Allied forces had stopped what turned out to be the final German offensive.

The five months between March and July 1918 was a period of combat testing for the Rainbow Division. The Rainbows were in the fight literally at every point, moving from the fighting around Luneville in March and April to the combat around Baccarat in May and finally to Champagne for the bloody days of mid-July. During the fighting in the Champagne sector alone on July 16–17, the 42nd Division sustained sixteen hundred dead and wounded.[7]

On February 20, however, all Vernon Kniptash knew as he departed Camp Coêtquidan for Luneville, was that he was leaving a life of relative safety and security to move to a place where the "cooties were biting and the bullets were sizzling."[8] Kniptash's experiences to come would closely match the following description: "To survive it would be necessary to go on beyond exhaustion, to march when the body clamoured to be allowed to drop and die, to shoot when eyes were too tired to see, to remain awake when a man would have given his chance of salvation to sleep. And we realized also to drive the body beyond the physical powers, to force the mind to act long after it had surrendered the power of thought, only despair and the strength of despair could furnish the motive force."[9]

Feb. 20   Well, we're on our way. There's 10 of us in one of these boxcars marked "Hommes-40 Chevauz-8."[10] We're not crowded, but I don't see how they can cram 40 men in one of these dinkies. We have passed thru Rennes and have just passed through Vitré.

---

7. Cooke, *Rainbow Division*, 110.

8. "Cooties" refers to the ever-present infestations of lice and fleas that afflicted the troops in the trenches. In addition to "cooties," the troops also contended with rats. See Farwell, *Over There*, 112; Sherwood, *Diary of a Rainbow Veteran*, 13.

9. Anonymous soldier, quoted in Gilbert, *First World War*, 52.

10. A "40 hommes et 8 chevaux" was a boxcar that carried forty men or eight horses. Traveling in such a fashion was particularly uncomfortable, and soldiers came to despise the experience. See Cooke, *Rainbow Division*, 53; Farwell, *Over There*, 302; Freidel, *Over There*, 46; Marshall, *Memoirs*, 16; Sherwood, *Rainbow Hoosier*, 45; Eisenhower, *Yanks*, 44, 53.

Stopped at Laval for 2 hours. French nurses brought us hot coffee. A train just pulled in loaded to the brim with the 107th Engineers from Wisconsin. They landed at Brest a week ago and were on their way to some camp. Another train pulled in from Verdun filled with French soldiers on leave. They were going home for 10 days after 3½ months of fighting. One of them spoke excellent English. He was from Montreal. His last words to us were "It's a helluva life, boys." The men looked pretty well fagged out and still the boys are "rarin" to go.

Feb. 21, 1918   Didn't sleep well last night. The boxcar rolled and pitched like the devil. Also, sleeping on hard boards isn't the most comfortable thing in the world. The country isn't as hilly as back at camp. Things are beginning to take on the aspects of war. We passed big munition factories, big assembly plants. Here you see big guns, 6" to 15", rifles all out of commish, waiting to be repaired. We had another hand out of hot coffee this morning. Sure reaches the spot. We expect to reach our destination at about 5:00 tomorrow morning. Stopped at Rommely on the Seine for five minutes. Were tendered a big ovation.

Feb. 22, 1918   Washington's birthday and me highballing across France in a boxcar. We've been passing French camps by the score. — Well, we finally arrived, Blainville is the name of the town. Started raining immediately, of course. Hiked H.M.O. for several miles to Dombasle, pretty big place. We are now 12 kil (7 miles) from Luneville, and about fifteen kil. from the front line. We're within easy reach of their guns if they choose to elevate 'em a bit.[11]

11. H.M.O. was a military term for "heavy marching order"; it referred to a circumstance where soldiers equipped themselves for "permanent field service with arms, accouterments, knapsacks, canteen and haversacks." See Farrow, *Dictionary of Military Terms*, 290. The Rainbows referred to Luneville as "Looneyville." The area had been taken by the Germans in 1914; its townspeople were subjected to numerous atrocities and destruction of property. See Gilbert, *First World War*, 52. The combat conditions in the Luneville sector were unlike those throughout much of the western front. As Colonel Henry J. Reilly, commanding officer of the 149th Artillery, put it: "The trenches were not quite what officers and men expected to find. The front was not always continuous." Quoted in Coffman, *War to End All Wars*, 150. See also Cooke, *Rainbow Division*, 53; James, *Years of MacArthur*, 1:154.

Feb. 23, 1918   Slept like a log last night. First real sleep I've had in 3 days. I've washed up at a faucet a half square up the street and feel like a white man again. Haven't had a chance to write home for a week and it may be another week before I get a chance. Hope the folks don't worry. They'll understand, surely.

Feb. 24, 1918   On guard last night at the stables. Pretty soft guard. Had hay to sleep on and that's more than the boys back at the quarters did. The French took the mattresses that were on the bunks and we are waiting for the hay to come so that we can fill our ticks. Till then we sleep on chicken wire. The name of this town is Dombasle and it's a good clean place. Saw several kids with arms and fingers off due to air raids. Kinda makes a fellow grit his teeth to see such things. Several German prisoners were taken yest[erday] and marched through the town to trains. This town is going to be the Regt'l H.Q. and Luneville will be Brig. and Divisional H.Q. Looks as if I won't get any closer to the front than I am right now. Sure hope the col[umn] moves up. Last night while on guard I could hear the guns plainly. They had quite an artillery duel between 7 and 9 and it wasn't target practice, either.

Feb. 25, 1918   A buddie of mine, acting as orderly to a lieutenant that was going to Luneville on business, told me that the road from here to that town is lined with graves and all the small villages are ruins. Says Luneville is a big town, but pretty badly shot up in places.

Feb. 26, 1918   On guard again tonight. Just caught it night before last. Pretty close to one another. Went over to the big Chemical Works in this town to take a hot shower and bath. The bath costs 2 cents and are worth 2 dollars. While waiting my turn I looked up and saw a hundred shrapnel bursts high in the air. Then I made out two planes soaring high in the air. It finally sunk through that thick skull of mine that they were Bosche planes and the French anti-aircraft guns were throwing a barrage around them. Finally, two French planes sailed up and those Germans turned tail and beat it for home. The Frenchmen chased them out of sight and I don't know what the final outcome was. I was in hopes they would mix things right above me, but I was disappointed. — Night — a squadron of Bosche planes just flew over this town on their way to raid Nancy. Nancy is just 12 miles from here and the fifth biggest town in France. I can see the shrapnel bursting, but can not see the planes.

Feb. 29, 1918   Found out that that air raid last night netted the Kaiser 11 victims, two killed and 9 wounded, something he can be proud of! Malcolm Cottingham of the 2nd Bn., stationed some 20 kil. from here, just came in and said the boys there are living like cavemen. Washing in gutters and sleeping in hay mows. Hasn't had his clothes off since he left Camp Coetquidan. We've got a palace compared to those conditions. Well, it all goes up to make this little war, and they do say war is Hell. We haven't signed the payroll yet and it's the last day of the month. I've got 5 francs left to last me to payday and Lord only knows when that will be. We've had nothing but red horse, beans, and hard tack since we left the old camp and I'm getting pretty sick of the menu. I've been going down to the Café de Chevaux Blanc for as many meals as I could, but now my money has dwindled down to a measly dollar, so I guess I'll have to put up with Army grub or starve.

Mar. 1, 1918   First day of March and it celebrates by bringing on a very wet snow. Very miserable outside. Am wrapped around a stove in a café connected with our quarters, but it doesn't throw out a whole lot of heat. Found out that our batteries have pulled into position and by this time are probably helping the big work along. Wonder which battery fired the first shot? Hope A Battery had the honor. Wonder how the boys are faring? I'll sure be glad when the Regiment gets together again so that we can swap experiences. The mail restrictions are more severe than ever now that we're at the front. Can't write a letter home that has a single military sentence in it. Just about leaves a fellow to hello and good-bye and no more![12]

x----------x

12. Once the soldiers reached the Luneville sector, AEF Headquarters placed severe restrictions on communications coming from the units. Diaries were prohibited, also. Obviously, in regard to keeping diaries, large numbers of soldiers (including Kniptash) chose to disregard the order. See Cooke, *Rainbow Division*, 84. Also, the first recorded shot fired by the 150th Field Artillery occurred on March 5, according to Rainbow Veterans Association, *In Memory of the 150th*, 4.

Mar. 2   On guard again last night. Cold and miserable. Plenty of firing between 7 and 12. Have had our wireless up for a couple of days now and have been getting all the news. Also get the medic report every four hours. It gives the windage, temperature, and barometric pressure and is necessary to firing data. We phone it out to the different batteries and they use it in computing their firing data. Had a big surprise just now. Part of the horse detail which left Camp Mills for Newport News just before we sailed for France arrived here today. Ran right into Sgt. [Karl] Moore and believe me it was just like talking to the States to talk to him. He was my old chief of section at Camp Mills and a very good friend of mine. He was granted a furlough while at Newport News and he headed back to Indianapolis and got married. All the boys said they had a wicked trip across. Were 30 days getting across. Had a mutiny in the engine room. Had a German spy on board. Got lost from the convoy. Engines went bad. Floated around for 36 hours at the mercy of old man Neptune. Sprung a leak. Drowned 241 mules. Bailed water for four and ½ days and finally landed in Ireland. Some trip, I claim. They were sure glad to see land. Carl said that, during that 36 hours they were drifting around hopelessly, he never saw as many soldiers reading the Bible at one time in all his life.[13] Capt. Miller paid the Colonel a visit and said that A and B Batteries are having their share of fun. Been working for 36 hours without sleep trying to get their guns into position and mud up to their waists. Said the men are all in. It must be a "hell of a life" as my French Canadian friend said back at Laval.

Mar. 4, 1918   The A Battery horse detail, which quartered here for a couple of days, left this morning for the battery. It is raining and snowing outside. Regt. after Regt. of French soldiers are marching through this town. Their bands usually play that inspiring march piece "Madelon."[14] It is a very stirring sight, but the

---

13. Kniptash refers to Sergeant Moore as Carl. Straub refers to him as Karl, which, according to military records, is accurate; see *Sergeant's Diary*, 53. Byron Farwell recounts the episode to which Kniptash refers in *Over There*, 85. Kniptash's diary entry for March 2, 1918, has been published in Ferrell, *Diary of Elmer Sherwood*, 171n2.

14. Kniptash here refers to a popular song sung by French troops during the war. Madelon was a fictitious young bar mistress who befriended the French soldiers throughout the conflict.

men look weary. It's still snowing. A wet, damp, miserable day. I'm chilled to the bone. Sergeant [Fred] Daniels and Corporal [Frederick] Stratton went out to the 2nd Bn. today and left [Edwin] Whitaker, [Joseph] Haley, and myself in charge of the station. Danny [Fred Daniels] put me in charge. First time I've been boss since I've been in the army. They will be gone for a week, picking up what dope they can.

Mar. 6, 1918   There's going to be something stirring. I can feel it in my bones. We've had two very fine days, and each one of them was marked by air raids. The mayor of Dombasle has posted bulletins all over town and one of my buddies who understands a little French says that the bulletins tell the people just what to do in case they get a hurry up call to evacuate. On every corner you see small groups of excited women, old women shaking their heads very solemnly, and all told there's a certain tenseness in the town that can be seen and felt, but can not be described. These poor people are sure sick of the war.

Mar. 7, 1918   Haley took the storage batteries to Luneville to be re-charged, and, having nothing to do till he got back, I climbed on a bicycle and rode over to St. Nicolas. It is a fairly good-sized town and is known to tourists because it boasts one of the oldest and most beautiful churches in France. This church was built in 1100. It's one of the best examples of architecture I've seen so far. Some of the smaller towns have fallen down and here and there one can see the effects of 700 years of every kind of weather, but as a whole it is wonderfully preserved. I sure thought of V + B while looking at it. They would understand it and appreciate it the way it should be appreciated. When I get back, I intend to pay this town another visit. Mail has been coming in, sack at a time, for the last three days and I've been getting a letter about every two hours. So far, I've collected 12 letters and most of them back letters dated January 9 to 11. However, they're just as welcome as they would be had they come at the proper time. Maude's letters have been read twice so far and after I finish writing this, I'm going to read 'em again. Just about the whitest, truest, bravest little girl in the world. Few fellows are as fortunate as I and she says that I never say in my letters that I wish I could see her again and that I never say that I long for her. I wish I wasn't so damn sensitive and had the heart to write these things in my letters. Lord knows I want to bad enough. I just can't write my real feelings toward her when I know that some flesh and blood censor is going to read the letters before she does. If they would only issue blue envelopes, I'd sure write her just how bad I do miss her. Oh, I'm longing for the time when we'll get to be together again. I sure sing the Blues around here enough. I just finished reading her letter for the third time when the big guns opened up and I came back to France with a bump. I sure was back in Indpls while reading those letters, though. The town "cryer" just beat his drums and made a speech and I was told that he was telling the people to be on the alert. There's going to be something doing around if things pan out the way they look. The Rainbow Division has been under fire for 2 days now and today's paper gave 'em a long write-up. Our Iowa infantry lost 14 men last night.[15]

Mar. 10, 1918   Our Division pulled off a little raid last night. Took some prisoners and brought back some information for the Intelligence Department. Iowa has lost some 19 men so far and New York has lost 16. I don't know how Alabama and Ohio has fared yet. We have had no casualties in the 150th so far and I don't believe Illinois or Minnesota has either.[16] I've collected 24 letters so far and am bubbling now. Last night at 11:00 o'clock all watches were moved up an hour, daylight saving plan.

Mar. 16, 1918   Well, lemesee what's happened worth mentioning. For one thing I took my weekly bath and it wasn't Saturday either. Another, we had an air raid last night. No damage done, but plenty of excitement while it lasted. A machine gun on the hill opened up and it sure sent a death rattle heavenward. The Bosche machine gave it up as a bad job and returned. The Sunset Division (41st) sent us a bunch of men to fill up vacancies in

15. The 3rd Iowa Infantry Regiment was the 168th Infantry Regiment, part of a brigade that also included the 4th Ohio Infantry Regiment, which became the 166th Infantry Regiment; the 4th Alabama Regiment, which became the 167th Infantry Regiment; and the 69th New York Infantry Regiment, which became the 165th Infantry Regiment. See Cooke, *Rainbow Division*, 247–48.

16. The raid on March 9 represented the first military action initiated by the Rainbows. See Coffman, *War to End All Wars*, 150.

our Regiment.[17] Fellows from Oregon, Idaho, Montana, and other Western states. Clean cut, well educated bunch and they were soon at home. Capt. [Edwin G.] Hofmann chose five of them to take up the wireless end of the game and I was elected to teach 'em the ropes. We had to empty the straw out of our ticks and I don't know when we'll get a new issue. Some of the boys have cooties and itch and the medics think the straw is the cause. The French are fumigating the room now. Stinks something fierce. We sleep on chicken wire tonight I guess. So far, I haven't been bothered with cooties and I hope and pray I never will.

Mar. 19, 1918   "Snow" has it that we leave this town in a few days. The Regiment is going to get together again in some town twenty miles from here and, from there, if everything works, we're supposed to hike to rest billets, some 70 miles from that town, where we join our infantry, have divisional maneuvers, and, after a month of this "Boy Scout stuff" we hit the front again and take over a sector.[18] This first trip up to the front has been a glorious success for the Rainbow boys and, with a little more seasoning, we'll be able to hold our own in the noisiest sector of the line. The French were not a bit backward in praising the Division. We had only 2 men wounded that I know of and none were killed. My friend [Charles] Hoover of A Battery was plunked on the forehead by a shrapnel ball while innocently cooking something in the kitchen. The other was a fellow from E Battery and yesterday he had his leg blown off at the knee. "Snow" also has it that our Regt. will be motorized. No more horses. Sounds good, but I guess we poor privates will still have to walk.

Mar. 24, 1918   Got up at 5 bells this morn'. Made packs and got underway at 8 o'clock. Started hiking H.M.O., but covering 5 miles, I relieved myself of everything but the clothes I had on. Covered 12 miles by now. Passed thru several towns where there was not a whole bldg. or house standing. Ruins and desolation at

17. The 41st Division (Sunset Division) was a National Guard unit made up of soldiers from the western states. It arrived in France in December 1917. See Coffman, *War to End All Wars*, 153.

18. Kniptash uses the term "Boy Scout stuff" to differentiate between life in the active sectors and the training done behind the lines.

every turn. Our town named Gerbersville was a mass of ruins. Made 14 miles this afternoon which means 26 for the day. Got to ride about 3 miles this afternoon and that helps some. That sure was an ungodly hike for a man to take when he was in the soft condition I was. The name of this little town is Fontenoy. Ran into the whole A Battery bunch and they were all in too. Had just pulled their guns out of position and hiked here. Got to see "Squirt" Lesh. We had a long talk. Gee, they had some wild stories to tell. I left them at 8:00 o'clock P.M. Washed up and made my bed! Am sleeping in a hayloft and a cow is stationed right under me. I'm so tired this place looks like the Hotel Severin to me. The boys are foot weary and some of their feet are in a bad way, swollen and blistered.[19] We only rested a ½ hour all day. It was almost too much. Don't know how long we stay here, but think it will be just for tomorrow, then we hike out again.

Mar. 26, <u>1918</u>   Well, we spent yesterday here and are still here today. Seems as if we are waiting for orders as to whether we go back to the front or go through rest billets. Saw Hoover today with his head bandaged up. He is recommended for Croix de Guerre.[20] It seems that this shrapnel knocked him out for two minutes and when he came to he walked up to the stove and

---

19. One of the most common complaints and ailments of World War I soldiers in was the problem of "trench foot." As one British writer, Philip Gibbs, described it thus: "Men standing in slime for days and nights in field boots or puttees lost all sense of feeling in their feet. These feet, so cold and wet, began to swell and then go 'dead' and then suddenly burn as though touched by red hot pokers. Battalions lost more men from the fighting line from trench foot than from wounds." See Gilbert, *First World War*, 219. Pete Straub complained of at least the beginnings of this problem in his diary entry of March 1, 1918; *Sergeant's Diary*, 45. Eventually, the men took to rubbing their feet two or three times daily with a special liniment, a treatment that seemed to prove effective. See also Farwell, *Over There*, 112; Marshall, *Memoirs*, 40. During his encounter with Lesh and others, Kniptash informed his Indiana friends about the extent of the German offensive; see Straub, *Sergeant's Diary*, 57–59.

20. Charles Hoover was the first member of the 150th Field Artillery to be wounded in action. He received the Croix de Guerre on April 1, 1918; see Straub, *Sergeant's Diary*, 53, 62. See also Charles Hoover, Roll No. 11, "Hodde, Harry F.— Hunt, Floyd F.," WWI SR. Hoover's service record documents that he was slightly wounded in action on March 16, 1918; it also notes that he received the Croix de Guerre but does not include the date. The Croix de Guerre was the most common of the French war decorations; see Gilbert, *First World War*, 234.

went on cooking slum just as if stopping shrapnel with one's fore-head was an every day occurrence with him.[21] It took guts and he earned the medal. Our communiqués tell us that the Bosche have started their much talked of "drive to Paris" business. It started Mar. 21 and, although he's gaining considerable ground, he's losing a terrible number of men doing it. They are pulling that old "wave" formation stuff and the French and English are mowing them down. Don't know when the offensive will come to a halt, but feel confident they will never reach Paris.

The Bosche has a new gun that has a range of 75 miles.[22] He is firing on Paris with it. Another attempt to frighten the French people into submission. That's a Hell of a poor way to go at it in my opinion. It will only tend to make them fight the harder.

Mar. 27, 1918   All kinds of "snow" flying around. Some say we are going up on the English front and help out. Others say that we will take over another quiet sector and relieve a couple of French Divisions so that they can go up there. That seems more logical to me because the French could handle it a whole lot better than we could.

21. The word "slum" refers to "slumgullion" stew, from the Irish. "Slum" con-sisted of a concoction of canned willy plus a mixture of vegetables. See Cooke, *Rainbow Division*, 29; Farwell, *Over There*, 302. In his memoir, Kenneth G. Baker, a Hoosier serving in the Wisconsin National Guard unit, described "slum" in the fol-lowing way:

Take a 35 or 40 gallon GI can, fill it about ⅓ full of water, preferably clean, and heat to boil. Into this put 40 or 50 lbs. of chopped up beef in chunks about bite size, to some as big as your fist, about half a bushel of potatos [*sic*] (this is the amount left over from a bushel, after a KP has peeled a bushel) these are cut into bite sizes also. Then [add] carrots and onions and any other vegetables that may be laying around. You boil this mess until a potato feels more or less soft. Then, you take a large iron skillet, put in a good supply of lard, melt it and get it hot, then add a goodly supply of flour to the grease and heat over hot fire, stirring vigorously until the flour is brown and dump into the boiling mess in this GI can. The result is a brown, gooey mess that will stick to your ribs, mess plate, clothes, or anything else it happens to touch. (Ferrell, "'Oatmeal and Coffee,'" 33)

22. This German gun was the fabled "Big Bertha," one of three specially man-ufactured weapons designed to hurl artillery shells over vast distances. The first of Big Bertha's shells was fired at 7:16 A.M. on March 23; it landed in Paris, thirty miles away, four minutes later. See Gilbert, *First World War*, 407; Keegan, *First World War*, 406. Also, as John Eisenhower has noted, the Germans amassed more artillery power for this offensive than in any prior action on the western front; *Yanks*, 105.

Mar. 27, 1918   Wednesday and we're still here. The German
offensive is still going on and they are gaining ground, but their
losses of manpower balances the scales. Haven't heard anymore
about moving.

Mar. 29, 1918   Everything was hustle and bustle this morning. We
were going to hike to Baccarat and when everything was loaded
and the men ready to move the order came down that we would
not move till tomorrow. Cussing on all sides.

Mar. 30, 1918   We got up at 5, breakfast at 6, and we're on our way
at 7. Got into Baccarat at 9 and it's quite a fair sized town. It's
badly shot up in some places. The Bosche captured it in 1916.
Regt'l H.Q. will be here, so I guess this is where I'm billeted for
some time.

Mar. 31, 1918   Easter Sunday and a rainy one at that. Stayed inside
our attic all morning and in the afternoon. Sgt. Daniels and
myself went out to find a room for our wireless station. Found an
old madame who had a big attic to rent and we took her up. Set
up the station immediately. We will sleep here too. One of the
largest glassworks in the world is located in this town. Makes a
specialty of cut glass. An old church across the river was hit pretty
hard, but the clock in the spire kept right on running. It's a freak.
The German offensive is still raging. They continue to advance,
but it's proving costly to them.

April 6, 1918   It's been just one year ago today that the U.S.
entered the war and she sure made wonderful strides. In another
year her weight will be the deciding factor and I'm sure the
higher ups in the German Army realize it. They are making a
grand stand play now in the hopes that they can accomplish their
end before America is strong enough to take hold. She'll fail
because I know the French soldier and his love for Paris. They
won't get to Paris and I'm as sure of that as I am that the Bosche
is going to come in at the short end of this war. The old lady that
owns this house tells some nice tales about the Germans when
they occupied Baccarat in 1916. She stuck thru the whole affair.
Said it was terrible. There were 200 German soldiers quartered
in this house alone and the town was run over by 20,000 of them.
The French were on the other side of the river and their
trenches are still there. She said the German officers beat and

cursed the men and dragged them around till they were scared to death. When the French finally drove them out, they demolished the sewage system in this house and carried off her silverware. She had a man and wife staying with her at the time and they took this man's wife away with them and they claim that everything they do is just because it has military value. I don't think they draw the line very sharply.[23]

April 7, 1918   Bosche aviators came over this morning and dropped some bombs. No damage done. A H-E shell from a French anti-aircraft gun failed to explode in the air and lit about 50 ft. from our station.[24] Made a terrific report and scattered fragments everywhere. That's the closest shave I've had so far and it's a joke compared to what some of the other boys are going through. Received three packages today; two cartons of Camels from Fred and Dot, a box of cakes and a carton of Camels from Bruck and John, and a can of cakes and jelly from Mumsey. Some joy day. Now for some letters thanking them.

Apr. 15   Working hard these days. Making a new tuning coil and haven't had a chance to get around much. The coil is sure a peach for a homemade one and represents many hours of begging, stealing, and hard work. Was talking to the man who had his wife abducted in 1916. He took us down to his room and showed us her picture. First time I've ever seen him sad. Said he used to get letters from her, but lately he has had no word. He is hoping for the best. This man is typical of all France. Under heavy sacrifices they are still chipper and confident as to the final outcome. A fellow can't help but admire them.[25] Our wireless

---

23. The Baccarat sector, like Luneville, had been the scene of fierce fighting between the Germans and the French throughout the war. Like Luneville, Baccarat, in the words of James Cooke, "attracted the seamier side of war—cheap bars, prostitutes, and speculators"; the Rainbows sustained an increase in their reported cases of venereal disease, and Division Headquarters staff came down hard on the offenders. See Cooke, *Rainbow Division*, 80; see also James, *Years of MacArthur*, 1:164.

24. "H-E" stands for high-explosive shell.

25. Kniptash's attitude toward the French was typical of Americans' sentiments toward their ally. At the time, most Americans considered France as a democratic, republican nation, like the United States, unlike the other monarchies that still existed throughout Europe. See Bruce, *Fraternity of Arms*, xvi. Carl Hixon, another member of the Headquarters Company of the 150th Field Artillery, was also highly

work is interesting, although a grind. We keep station open day and night and are working in reliefs of four hours on and eight hours off. Have to get the weather reports every four hours and keep an ear open for any S.O.S. that might come. We are now catching the communiqués from every country in Europe. We are ambitious to catch the States.

x----x

Apr. 28, 1918   We're going to pull off a little party in this sector in a few days.[26] The road through Baccarat leading to the front is lined with guns, ammunitions, trucks, and supplies. French Marines are installing their big naval guns. We are going to try and find out how much the Bosche robbed this sector down here to get men for his drive to Paris, and also try to avert his attention down this way in hopes that it may slacken the pressure farther north.

April 30, 1918   Everything is tense. Tomorrow at 1:15 the artillery opens up and keeps firing steadily till May 3. Then 700 doughboys are going over and finish what the artillery missed.[27] It is the first time that the 42nd Division has taken the initiative on its own foot. It means make or break and the boys are satisfied that it will be <u>make</u>.

---

complimentary of the French. "We made very good friends with the French soldiers," Hixon recalled. "A French corporal taught me French [and] I taught him English through the medium of German." Carl Hixon, Military Survey, World War I, September 22, 1983, U.S. Army Military History Institute, Carlisle Barracks, Pennsylvania, 8.

26. Kniptash often used the word "party" to describe any type of offensive undertaken by the Rainbows. The term might refer to a small raid, a minor skirmish, or a major encounter.

27. The term "doughboy" originally applied to American infantrymen in World War I but later was used to describe any American soldier. The origin of the term may be traced back to the Philippine insurrection during the early years of the twentieth century when American infantrymen would be covered with dust after long marches on dusty roads in the oppressive heat and humidity of the jungle. The thick dust that was caked to the soldiers resembled flour—hence the term "doughboys." As Thomas Fleming explained, British and French newspapermen referred to American troops as "Sammies" at the outset of U.S. involvement in the war. General Pershing disapproved of that term, however, and instructed the U.S. Army newspaper *Stars and Stripes* to refer to American troops as doughboys. See Fleming, *Illusion of Victory*, 123; Farwell, *Over There*, 304.

May 1, 1918   At 1:15 to the second all the guns opened up as one gun. We gave them the correct time and all the watches were synchronized. They are firing at regular intervals and there's never a lull. This eve a Bosche plane came over to find out what made us so angry, but our anti-aircraft guns chased him back. Our bunch is working with Brigade wireless and the two of us are working with the Division plane. It scouts around looking for unexpected targets and reports by wireless to Brigade.[28] Our bunch is running the panels. The guns kept it up all last night.

May 2, 1918   Still at it this morning and going strong.

May 3, 1918   Thru up an intense barrage at 4 A.M. and the doughs went over. Don't know the results yet.

May 4, 1918   Our little party yielded plenty of information, but few prisoners. All trenches and dugouts were smashed and several Bosche taken that proved they had stolen heavily in this sector to furnish men up north.[29]

May 7, 1918   We are expecting the Bosche to return the reception we handed him but don't know just what day he's chosen.

May 27, 1918   Several things have happened since the last writing. A counter attack by the Bosche put 44 E Battery men in the hospital. Victims of gas. The attack was repulsed. Things here are fairly quiet.

The wireless boys have been very busy building a wireless set and right now it is completed with the exception of one condenser. It's quite a neat looking job. We turned in our overcoats, two blankets, rubber boots, and bed ticks this morning. This looks as if we're going to do some tall soldiering this summer. There's talk of our moving any day now and we know we got a three day train ride ahead of us. That looks as if we're going to help in

28. In his position as a wireless operator, Kniptash personally encountered one of the significant tactical innovations of World War I—that is, using aircraft and balloons to communicate with the ground forces for the targeting of artillery fire. See Cooke, *Rainbow Division*, 85.

29. The results of the Rainbow Division's raid on May 2–3 showed that the Germans had moved soldiers from the Baccarat sector, probably to combat positions closer to Paris. The Germans were essentially holding off the Rainbows with artillery fire and gas, with horrifying consequences for the Americans. See Cooke, *Rainbow Division*, 89.

some sector up north. General Pershing was in town today, but I didn't get to see him. The Bosche pulled off a little party last night and our Div. suffered 200 casualties as a result. We're going to give 'em Hell tonight to the tune of 30,000 gas shells. The guns are firing now.[30]

June 1, 1918   The order for our moving was cancelled so we stay here three weeks longer anyway. Went up to the $2^{\underline{nd}}$ $B^{\underline{n}}$ yesterday and heard the shells whine, great life up there, plenty (of) gas and lots of excitement. Another big German offensive has started and things are pretty serious. The French division that was to relieve us had to stay where they were and fight.

x---x

June 20, 1918   Several things have happened since the last writing. The Marines got a big write-up because of their work at Belleau Wood close to Chateau-Thierry. The wireless station now ranks a sending set. We're going to move out of here either this afternoon or tonight. The biggest part of our division, with the exception of the heavy artillery has already left. The 77th Div., the first draft division to reach France, is going to relieve us. They hail from little old New York and that's all they talk about. Their artillery is still in training so a French brigade is going to take care of the big gun work. When we came to Baccarat three months ago we saw pictures of these drafted boys in the New York Herald. Showed 'em marching down Fifth Avenue cheered by enthusiastic crowds. They landed here in April and from the way they blow about themselves it would lead us to believe that they've been over here ever since the war started.

The Rainbow boys told 'em a few things to help 'em out but they knew it all, didn't need any pointers, said they could take care of the Bosche alright. Last night a long column of them, four regiments, passed our station on the way up to the trenches for the

---

30. Ibid., 90–91. The German attack on May 25–26 on the Rainbow Division trenches was especially fierce and resulted in numerous American casualties. The Americans were surprised by the German assault, and though they repulsed it, they paid heavily. Troops who suffered from the gas attacks were in particularly serious condition. German activity was heightened during this period, in preparation for another major offensive that was to come six weeks later. See Marshall, *Memoirs*, 94, 99.

first time. They tried to kid us but didn't have much luck. They yelled, "Fall in line and fight for your Uncle." I called back, "You fellows ought to have come over when the soldiers did," and they shut up like a clam. They went up singing but it's an easy matter to sing on the first time up. If they can keep it up I'll hand it to 'em but right now they look like very poor soldiers to me.[31] The 1st American Army is about formed now and the Rainbow Div. is part of the 1st Army Corps. I think the 1st Army Corps comprises the 1st, 2nd, 26th, 28th, 32nd and 42nd divisions. It's quite an honor. The French division that is relieving us and at the same time doing the Artillery work for the 77th is the one that was supposed to relieve us three weeks ago. The offensive came up and they had to stay on the Somme. They lost three out of every four men but they held the Bosche. They had about 2500 men left in the division when the offensive finally petered out yet they came singing into Baccarat. Lord, but these French are soldiers.

The Americans are sure strong for them. That same feeling is felt by the French toward the Americans.[32] Differences in language

31. There was a natural rivalry between the 165th Infantry Regiment (National Guard) and the 77th Division (National Army) since both came from New York. The soldiers in the 165th obviously believed that they were military superiors to the draftees in the 77th. Edward Coffman gives a version of the scene on June 20: "On one moonlit night in June, [the 77th] passed the Rainbow Division behind the lines. As the columns marched past in opposite directions the soldiers in the 77th and the New York Irish (the 165th) regiment yelled out their sections of the city and listened for response. Inevitably someone started singing 'Sidewalks of New York' and one man in the 77th sighted his brother in the Rainbow." *War to End All Wars*, 258. See also Slotkin, *Lost Battalions*, 160–61.

32. Kniptash gives an accurate description of the close relationship that existed between the French and American soldiers. Pierre Teilhard de Chardin, a French soldier in World War I who became a prominent author and theologian in the 1920s and 1930s, offered an opinion of the Americans: "We had the Americans as neighbors, and I had a close-up view of them. Everyone says the same: they're first-rate troops, fighting with intense *individual* passion (concentrated on the enemy) and wonderful courage. The only complaint one would make about them is that they don't take sufficient care; they're too apt to get themselves killed. When they're wounded, they make their way back, holding themselves upright, almost stiff, impassive, and uncomplaining. I don't think I've ever seen such dignity and pride in suffering. There's complete comradeship between them and us, born fully-fledged under fire." Quoted in Coffman, *War to End All Wars*, 246; see also Farwell, *Over There*, 185–86. In another valuable account, historian Robert Bruce notes, "American soldiers respected the experience and professionalism of their

and customs offer no barriers to that sort of friendship. — Sent 20 dollars home to Mumsey today.

June 23, 1918   We're resting here in Hallainville for a couple of days and tonight we leave for Charmes. There we entrain and leave for a real live fort. Made the hike from Baccarat to here, 20 miles, in about 5 hours. Albert [Wright] and myself are the only two to finish with packs on our backs. We started at 7 in the morning and got here at midnight. I was so tired I was numb. Tonight we take a 16 kil. hike to Charmes. Gen. Pershing was in town today. First time I've ever had a chance to see him. We were at mess and when he steamed through we all snapped to attention. He held his salute till he had passed the last man. He's every inch a soldier.

June 24, 1918   Highballing across again in a "Hommes 40, Chevaux 8". Hiked to Charmes last night (16 kil.). Started at 6 P.M. and at 4 A.M. the train was landed and loaded and pulled out. There are 19 in this boxcar. Passed thru Nancy and Toul and are headed for Neuf-Chateau. Don't know whether we're going to Chateau-Thierry or not. Maybe going to Italy for all I know. Care less. Finally, put on the brakes at Chalons-Sur-Marne. A big town, but practically deserted because of Bosche air raids. Unloaded in quick order and hiked 22 kil. to this town of <u>Dampier</u>. Have carried my pack all the way now since Baccarat and, believe me, it's a grind. Understand that dismounted men don't have to answer stables anymore. It's no more than fair. This idea of going to stables week in, week out, grooming and taking care of horses and then when a move is made have the privates walk and carry packs while the sergeants and corporals ride isn't what it's cracked up to be. Got some new "snow" that the 42nd Div. will be a shock division and will be attached to the 1st Army Corps, stay back of the lines fighting a "boy scout" war till some trouble on the line needs attention. Then we pull in, put on the grips, and pull out. Sure hope this is "snow" and not the truth.

French trainers, and the French admired the enthusiasm and fighting ability of the American soldiers. Many of the Americans developed close personal friendships with their French counterparts." *Fraternity of Arms*, xvi, xvii.

June 27   Left camp today with Sgt. Daniels and Cpl. Stratton and came to St. Jermaine. We came here for a ten day school in radio, and no sooner had pulled in, than we were told the school had closed and that we were to stay here and move out with the Signal Corps. Understand that the school will open again at some little town back of Reims. Started hiking at 9:00 o'clock P.M. and reached Vadena at 3:00 o'clock A.M. The hike totaled 27 kil. and the boys were all in. I hiked so much lately that 27 kil. is getting to be a little saunter to me.

June 28, 1918   Rested all day today. Some of the boys' feet are in pretty bad shape. School starts tomorrow.

June 29, 1918   Started school this morning and at 10:00 o'clock we were told that it was again called off and we were to report to our organizations. Hopped in a truck for a change and came to this berg of Sommeville. Lord only knows where we go from here. This business of being held in Reserve is sure strenuous on the private soldiers. I've walked 80 miles since Baccarat with a 60 lb. pack on my back. However, I'm hardening up to it now and it doesn't bother me much. Boys say we pull out of here tonight.

July 4, 1918   The glorious fourth and we celebrate it by hiking 24 kil. The telephone and radio details pulled out at noon and the rest follow tonight. Reached this place at 9 o'clock P.M. Immediately set up communications. We are a few miles out of Suippes and in country where civilians are not allowed to stay. The country is fine for tanks and open warfare. The French are expecting the 5th offensive to strike here.

July 5, 1918   Had a gas alarm last night, but it fizzled out. Our division is the only one east of Reims and we are part of Gen. Gouraud's 4th Army. He's a one-armed general, and greatly beloved by the men under his command.[33]

33. General Henri Gouraud commanded the French 4th Army, and the 42nd Division was placed under his command in preparation for what would be the fifth, and final, German offensive of 1918. Gouraud had lost an arm in the fighting at Gallipoli earlier in the war, and he soon became a favorite of the American troops. After the war, he became the honorary president of the Rainbow Veterans Association. See Cooke, *Rainbow Division*, 97–98; Farwell, *Over There*, 177–80. By this point, the Rainbows had moved to the Champagne sector and had been holding the sector for more than a hundred consecutive days, a record for U.S. troops

July 8, 1918   Moved our station to a big dugout last night. Haven't had 10 hours sleep in 3 days. The wireless communications works O.K. This is a very large dugout, capable of sheltering 2,000 men. It's 60 ft. underground and has rooms and cots. The boys are sleeping back in cantonments, but in case of a bombardment, are to come here.

x---x

July 13   This sector up here is the Champagne sector and before the war was used by the French Army as a review ground and for maneuvering. Many historic battles have taken place here. The sector to our left, west of Reims, is catching Hell all the time. Big barrages every so often. Our sector was moving the first night, but there's been a lull ever since.

July 14, 1918   Bastille day in France and it was like any other day for the boys at the front. Those back of the lines got a holiday, but not us. Got to read a notice Gen. Menoher sent out to the officers of the 42nd Div. and there's sure going to be Hell popping in a couple of days. The bulletin started out by saying that the 5th German offensive was not even trying to be kept secret by the Bosche.[34] The French have got all the dope in regards to the number of men facing them, the size of the guns, etc. Gave the names of the Divisions and it showed that Germany has her best troops in this sector. The Austrians have pulled up several batteries of "minniewurfers" (about 30.5 mm). The 5th German offensive will cover a front of 60 kil. The objectives are Chalons, Epernay, and Reims. We're in a direct line to Chalons so we'll see our share of the fun. While our Artillery will take care of theirs, and I'll let our doughboys from Alabama, New York, Illinois, and Iowa take care of all the Prussian Guards the Kaiser's got. It takes

---

in France. See Cooke, *Rainbow Division*, 93; Straub, *Sergeant's Diary*, 97; Bruce, *Fraternity of Arms*, 227.

34. In reality, the Americans had captured several German prisoners-of-war who revealed the plans of the German offensive. Gouraud had devised a masterful plan of "defense-in-depth" where the first line of trenches was lightly manned to confuse the German attackers. The French and the Rainbows began making their preparations for the offensive on July 6–7, and then they waited. See Cooke, *Rainbow Division*, 103; James, *Years of MacArthur*, 1:174–77; Sherwood, *Rainbow Hoosier*, 74.

more than a Prussian Guard to beat an Alabama dough.[35] The date of the offensive is given as close to July 15 according to the statements of German prisoners taken today. We moved back to a smaller dugout. Have the stations set up in there, but are sleeping out in pup tents. Taking a big chance, but such is open warfare. We got a good view of the front from here and I never saw so many guns masked before. Every step you take you run into a battery. There's no attempt at camouflage. The orders are to fight till the last man, and in no case, to let the Bosche through. Everything is tense, waiting for things to start.[36]

July 15, 1918   At 12:17 this morning the German Artillery opened up as one gun. We had been bombarding them for two hours and when they joined in on the chorus the noise was deafening. I'm sure I'll never hear the like again if this war lasts 30 years. It kept up till 5:30 A.M. and then the German Infantry came over the top. In the meantime the French and American infantry had dropped back to intermediate positions and the Bosche was unaware of it. He did a good job of destroying our frontline trenches and, of course, so he reasoned, had killed all the Infantry we had. Their Infantry came over in three huge waves and our 75's machine guns and trench mortar batteries fired at 'em point blank. The first wave was just naturally killed standing

---

35. The Alabama Regiment, the 167th Infantry, had the task of meeting the first wave of German attackers. Kniptash was correct: their foes were the German army's elite Prussian Guards, and the "Bloody Alabams" were more than equal to the task. The Alabama regiment also had a swagger characteristic of its reputation as a unit of ruthless killers. See Farwell, *Over There*, 114. After the battle ended, one Alabama soldier wrote home: "All you can cheer up and wear a smile. I'm a little hero now. I got two of the rascals." Cooke, *Rainbow Division*, 111. See also Farwell, *Over There*, 174; Straub, *Sergeant's Diary*, 126. Kniptash's reference to "minniewurfers," or "minnen-wurfer," meant a German-made, muzzle-loading trench mortar. See Farwell, *Over There*, 303.

36. Cooke, *Rainbow Division*, 105. Through an interrogation of a German prisoner, Gouraud learned the exact time of the beginning of the German offensive, a few minutes past midnight on July 15. Gouraud devised a code, "Francois 570," that he gave to his subordinate commanders, indicating that the attack was imminent. The Rainbow headquarters received the code on the afternoon of July 14. In response, the 150th regiment opened fire on German positions at 11:30 P.M. on July 14. See Sherwood, *Rainbow Hoosier*, 74; Coffman, *War to End All Wars*, 223–24; and "Log Book, June 4–October 10, 1918" in 120/AEF/42/FA, Box 38.

up. They came over shoulder to shoulder and couldn't find room to fall down. The second and third waves suffered the same fate. Then our doughboys went out and took prisoners or finished up the ones that the artillery didn't get. It's the first time since the war started that a big offensive ended without a foot being gained. Shells have been landing fairly close. One killed a horse about 100 feet away.

Air battles galore and I saw one French aviator bring down eight sausage balloons in one afternoon. The offensive has stopped so far as the Germans are concerned. They've decided that, after all, they'll let the French keep Paris. Six New York boys were killed by a shell on the spot where our station used to be. Could have been us just as easy.

x---x

July 16, 1918   I've read some official reports of the battle. The German offensive was a complete failure. They made one slight advance west of Reims. In this place they gained some 8 kil. on a 4 kil. front but were met at the point by an American division who not only chased them back, but chased them back three kil.! Farther than the point where they started. On the rest of the 60 kil. front, they didn't gain a foot and they lost an enormous bunch of men for their trouble. We pull off a little raid tonight. I'm on shift now (11:45) and a squadron of Bosche avions just came over to hinder our bringing up reinforcements. They flew low and fired their machine guns at our men. Also dropped several bombs.

July 17   Our little raid netted us 58 prisoners and "beaucoups" information.[37]

July 18   Have read the final, official bulletins about our work. Said it's the biggest defeat the Bosche has suffered since the first Battle of the Marne. The main attack was delivered in our sector. Our Artillery and Infantry broke up all formations. One whole German Division was completely massacred before the real battle began.

37. *Beaucoup* is a French word that, simply translated, means "much" or "a lot of" something.

The Rainbow Division has gained a better rep. than the Marines ever will earn.[38] Our Artillery kept the German tanks from reaching their own frontline, letting alone coming across to ours. Our 117th Trench Mortar battery got five tanks by direct hits. The French Blue Devils (cheaussers) [sic] stopped dead in their tracks with their eyes like saucers and mouths wide open and watched our doughboys go after 'em. The spirit of their fighting was contagious and the Blue Devils fought doubly hard. The French morale has gone up a 100%, and the 42nd is A-number one in their eyes.[39] Now Gen. Foch has started another row.[40] A big Allied counter-offensive has started at Chateau-Thierry with the 26th Div. opening up. The communiqué makes no bones in saying that it was due to the 4th Army's efforts (and we are all a part of that Army) that this counter-offensive is possible. The boys are tickled to death and hoping that the higher-ups decided

38. Like most Rainbows, Kniptash had little respect for the Marine Corps, believing that the marines had embellished their initial combat with the Germans in early June in the battle for Belleau Wood. The marines of the 2nd Division and the Rainbows jousted verbally repeatedly during their time in France. See Cooke, *Rainbow Division*, 97; Coffman, *War to End All Wars*, 214–22; Farwell, *Over There*, 169, 172, 176; James, *Years of MacArthur*, 1:176–81.

39. The significance of repulsing the German offensive was noted immediately by the Americans. Elmer Sherwood wrote of the German failure as "the Kaiser's Waterloo"; *Rainbow Hoosier*, 74. See also Straub, *Sergeant's Diary*, 126. For the 150th, the fighting on July 15–16 was terrific. As its semiofficial history recorded, the 150th "fired as it never had before, continuously for fourteen hours until the word came that the Germans had failed and withdrawn"; Rainbow Veterans Association, *In Memory of the 150th*, 5. George C. Marshall considered the German failure in mid-July as the "turning point of the war." Quoted in Farwell, *Over There*, 184. The ferocity of the American resistance was not lost on the Germans, either. In his journal entry for July 15, 1918, the German officer Kurt Hesse made the notation, "The American . . . had nerve; we must give him credit for that; but he also displayed a savage roughness. 'The Americans kill everybody!' was the cry of terror of July 15th, which for a long time stuck in the bones of our men." Eisenhower, *Yanks*, 161. As a final note, Major General Charles T. Menoher, commanding officer of the 42nd Division, praised the Rainbows for their action in "crush[ing] the German assault"; see letter, Charles T. Menoher To The Officers and Men of the 42nd Division, August 13, 1918, Kniptash family files (see fig. 12).

40. Marshal Ferdinand Foch, commanding general of the French armies, was placed in command of all Allied forces on March 26, 1918. Following the failure of the German offensive in mid-July, Foch launched a counterattack on July 18. See Gilbert, *First World War*, 442; Cooke, *Rainbow Division*, 118.

to send us up there to help out. A Bosche avion came over last night and dropped eight bombs and I was the closest man to 'em. I was just hitting dreamland when the first one fell. The last one hit just 100 steps from my pup tent and dirt and fragments covered the tent. I flattened out thinner than the blanket wrapped around me and hoped for the best. The best finally came when the Bosche finally made up his mind to return and the dying out sound of his motor as he got farther away was the best thing my ears have heard since they've been in the Army.

July 19   The Bosche is still retreating. Has evacuated Vaux and Chateau-Thierry.[41] We moved to a small camp today and it looks very peaceful and gives me visions of a much needed rest.

July 20, 1918   A good night's sleep last night and I feel panilla this morn. Saw [Elliot B.] "Doc" Hadley this morn. He went up to an Officer's Training School and got a 2nd Lieut. commission, but lucky enough to get assigned to this Regt. again. Lots of the sergeants have gone to this school, but he's the first one to come back. Looks snappy. The "snow" is that we go to Chateau-Thierry and help in the big push.

---

41. Actually, the American 2nd Division had successfully taken positions at Vaux (but not Château-Thierry) on July 1. See Farwell, *Over There*, 173. See also "Daily Operations Reports 1918, May 10–June 20," in RG 201/AEF/42/FA, Box 38, for reports on military activity during this period.

CHAPTER 3

From Château-Thierry to the Armistice, July 21–November 11, 1918

Life's just a bubble, don't cher know,
Full of trials and troubles, don't cher know,
You can only wear one tie
And one eyeglass in your eye
And have one coffin when you die,
Don't cher know.

From Sherwood, *Diary of a Rainbow Veteran*

AFTER PARTICIPATING IN THE SUCCESSFUL EFFORT TO stop the fifth German offensive in mid-July 1918, the Rainbow Division began to move out from the lines that they held in the so-called Champagne defensive on July 18, 1918. By July 21, the Rainbows had received their orders to join the French 6th Army to participate in the new offensive scheduled against the Germans along the Marne.

By this time, the Rainbows, Vernon Kniptash included, were near exhaustion from battle fatigue. Yet there was to be no rest, not until the Allied armies finally had pushed back the German forces to the point where an Armistice was declared and the fighting came to a stop. For the Rainbows, bitter fighting still lay ahead—at Château-Thierry in July and August where they sustained their worst casualties of the war; then in the action at the Saint-Mihiel salient in September; and then in October in the Meuse-Argonne offensive.

During this four-month period, Kniptash revealed a variety of emotions in his diary entries. He recorded moments of great exhil-

Epigraph. Taken from an American song popular on the western front. Sherwood, *Diary of a Rainbow Veteran*, 101.

aration, as when he understood that the Allied forces had forced the Germans into retreat. He betrayed moods of skepticism, as when he learned of the prospect that Germany's allies—Austria-Hungary, the Ottoman Empire, and Bulgaria—were about to pull out of the war. He wrote of the fear that enveloped him when his unit came under intense German artillery fire and aerial bombardment. He wrote proudly of the skills he was developing as a practitioner of communications and of the combat effectiveness of the Rainbow Division. He wrote movingly of the wretched conditions faced by the soldiers as they battled not only the German enemy but also mud, rain, lice, disease, and the squalor of life on the western front. During this period, Kniptash continued to encounter the death and destruction caused by the war. During periods of low morale, Kniptash was sustained by the knowledge that the Allies were poised to end the war victoriously and that the fighting would not last indefinitely.

July 21, 1918   Hike to Chalons this morning. Entrained and we're on the way at 3:00 o'clock P.M. Traveled all night and reached a point 2 kil. out of Paris at 2:00 o'clock P.M.. Got orders there and speeded up toward Chateau-Thierry way. Good bye Paris! It's about as close as I'll ever get to you. Got off at Lizy-sur-Ourcq. Hiked to Dhiesy. The French civilian population evacuated in a hurry and everything is just as they left it.

x-----------------------------x

July 23   Still here and don't know when we leave. Chateau-Thierry is 20 kil. farther up. I think we are being held in Reserve.

July 26, 1918   Hiked to Chateau-Thierry this morning. Reached there at noon. Passed through Vaux and there's not a wall standing. I saw my first dead German soldier there. He was about five days dead then. Chateau-Thierry was pretty badly shot up in places, but altogether got out of it pretty lucky. Saw "beaucoup" Bosche material here; guns, ammunition, etc. Hiked to Belleau Woods this afternoon and are now camping on a spot that the Marines fought so hard for.[1]

1. During their march to Château-Thierry, the Rainbows routinely passed troops from other units. As the soldiers passed, they asked each other the identity

July 27, 1918   Moved up closer, i.e., the telephone and wireless gang, to a big shell torn chateau. Bosche dead everywhere. Material galore. Grabbed onto a Bosche cart and will use it to haul our wireless material and packs from now on in.

July 28, 1918   Moved up still closer to this shattered town of Beauvardes. Are about 4 kil. from the front now. Have had several narrow escapes. They are shelling this town. If it gets much hotter, we will have to move out. There is no protection. Our immediate objective is Fere-en-Tardenois and our final one is Fismes-on-the-Vesle. We are steadily pushing them back, but their resistance has increased considerably. Lieut. [Jesse] Fletcher's horse was just killed by a shell. That happened about 30 ft. from where I was standing. I fell on my belly "toute de suite" and spare parts flew thither and yon hunting some place to plant themselves. I've been ducking shells for three hours now and it's getting hotter every minute. — Well, they finally made it so hot for us we had to move. Dropped back ¼ of a kil. to a couple of houses and a barn and established the P.C. there.[2] We were sure lucky to get out of that mess with a whole skin. Have seen some awful sights. Waste and desolation everywhere. Dead horses. Dead Americans. Dead Germans. Ambulances tearing back filled with wounded. Long columns of German prisoners under the guard of a couple of M.P.'s trudging back. Air battles every minute of the day. Stacks and piles of Bosche ammunition. Saw one stack of 105's that was one square and a half long, 16 feet wide, and 8 feet high. Under every bush and tree was a stack of shells. Then there was guns ranging from 210's down to 77's and thousands of machine guns. It has been a rich haul so far and the booty will grow larger as we push 'em back. There is only one road leading to the front and it is jammed terribly. Two columns of troops, guns, and supplies going forward and one column of empty wag-

---

of their divisions. "What outfit?" one soldier asked. "42nd," came the reply. Then, another reply, "Oh, Rainbow, now there'll be some hell raised." Sherwood, *Rainbow Hoosier*, 81. See also *Diary of a Rainbow Veteran*, 37; James, *Years of MacArthur*, 1:183, 185; Ferrell, *Diary of Elmer Sherwood*, 62.

2. "P.C." is an abbreviation for the French phrase "poste de command," or command post.

ons and loaded ambulances going back. Bosche avions come over every so often and sweep from one end of the road to the other, dropping bombs and shooting their machine guns. They are doing no damage, however, and the boys have fun shooting their rifles and pistols at them. We had a flock of them come over when we were at Beauvardes and shoot machine guns at us. They flew so low that the Iron Cross on the bottom of the wings looked as big as a ten acre field. The boys had all confiscated German rifles and we formed an anti-aircraft battery. We had a picnic answering the fire of those Bosche avions.

Aug. 4   Since the last writing things have been more or less a nightmare and I don't remember any of the events in the order in which they occurred. It's been days of fighting and nights of hiking. We just can't keep up with the Bosche; he's retreating so fast. A night hike is terrible. The roads are jammed with traffic and when the column does move it's a snail-like affair. A kilometer an hour is good time. You walk ten minutes and then you're held up for twenty. It's sure aggravating, to say the least. Men are continually getting lost from their organizations and there's confusion everywhere. The nearer you approach the fighting, the worse these conditions become. Here the Bosche try to come as close as possible to the road without hitting it. It's anything but pleasant but it's a whole lot better to know that you're moving forward and not backward. I can't imagine retreating, the confusion must be doubled. We stopped at Sergy. Our fire didn't leave a house standing. Every place strewn with dead, both friendly and unfriendly. Can see Fere-en-Tardenois from here and it is in the same condition. We started to establish our P.C. and found out that the Bosche was out of range. We moved, as a consequence, to a farm 5 kilometers nearer where they ought to be. There we found out again that we were out of range. Just can't keep up with those "Kultur boys."[3] We moved up another five kil. and are going to establish Regtl. H.Q.'s at this big farm. Known as Chateau Farm. That makes three moves in

3. Here the German term *Kultur* (culture) refers mockingly to the alleged superiority of German civilization as contrasted with that of the French, British, or Americans.

one night and I'm all in. Shells have been dropping around us at regular intervals, but I'm not too tired to pay much attention to them. We put up our station in a downpour of rain. Getting supplies to us is proving the big problem and we're lucky if we get our three a day. Now that we have Fere-en-Tardenois (which, by the way, was captured by our division) conditions ought to better themselves considerably. Although there is only one road leading to it, there are three from there up to where we are. So that will divide the traffic three ways.[4]

Aug. 6   Still fighting like Hell and no relief in sight. The boys are dead tired. Our doughboys were relieved when they captured Fere-en-Tardenois but our Artillery kept on going. The 26th division doughboys were relieved by ours at Beauvardes and now we are relieving their artillery. Lord only knows when our relief comes. That New England bunch was sure happy to leave this section of France. They've seen "beaucoup" fighting since they left Coetquidan but not any more than we have.[5] We've been on one or other front now since last February and we've earned a rest. The 4th Div. Regulars pulled in yesterday and the boys think it is our relief. Our officers are giving them pointers and yesterday they fired their first shot at the Bosche. We have been supporting their Infantry ever since we left Sergy. Part of their wireless boys are practicing under us. Pretty good scouts but green as grass. Don't know how long it will be before their Brigade will be able to relieve ours. The filth around our station

4. The village of Fere-en-Tardenois was almost completely destroyed by the fighting that raged between July 18 and 25. The town was virtually ruined, and the bodies of dead and wounded soldiers filled the streets. See Gilbert, *First World War*, 445–46. Pete Straub recorded the scene at Fere-en-Tardenois thus: "We pulled half-way into the town of Fere-en-Tardenois and could go no further as the place was in complete ruins from shell-fire, and we could go no further. Buildings had fallen right across the streets." *Sergeant's Diary*, 144. Also, Vernon Kniptash recorded no diary entries between July 28 and August 4, perhaps because his unit was engaged in virtually perpetual combat over that six-day period. Over eight days of fighting at then end of July and beginning of August, the 42nd Division suffered sixty-five hundred casualties; see Coffman, *War to End All Wars*, 255; Cooke, *Rainbow Division*, 118–22; James, *Years of MacArthur*, 1:186, 188, 191.

5. Kniptash refers here to the 26th Division Infantry, also a National Guard unit composed of troops from New England, referred to as the Yankee Division.

and vicinity has just about got the boys down. Millions of flies. Most of the boys are sick. Cramp and diarrhea. The Bosche polluted all the water before he evacuated. Everything was made just as unpleasant as possible for us. Of course, this is all fair enough in warfare but that doesn't relieve the situation. One thing that they did do that didn't look just exactly fair was to blow up the chateau connected with this farm. I can't figure out the military value gained by that trick. On the farm we just left they had a neat little trap set but the Frenchmen around there caused it to be a fizzle. They had an innocent looking box setting innocently in a corner of a big silo. Wires led off in all directions. I don't know what had to be done to set the box off but the French cut all those wires and then opened the box. It was full of dynamite. Cute little trick but it didn't work. — The battle has come to a deadlock at the Vesle River. They tried a counter-attack last night but it was repulsed. We got too many guns on this side for them to pull off anything. Found out that A Battery had some casualties. [Orel] Dean was killed and Sgt. [John] Skidmore, [Egleasheao] Dill, and [George D.] Secrist were pretty badly wounded.[6] They've been dropping shells around us for two days now but so far they haven't got our number. Those shells sure have a sickening whine as they come toward you and the crash that follows is a relief as it lets you know just how far or near they're hitting. Our Brigade alone put over 23,000 shells last night. The Bosche has gotten a good foothold on the other side of the Vesle and so far we've been unable to oust him. — I haven't had a bath for a month now and I've got cooties, itch, bumps, diarrhea and Lord knows what else. I know I've lost weight and I'm feeling mighty low. We'll sure be glad when the relief is turned on. — The Stars and Stripes devoted a whole column to the Champagne battle and that means us. The boys read

6. Orel Dean was reported as killed in action on July 28, 1918, and Egleasheao Dill was reported as severely wounded in action on July 26, 1918. See Orel Dean and Egleasheao Dill, Roll No. 6, "Crose, John O.—Dulin, Hale M.," WWI SR. John Skidmore died on August 31, 1918, of wounds received in action; see John Skidmore, Roll No. 28, "Shore, Dave—Smith, William G.," WWI SR. George Secrist was reported as severely wounded in action on August 9, 1918; see George Secrist, Roll No. 27, "Schnell, August J.—Shore, Dave," WWI SR.

it with pardonable pride. — Saw two Bosche planes bring down two of our observation balloons just now. One of them attracted the fire of our anti-aircraft batteries while the other did the job. One of the balloons was anchored close to our station and I saw the observers make their parachute. The Bosche aviator fired at them with his machine gun while they hung helpless to their parachute. It was a brave thing to do.

Aug. 7   The Bosche are getting the why and wherefore of this farm. They just dropped a 77 right in the center of the court-yard. We catch Hell tonight. — Night — Well, they started dump-ing them in, but they've missed us so far. Hitting all around us and too close for comfort. It's little sleep the boys are getting these days. Can't sleep in the daytime because of the flies and can't sleep at night because of shells. I guess you're just not sup-posed to sleep in this open warfare game.

Aug. 8, 1918   Well, I got thru that night O.K. so I'll live to be twelve hours older anyway. Your life is counted in hours at the front. Lord, what a sickening whine those incoming shells have, altogether different from the ones going Bosche-ward. Makes a fellow want to run, run, run or dig a hole and keep digging till you see little yellow chinks running around.[7] One consolation is that the Germans are getting 5 of our shells for every one they put over. Just a steady roar of guns all the time. There are no dugouts and trenches and a fellow has to take his chances in the open.

Aug. 9, 1918   Same filth, dirt, and shells and a hope for a relief soon. Our Brigade is just about frazzled out and will have to be relieved shortly or something will bust. The strain and grind is too much.

Aug. 10, 1918   Still here in the Bosche fire getting hotter and hot-ter. We've been running our station thru it all and it's pretty hard to concentrate on your work with those whizbangs flying

---

7. According to Edward Fraser, comp., and John Gibbons, *Soldier and Sailor Words and Phrases*, 54, the word *chink* used in World War I referred to "any China-man." Also, apparently other soldiers in the 42nd Division used the word, as James Cooke recorded an entry written by Leslie Langille, a member of the Illinois unit in his account, *Men of the Rainbow*, 62. See Cooke, *Rainbow Division*, 67.

around.[8] — Night — The Bosche has commenced his strafing again and we've just got orders to move. We've finally been relieved. We've just had an hour of sneezing. Bosche sent over sneezing gas and I've just about sneezed my head off.[9] We finally pulled out. They are shelling the road just behind us. Narrow escape number 1, 756, 832. Passed thru Fere-en-Tardenois, Beauvardes, etc., and are now resting here at the same chateau we stopped at on July 27. Hit hard at 6 o'clock this morning after hitting all night. Don't know how long we stay here, but believe it's the beginning of a good long rest. We've sure earned it.

x---x

Aug. 12, 1918   Have taken a bucket bath, washed some clothes, slept "beaucoup," feel pretty good again. The "Stars and Stripes" gave the battle a big write up and we recognized some of our Division's jobs. The boys are all happy and proud of the old 42$^{\underline{nd}}$.

Aug. 13, 1918   Am pretty well rested up now and am receiving heaps of mail from home. They are all enthused back there about the Allied successes. (English are pushing them back all along the line west of Soissons.) And I expect the final results will knock 'em a complete curve. — Went over to see that big gun base. Its picture was in the "Stars and Stripes." It's an enormous piece of work and must have cost a mint of money. The Bosche managed to get away with the gun proper, but he didn't have time to destroy the base. He tried hard enough too, alright. The base revolves on a big circle formed of 8" steel ball bearings and the whole thing resembles a turntable in a roundhouse. Quite a neat prize. Paris will rest easier.[10]

8. A "whizbang" was a shell fragment from a large artillery piece, particularly from an Austrian 88 mm gun. See Farwell, *Over There*, 305.

9. In World War I, Kniptash lost his sense of smell, permanently, perhaps after this encounter with sneezing gas. See also Kniptash's diary entry, November 28, 1918, for a reference to Burl Johnson, who was wounded, degree undetermined, on August 9, 1918, perhaps from mustard gas; see Burl Johnson, Roll No. 12 "Hunt, Floyd F.—Johnson, Walter A.," WWI SR. Also, portions of Kniptash's diary entries of August 7, 8, and 9 were published in Ferrell, *Diary of Elmer Sherwood*, 173n3.

10. Kniptash refers here to "Big Bertha" and the amazement the Rainbows expressed as to its size. Both Straub and Sherwood also recounted their recollections about the size of the weapon, and Sherwood even included a photograph of

Aug. 14, 1918   We pull out of here this morning. Haven't any ideas as to where our destination will finally turn out to be, but the good old Army "snow" has several places picked. Some say we are going to a quiet sector. Some say we are going to Italy, and the rest say we're going way back of the lines for a complete rest. So there you are. I'm inclined to think the latter is the most logical. We need the rest and now would be a pretty good time to take it. We'll see though. — We hiked to a big orchard 5 kil. back of Chateau-Thierry. Reached here at noon. Will move again tomorrow morning. Had to make this hike in a baking sun with blouses and helmets. We must have discipline, you know.

Aug. 15, 1918   Moved still farther away from the front to this town of Montrieul aux Lions and stay here a couple of days, I guess. The non-coms get passed to LaFerte, but the poor privates had to stay to learn. Heard that the 26th Div. took up their old positions in Toul. Some say we are going back to the Baccarat sector and do the same.

August 16, 1918   Left this burg at 6:00 P.M. and reached Lizy-sur-Ourcq at 11:00 P.M. A Bosche plane came over and we had to hold up on our loading till he decided to leave. He dropped his bomb at the LaFerte railroad yards. Finished loading at 2:00 A.M. Had to pull out via Chateau Thierry because that Bosche blew up the track at LaFerte.

Aug. 17   Rode all day, passing thru Epernay, Chaumont, Rolenport (where our ditty bags are), and finally, reached our destination at 12 at night. The station lights were all lit up like a million dollars and from that the boys knew that there was no war back here. Hiked a few kilometers to this town of Meuvy. Pitched pup tents.

---

the emplacement in his published account. See Straub, *Sergeant's Diary*, 154; Sherwood, *Diary of a Rainbow Veteran*, 69; and *Rainbow Hoosier*, 95. Also, in reference to his comment that the "English are pushing them back," Kniptash was commenting on the successful drive of the British against the Germans that began on August 8, what General Erich von Ludendorff, the commander of the German forces, would later call "the black day of the German Army." It was at this point that Ludendorff placed the German army in a permanently defensive position, convinced that his nation could not win the conflict. See Farwell, *Over There*, 246–47; Gilbert, *First World War*, 450; Keegan, *First World War*, 412.

Aug. 18   This town is so insignificant that it's not even on the map. At least, we failed to locate it. "Snow" has it that we stay here for a month and drill, drill, drill. Helluva place to bring a man who's been at the front for 7 mos.

Aug. 19   Paid today. Was June's pay. Understand we get our seven day passes while here. I am from Missouri on this pass business. I don't believe there is such an animal.

Aug. 20, 1918   Boys were all "lickered up" last night and there was "beaucoup" crap and poker games. Can't blame the boys much for getting lit up. It's about the only thing left for a man to do in this one horse town. I went to bed myself. Don't appeal to me. — Am going to write home and tell 'em I'm still alive. I know they're worrying.

Aug. 23, 1918   Went over to "A" battery and bid [Byron C.] Bibe Young good bye. He's going back to the States as an instructor. Lucky devil.

Aug. 24, 1918   Left for a school in radio this morning. Rode over with the rest of the wireless boys to this town of St. Thieubault [sic] and is only a step over to Beaumont. This school is going to be stiff doings. Something to do from 5:45 A.M. till 10 P.M. Listened to a very good lecture given by Dr. Jenkins of Missouri.

Aug. 25, 1918   Sunday and I'm "baking 'em." School opens tomorrow.[11]

Aug. 26, 1918   School opened with a bang and things are running fairly smoothly. — School is again called off and we are to report to our organizations. Major Garrett gave a long talk on communication and ended up by saying that it was again called off and we were to report back to our outfits. — That looks like the front again. Left school in trucks and reached Meuvy again this eve. Learned that Capt. [Wilmer] Kashmer goes back to the States as an instructor.[12] Cap[t]. Hofmann will take charge of the H.Q. Co. again.

11. "Baking 'em" was apparently a term for remaining in bed where one was warmed by the blankets.

12. Kniptash was apparently mistaken about the orders regarding Capt. Wilmer Creighton Kashmer. His service record indicates that he served overseas continuously from October 18, 1917, to July 18, 1919, rather than being returned to the

Aug. 27, 1918   Doing squads east and west and hoping for the move.

Aug. 28, 1918   Took a 30 kil. ride on a horse today. Some scenery.

Aug. 29, 1918   Moves this morning. Started at 8 A.M. and arrived here at 5:00 P.M. Some 30 kil. We passed our doughboys on the way. The whole Division is concentrated around here. The general "snow" is that the American 1st Army will make a drive on the Lorraine front. Name of this town is Bulgneville. Several fellows from the Lily Base #32 were over to see us. Said they had heard the same "snow." They said Gen. Pershing's H.Q.'s had been moved from Chaumont to Neufchateau for the drive. Base #32 will be an evacuation hospital instead of a base. They must be expecting "beaucoup" wounded. The #32 men are sure fighting a wicked war. Was talking to my old friend Kenneth Fisk and he said he played tennis every day. Said they had wonderful courts. Have pie every so often and eggs every day. Nothing to do but look pretty and wait for the wounded to come in. Of course, when they get a trainload of wounded they are kept busy, but this only happens when there's an offensive. I wouldn't change places, though. They miss the fireworks.

Aug. 30, 1918   Made a night hike of 15 kil. to Landeville. Are here till further notice.

Aug. 31, 1918   Still here and expecting to move any day.

Sept. 1, 1918   Paid Neufchateau a visit today. Had some real Honest to goodness ice cream and mixed with white people again. Had a long talk with Mr. Craig. He's an actor playing the lead role in "Baby Mine." Owns a theatre of his own in Boston. Had one son killed at Verdun two years ago and his other son a lieut. in the French Army. We must have talked for an hour.

Sept. 2, 1918   William H. Cressy, my old friend at Keith's [theatre], came to our town last night with his wife and others and entertained the boys. His wife and himself put on their famous "New Hampshire lawyer" and it went big.

United States for a different assignment. See Wilmer Creighton Kashmer, Roll No. 13, "Johnson, Walter A.—Kerr, Roy," WWI SR. In the same vein, Capt. Edwin G. Hofmann served overseas from November 18, 1917, to April 25, 1919; see Edwin G. Hofmann, Roll No. 11, "Hodde, Harry F.—Hunt, Floyd F.," WWI SR.

Sept. 3, 1918   Paid <u>Neufchateau</u> another visit. Got a poncho, underwear, socks, etc. from the Red Cross.

Sept. 5, 1918   Got off lucky for once in my life. We had a 40 kil. hike scheduled for last night. Started hiking when a big truck steamed up and said it wanted about 20 men to help unload hay. I was one of the twenty. We coasted the 40 kil. and unloaded the hay in ten minutes. Then we made our beds and went to sleep. The boys started at seven and got here at 5:00. They were all in. We pull out again tonight.

Sept. 6, 1918   Marched all night, passing thru Toul and stopping some 11 kil. on this side of it. Pitched a tent in a big woods and used a couple of buckboards as a bed. The ground was too wet. — Pulled to another spot in the woods today. — The P.C. is getting ready to move to the town of Ausanville.[13] This town will be Regt'l H.Q. — I guess this drive will be a long one. There's one of two objectives and I don't know which one it will be. One of them is the taking of Metz and the other is working out the St. Mihiel salient. This terrain is massed with guns and everything points to a surprise attack. The 28th Engineers have been working on Mount Sec for ten months now. They have got it completely mined now and in case the Bosche resist too much will probably blow it off the map in this drive. — Move to the town of Ausanville this afternoon.

Sept. 7   Mumsey's birthday.

Sept. 7–11, 1918   Waiting for the word to open up. All the civilians have moved from here so the zero hour is not very far off. This quiet sector is a relief to what we've just gone through. The 89th Div. of drafted boys has been holding the line here, and, although they're a whole lot better than the 77th Division, still they don't look the part of soldiers. They try to make this sector out as a bad one, but they don't know what bad is. I've only heard one shell come over the 4 days I've been here. Things are going

13. Kniptash is referring to the impending American attack on the Saint-Mihiel salient, a segment of the western front that had been held by the Germans since 1914. The successful American campaign against the Germans in the Battle of Saint-Mihiel was a notable event in the war. See Farwell, *Over There*, 208–17; Marshall, *Memoirs*, 131–47.

to change, though, "tout de suite," and these 89th boys will see what we mean by a bad sector.

Sept. 12, 1918   This morning at 1:00 A.M. the guns opened up and at 5:00 A.M. the doughs went over. Started taking prisoners immediately. They passed thru this town on the way back to the pens. Must have been 2,500 for the day's work. Found out that the objective is to bite off the St. Mihiel salient and not try to take Metz.[14] Our doughboys are working northwest and the 1st Division is working southeast. A French Division is pushing at the point of the thumb. Things are working very successfully and, outside of a few scattered places, the resistance is negligible. [Editor's note: At this place in the diary, Kniptash drew a diagram of the St. Mihiel salient, showing the respective positions of the French troops and the troops of the 42nd Division.]

Sept. 13, 1918   French refugees that have been in German hands for 4 years are coming back to this town. They sure tell some horrible tales. Told of brutality and drunkenness. Sure didn't help the Germans "rep" any. Nearly every woman had a child, and, in every case, its father was a German soldier. Also said that the Bosche knew of our drive for eleven days, but couldn't get the men and guns up here to stop it. The German prisoners I saw were in the best of health, but their morale was very, very low.[15]

14. The success of the Allied advance had convinced Colonel Douglas MacArthur that the Rainbows should attempt to capture the key town of Metz before the Germans could bring in reinforcements. As MacArthur later wrote:

Metz was practically defenseless for the moment. Its combat garrison had been temporarily withdrawn to support other sectors of action. Here was an unparalleled opportunity to break the Hindenburg Line [the heavily fortified line of defense that protected German positions in the rear] at its pivotal point. There it lay, our prize wide open for the taking. Take it and we would be in an excellent position to cut off south Germany from the rest of the country; it would lead to the invasion of central Germany by way of the practically undefended Moselle Valley. Victory at Metz would cut the great lines of communication and supply behind the German front and might bring the war to a quick close. See Manchester, *American Caesar*, 102. MacArthur was overruled by his superiors, however, in his enthusiasm for a fresh offensive upon Metz. While sound tactical reasons existed for not pressing the offensive, the failure to exploit this opportunity probably lengthened the war. See Cooke, *Rainbow Division*, 156; Smythe, *Pershing*, 88–89.

15. By this point in the war, German morale was turning increasingly pessimistic. As Joseph Persico wrote, "Intelligence officers of the 42nd Division were

They were sure glad to be taken prisoner. We are waiting for the congestion on the roads to clear up before we move the P.C. up. We are in the S.O.S. so far as the battle is concerned. Our dough-boys captured a Bosche commisary [*sic*] at Pannes and stocked up on cigarettes, cigars, beer, and whiskey. The two divisions (1$\underline{st}$ and 42$\underline{nd}$) met and cut off about 150 square miles of France. The American communiqué credits 8,000 prisoners to the Americans for the first day's fighting.

Sept. 15, 1918   Moved this morning to the town of Essey. We are now 9 kil. from the front line. The Bosche is shelling the town as I write this. It's a big one and is hitting close. — Our prisoners so far total 13,300. The objective has been reached and we are now organizing the line. The doughs have dug in. — This drive was the biggest thing the Americans have tried yet, and it was marked because of the few casualties we suffered. Our division had only 20 killed and about 150 wounded. Don't know how the other divisions fared, but they didn't encounter any more resistance than we did. The Bosche just wouldn't fight. In many cases they had their personal belongings all packed and waiting for some doughboys to take them prisoner. It was a joke as far as fighting was concerned.

Sept. 16, 1918   Nothing much new. Understand we stay here till this sector is organized and then pull out. — Went up the line a piece and collected some souvenirs. — 10:30 P.M. — The Bosche is dropping his ten shells in the town again. Come in at 4 minute intervals. Methodical as a machine. He's firing at random and it's what is known as harassing fire. We've got our station in a peach of a dugout so have got little yet to worry us.

---

sure that they had discovered deep fissures in German morale. They found a sack of unmailed letters stowed in a command post previously occupied by the once elite, now battered German 16th Division. In one letter, an infantry man complained, 'We few fellows cannot hold up to this superior might and must go helplessly into captivity and of course most of the prisoners are murdered.'" *Eleventh Month*, 273. While the German soldier's fear of captivity was understandably real, the chance of his being killed as a prisoner of war was slim. In response to a question as to how enemy prisoners were treated by American forces, Carl Hixon responded, "We treated them with respect. I talked with a number of prisoners and they were humans just like me." Military Survey, U.S. Army Military History Institute, 9.

Sept. 17, 1918   Same old story. Repulsing Bosche counter-attacks most every night, but, outside of that, there's little excitement. Boys all say they saw in yesterday's paper where Austria is suing for separate peace. Haven't seen the paper, but hope it's so. Yesterday brought me 12 letters! Have answered all of them and got 'em on the way. — Just read that paper telling about Austria's sue for peace and see where the Allies say nothing doing.[16] Well, that's the idea. No peace until we dictate the terms. Germany's word has been violated by her so often that the Allies won't believe a thing she says. The Allies are now in a position to push things to the limit and they're going to do it. — Found out a couple of days ago that our old friends, the 77th Div., had some of their confidence knocked out of them. The very night they reached the trenches in the Baccarat sector the Bosche cut loose on them and drove them back from 5 to 8 kil. Even Baccarat had a couple of shells dumped into it. It took a French Div. a day to gain the ground back again. Guess now the 77th wished they had taken some pointers from the Rainbow boys.[17]

Sept. 18, 1918   Nothing much to report. The Bosche failed to shell this town tonight and our guns may have got him after all. One of our batteries has been trying for two days to silence him. He's railroad artillery and drives in from Metz every night to shoot his shells here and there over the ground he owned for four years. Towards morning he goes back to Metz to wait the next night. Doesn't take a chance in the daytime. "Snow" has it that we get paid in a few days. This pay will be for July and August. Well, it can't come any too soon. I've borrowed 40 francs already and am broke now.

Sept. 19, 1918   Same old story. Sector very quiet. We fixed up our dugouts and it makes a neat little home. Wouldn't mind spending the winter right where we are. The dugout has a wooden floor, tables, a spring at the entrance, and ten bunks. Then there's a daisy stove. Sure could live panilla. However, we fall out

---

16. Austria-Hungary continued to send out peace feelers, unsuccessfully, until the war ended in November. See Gilbert, *First World War*, 487.

17. The 77th Division, a National Army unit made up of draftees, had relieved the Rainbows in early August. Cooke, *Rainbow Division*, 163–64; Coffman, *War to End All Wars*, 315–16; Slotkin, *Lost Battalions*, 1–11.

of here from all indications. Another Div. is coming into the line and the last of it pulled in tonight. Don't know whether they're draft boys or not. Am on from 2 A.M. to 6 A.M. and the claxons are shrieking. Gas alert. They must be a panicky bunch of fellows or else the Bosche is pulling a little hate party. Am going to leave the rest of the fellows asleep until the alert turns into real gas. This "claxon gas" isn't a very bad gas and there's no use waking up for it. We had "beaucoup" of it on the Champagne front. The boys were up there and woke up each time. Finally, after a few days, they decided sleep was a whole lot better and gas alerts didn't "mean" much to them. They left it to the guard to smell the gas and it was time then to put on our masks and not before.

Sept, 20, 1918   Payday today and we drew our July and August pay. I drew two hundred and ninety-nine francs. That included my allotment. Am going to send 30.00 dollars home at my first chance. Bosche avion came over and dropped a few "eggs."[18] They hit the edge of town.

Sept. 21, 1918   Found out the true facts about that gun that was firing on this town. The Bosche slipped a 150 thru our lines when they run through a dense woods. He sent six men over and every night, beginning at 10:30, he dropped shells in the different towns in our vicinity. We finally found them out and Alabama sent out patrol and captured them. Today, Cpl. [Elmer] Bell is going to take a detail up and bring the gun back. It was a very nervy piece of work on the Bosche's part, but, as far as I know, the shells didn't claim a single casualty.

Sept. 22, 1918   The Bosche bombarded this town with long-range guns last night. Its first shell got 9 fellows and after that the shells didn't claim a single victim. The nearest one to our dugout was some 50 ft. and the concussion made the candles flicker. It's a big shell and its "crump" is enormous. Those 9 fellows were only slightly wounded. So far, his long-range sniping hasn't netted

18. Kniptash and his fellow soldiers referred to the bombs dropped from German aircraft as "eggs," distinguishing them from shells launched by German artillery. Bombardment from the air was much feared by American soldiers. Elmer Sherwood described the experience as akin to being "a rat in a cage. The crash of bombs is terrific and causes the sweat to pop out on one's forehead." *Diary of a Rainbow Veteran*, 77.

him much. The Bosche must be getting peeved because we're dropping a few shells in his pet city of Metz.

Sept. 23, 1918   Sent 30.00 home to Mumsey via a Y.M.C.A. money order. The P.C. detail moves to a big forest some 8 kil. from here. Passed thru Pannes, Nonsard, and finally reached the forest. It is known as the Bois de Nonsard (Forest of Nonsard) and it is full of Bosche shocks and stables. We're sleeping in a big theatre tonight. Will know about the lay of the land tomorrow.

Sept. 24, 1918   The Bosche called the theatre the "Lichtspiele Nonsard." Have been tramping around the woods and visiting the different shacks and looking for a suitable place for our wireless station. All of them are in first class shape, but we're having a hard time finding an open space for our antenna. Finally found this place. Has two rooms, a stove, two windows, wooden floor, and with the exception of water, has all modern conveniences. We cleaned house, built bunks, set up station, and things are looking like a million dollars. Cozy as a den. The boys all hope we spend the winter here. We sure could fight a wicked war this winter. Suppose now that we've got everything looking panilla we'll pull out of here. The Bosche has dropped a few shells to our left, but he hasn't got the range on this place yet.

Sept. 25, 1918   The rest of the Regt'l Detail pulled in today. The Americans pulled off a little party last night. Intense artillery bombardment. Don't know the results as yet, but the operation was more than a raiding party.

Sept. 26, 1918   There's a heavy artillery barrage taking place to our left. A regular miniature Champagne battle. The Americans have sure got the Bosche guessing in this neck of the woods. Our Intelligence Department tells us that the Bosche has massed troops around the fortifications of Metz and are sending out raiding parties two and three times a night to find out what American troops are facing them. They're afraid we're going to try for Metz before winter sets in. They are shelling a battery to the left of us and this woods carries the sound so clearly that it sounds as if the bursts are right outside the door. Danny went to Toul and Sonny and I hitched up old May with the intention of going to Essey to visit the commissary. We got almost to Pannes when May shied at an engine, turned clear around, shook herself clear of Sonny and

I, and highballed back toward Nonsard. The last we saw of her she was vanishing over the top of a hill and all four feet were off the ground. Hiked back to Nonsard and a boy told us that she got off the road and stopped in a big field. Some fellow caught her there. Hopped in, and drove off thru Nonsard. There's five roads leading out of Nonsard and we didn't know which one to take. Hunted for her all afternoon and had to come back empty handed. Hate to face the captain. Will saddle up tomorrow and hunt for her again. If we still have no luck, we'll tell Division about it and let them put out a lost, strayed, or stolen order. That usually brings them in. All the boys are kidding us now and I admit I'm worried. About that barrage last night. Found out that the French and Americans are bucking the line from Verdun down to Lorraine. Just won't let the Bosche rest. Don't know whether the attack was successful or not.

Sept. 27 2:00 AM   Just relieved Sonny at the set. He copied the 1:00 o'clock French and American communiqué and it turned out to be 405 words of good news. Can't read the French communiqué, but it tells about successful operations around <u>Verdun</u>. The American communiqué even goes so far as mentioning the names of the divisions taking part in the drive. It reads: — September 16–9pm — This morning northwest of Verdun the 1<u>st</u> Army attacked the enemy on a front of twenty miles and penetrated her lines to an average depth of seven miles. Pennsylvania, Kansas, and Missouri troops serving in Major General [Hunter] Liggett's 1<u>st</u> Army Corps stormed <u>Varennes</u>, <u>Montplainville</u>, <u>Vauquois</u>, and <u>Cheppy</u> after stubborn resistance. Troops of other corps, crossing the Forgesbrook, captured the Bois de Froges, and the towns of <u>Malancourt</u>, <u>Bethencourt</u>, Montquaselon, Cuissy, etc., etc. The prisoners so far reported number over 5,000. — A.R. — Well, there's one drive the 42<u>nd</u> missed by golly. Don't see how they could try such a thing without us to start things. The sector to our left is the end of the drive and they've kept up a steady bombardment since the drive started Sept. 26. It's going on right now. Well, I hope that 7 mile penetration increases to 20 miles by tonight. I suppose, before it's all over with, the Rainbow boys will be yanked away from here and then sent up there as we leave. — Hunted all day for May and the little cart, but couldn't find a trace of her.[19] Danny and I were on horses and I know we rode 50 kilometers looking for her. I'll have to get my meals standing up for a few days. I'm raw. Don't know whether we'll ever see her again or not and care less. She'd driven us nuts in time. Shied at everything and didn't have an ounce of sense.

Sept. 28, 1918   "Snow" has it that we move shortly. Some say to Baccarat. However, it is only "snow" and can't be relied upon. Our doughboys have been relieved and that usually means a move. — Have heard nothing concerning May's whereabouts. Guess we've seen the last of her.

Sept. 29, 1918   Signed the payroll today. My allotment will not be taken out this month either, so I'll draw something like 164 francs. — The Allies are still advancing. On the eastern front, they captured Veles and on the [western] front the British are menacing Cambrai. Also, Bulgaria is crying for peace. Peace negotiations are on the way and seem to be progressing much more successfully than Austria's attempt. If Bulgaria drops out, Turkey will have to. Then, poor old Austria will be up against it right. Sure hope Bulgaria gets her peace. — Made a bet of 20 francs with Albert that hostilities would not cease by January 1, 1919. I'd gladly lose the twenty in case it should come true, but I can't see peace until after the spring drive.[20]

September 30, 1918   The escholon [echelon] moves out tonight and we follow tomorrow, probably in the morning. "Snow" has it that our immediate destination is some 20 miles south of Toul. The French communiqués don't sound quite as encouraging as

19. The "little cart" to which Kniptash refers was a piece of German equipment that he obtained after the Germans retreated in late July. Most American units made extensive use of German equipment that had been left behind once the German army began its retreat.

20. Kniptash makes a reference to the "spring drive" in this diary entry. Like other American soldiers, Kniptash also believed that Pershing planned to make the major American effort against Germany in 1919, probably a military action that would strike into German territory. Kniptash's reports also revealed that the major Allied campaign for the Meuse-Argonne had begun. This offensive was the greatest military effort in American history, to that date. The Meuse-Argonne action was, in fact, considerably more than a resumption of the Champagne experience, as Kniptash indicates in his entry of September 27. See Farwell, *Over There*, 223–28.

they did. They talk of meeting resistance here and violent counter-attacks there and, although they made gains on the Argonne battle, still they didn't reach their objectives. That's why I think the 42nd is going up there to help stir things up again. — The Bosche is shelling this woods and the shells are hitting about two squares from here. He just shot over 14 in as many minutes and 7 of them were duds. Up on the Vesle the number of his shells that turned out to be duds was very noticeable. One fellow up there counted 86 came over, and, of this total, 46 were duds. Hope they continue having the same bad luck.

Oct. 1, 1918   We wrecked our happy home this morning and have got our stuff all packed in the telephone wagon. Sure miss the Bosche cart and old May. "Snow" has it we pull out tonight. — Hung around all day and pulled out at 8:30 P.M. Just before we started, Chaplain Nash said that Bulgaria had finally got the peace she was yelling for. She's out of the game now, and I think Turkey will be the next to fall. From then on, goings will be easier. We waited at the edge of the woods till 10:00 P.M. for the rest of the company and like to froze to death doing it. The roads were muddy and the air was clammy and cold. Hiked to this town of Troyon and it was the most miserable hike I've taken so far. There was 32 kil. of this misery, and, believe me, I wasn't a bit sorry when we reached the billets. Reached here at 6:30 A.M. Probably hit the trail again tomorrow night.

Oct. 2, 1918   Stayed in bed most of the day, but couldn't sleep. It is raining now, and a cold, damp air penetrates clear to the bones. We pull out again tonight. — Started hiking again. Started at 7:00 P.M. and reached this place at 9:30 P.M. About 12 kil. We are now some 20 kil. south of Verdun and about 30 kil. from the front. I think our next sector will be west of Verdun between Verdun and the Argonne. The "snow" is that we relieve the 1st Div. The 1st relieved the 35th Division. Read in the papers today where the French entered St. Quentin and the British are on the outskirts of Cambrai. It will be just a question of time before Germany will have to evaluate her once invulnerable Hindenburg line. Then, it's fairly easy sailing clear through Belgium and to the border line. The German people sure haven't got much to cheer 'em up through this coming winter. They'll get a taste now of what the French people had to put up with for four long years. — We are quartered near the town of Ramboullet [indeciperable]. Guess we stay here a few days.

Oct. 3, 1918   Sticking around all day. Sleeping and eating. The cannonading at the front is very intense and there are several big guns in action. We are some 30 or 40 kil. from the front, but the bombardment can be heard very plainly. Now, I believe the story that the people in Paris heard our bombardment on the Champagne battle. Some new orders came rushing down and we pull out of here tomorrow morning. "Snow" is that we relieve the 1st Div. as it's been shot up pretty badly. I'm leery of this front because it's close to old battle-scarred Verdun.[21]

Oct. 4, 1918   Left here at 3:30 A.M. Passed thru Thiacourt, Souilly, etc., and finally reached this woods at 12:00. We are close to the town of Dombasle. We are some 30 kil. back of the town of Mont-faucon, the town the Yankees first captured when the drive started.[22] This hike covered 26 kil. of France. The horses were all in, down and out. They had nothing on the men. They say we hike another 10 after dark. Don't see how it can be done. The men can stand it, but the horses won't be able to make the grade. Slept all afternoon up till 7:00. Missing my supper. Found out that we don't move out tonight, so it's me for some more bakin'.

Oct. 5, 1918   Slept cold last night. I'm sure going to get some more blankets the next salvage dump I hit. The cannonading is more distant this morning, which means that the Bosche must have retreated some more last night. Don't know when we pull

21. Verdun was the site of one of World War I's most vicious and sustained battles. The Germans had attempted, on numerous occasions in 1916, to take the city and even laid siege to it. The French held out, however, in one of their notable moments of the war. See Gilbert, *First World War*, 233–35. The best single account of the Verdun campaign is Horne's *Price of Glory*. See also Keegan, *First World War*, 278–86.

22. The "drive" to which Kniptash refers began on October 4 and represented the Allied attack to smash the Hindenburg Line and break the German defenses. This period in the fighting gave Pershing "the greatest strain" of any point in the conflict. See Coffman, *War to End All Wars*, 320–21; Farwell, *Over There*, 228. Kniptash also mentions the capture of Montfauçon, which occurred on September 27 after a fierce battle with the Germans. See Farwell, *Over There*, 228; Freidel, *Over There*, 154; Marshall, *Memoirs*, 161.

up, but it had better be shortly, or we'll never reach the line. However, this S.O.S. [service of supply] business is pretty panilla for a change. Was tickled at some of the things I heard while taking that hike yesterday. Whenever we passed a group of soldiers, they'd whisper to one another, "Those boys belong to the Rainbow Division" or "He's part of the gang that whipped 'em at Chateau-Thierry." They didn't intend for us to hear, but I made it a point to find out just what sort of a name the Rainbow Div. has got behind the lines. We appear to be well known from what I heard yesterday. — An avion came over tonight and dropped 20 eggs. They hit close, but I've had 'em come closer.

Oct. 6, 1918   We moved this morning. Started hiking at 9:00 A.M. and reached this woods at 4:00 P.M. The going was hard as the roads were shot up terribly. The Engineers have been working on them, but it will be some time before they'll be fit for heavy traffic. We are now in the woods where the Crown Prince massed his forces for his bombardment at Verdun. The woods itself is shot to pieces. — The P.C. moves up tomorrow.

Oct. 7, 1918   Part of the P.C. moved up this morning and the rest of us follow later. Heard the "snow" that the Bosche is retreating on a 45 kil. front around Reims. Sure hope it's true. We are now five kil. south of Montfaucon. The New York Herald read good this morning. Said Turkey and Austria were ready to accept all of President Wilson's peace terms and Germany will accept eleven of them. She wants to discuss the three concerning Alsace-Lorraine, Belgium, and Russia. Hope some agreement is reached. — We moved at 6:00 P.M. Passed through Montfaucon and the P.C. is in a ruined village about a quarter of a kilometer out of this town. The Bosche is shelling both places heavily. There's no dugouts and it's another Chateau-Thierry affair. Take your chances in the open. Reached here wet and miserable and didn't set up station. Made our bed in what was formerly a house, but is now only two walls and a couple of rafters. It turned the rain, however, and that's all we asked. Sgt. Major [Paul] Bonham almost had a leg taken off. A fragment ripped through his pant's leg and barely grazed the skin. This is the worst place we've been in so far.

Oct. 8, 1918   Set up station in an old, tottering archway. Was just about ready to fall down, and if a shell lights too close, I'm afraid we'll have to dig ourselves out. The Bosche has been shelling this place "toujours" [always or often] and they're big ones. I'm afraid the Colonel has chosen a bad place for his P.C. There's a crossroads and a food supply dump some 150 yards behind us and this is what Fritzie is trying for. We get the benefit of all his shorts. Was standing in the mess line this evening and he dropped three so close that all of us laid down in the mud. Followed these 3 up with 17 more and by that time the boys decided there were several things worse than going hungry and everybody beat it to get out of the line of fire. This is the worst front we've been in on so far. Not so much the bombardment, although a heavy one goes on night and day, as it is the accommodations. There is absolutely no protection and so far we've been lucky to keep dry. It's getting terribly cold at night, and the boys haven't been issued any of their winter clothing. They're going to have a bunch of sick soldiers on their hands if they don't remedy the situation soon.

Oct. 9, 4:00 A.M.   Fritzie dropped his encore "twenty" at 2:30 this morning. They're hitting too close for comfort. Climbed out of a fairly warm bed at 4:00 A.M. to do my three hours at the set. I'm sitting here slowly, but surely freezing to death. — The Colonel is putting out the "snow" that in a couple of days the Allies are going to try to pull off the biggest thing the world has ever known. Says we are going to hit the entire front from Switzerland up to the sea. It's going to be the Allies's [sic] last bid for peace this year, and, if it fails, they are going to dig in for the winter and stake everything on the spring drive.[23] Sure hope it succeeds in bringing about peace before winter. Gen. Foch ought to have plenty of Americans to carry out his scheme. The U.S. sure must have some of her artillery over here by now and with the Bosche minus that big bunch we captured from him in the last three months, we ought to have superiority in guns. Then we got

23. The "snow" to which Kniptash refers was for the Rainbows to participate in the fourth phase of the Meuse-Argonne offensive, which lasted from October 12 to 16. See Cooke, *Rainbow Division*, 168. Also, Robert H. Ferrell gives an account of the Rainbow Division's role in the Meuse-Argonne offensive in his *America's Deadliest Battle: Meuse-Argonne, 1918*, 102–109.

his morale way down to zero so I believe the big drive will be a success. They want peace so bad now they can taste it and a big surprise like this would certainly hasten matters. Our doughboys are being held in reserve and suppose will be in this sector when the fireworks start. — Batteries "B" and "D" had some wounded and killed yesterday. Also heard that "A" suffered, but don't know for sure. This is sure a bad front. — Later — 4:00 P.M. Whoopee! We finally ousted him out of his hole and got him going once more. The doughs went over at 8:30 this morn' and are still going. Just copied the communiqué but interference was so bad the thing as a whole didn't make sense. "Beaucoup" Allied planes are up adjusting batteries onto retreating Germans. Made enough out of the communiqué to know that we took 3,000 prisoners today and are still advancing. Lieutenant Fletcher says that at 8:30 A.M. every doughboy from Switzerland to the sea went over the top. The communiqué didn't mention the fact so I can't see it. Sure know we're back in the S.O.S. here, though. Haven't heard a shell since that 2:30 party. "Mack" says the P.C. pulls out of here tonight and moves forward. Waiting for the orders to move now. — Got the orders to tear down the station and pack. While doing so, a chain of exciting events happened so quickly that it left me completely and gloriously bewildered. I looked up in the sky and counted 104 aeroplanes at once. Never saw so many before in one place in my life. Just like bees. Then, all of a sudden, I saw one make a straight dive for our observation balloon, and set it on fire. He was a Bosche and had painted his plane a dark brown so as to hide his markings. He sure had the guts to tackle that job with better than a hundred Allied planes flying around. As soon as it was discovered that he was a Bosche, five of our planes hopped onto him and brought him down. He was making a beeline for his lines all the time and everybody on the ground was firing at him. Excitement galore. It's miraculous how everybody came out without a scratch. The five planes finally made him do a nosedive to earth. His partner was brought down by anti-aircraft fire, and everybody let out a shout. I've been at the front for quite a few months, but never saw anything that equaled this. To top it all off, Charlie came up with a mess and a big bag of mail. I drew 14 letters. That was the climax almost. It finally came when the Col. said we wouldn't move till morning and I got a chance to read my letters! They were from Mumsey, Maude, Louie Fehrenbach, Ott Roos, Louie Bruck, Aunt Kate, Bertha Coffman, Daryl Glenister, Claire Annette and Clyde Wolfe, Jake Walbrandt.[24] Never read such an enjoyable bunch of letters.

Oct. 10, 1918   A few shells dropped around last night, but they were not close. — Re-read all my letters this morning. Am going to answer 'em as soon as the chance comes. Right now, we don't know whether we move up or not. Charlie came up with the mess this morning and said that [John] Peterson was shot through the heart by a machine gun bullet. That avion that shot down our balloon yesterday opened up on our eschelon at the same time and got Peterson as he was coming back from watering his horses. Charlie got back just as [David J.] Davis was blowing taps over Peterson's grave, and he said it cut deep. Everybody from Capt. Hofmann on down are greatly moved as it is the first casualty that H.Q. Co. has had and I was talking to Peterson a couple of days ago. Just a kid.[25] Well, it all goes to make the war, but I hate to see Peterson killed. One consolation is that they killed the Bosche avion. — Had another exciting one half hour. Two more Bosche tried for our balloon, but didn't have any luck. One of them managed to get back to his lines, but the other was shot down. — Been showing around this place all day despite the fact that they were driven back a considerable distance yesterday. It must be long range stuff. Latest "snow" has it that the whole German 4th Army surrendered to the British and that Austria and Turkey have dropped out. This is almost too much to swallow, but the boys say they got the dope straight from Brigade Headquarters. We'll be finding it out soon enough if it's the truth. I don't believe it.

24. The letters described here covered a wide range of Kniptash's friends and family. Louie Bruck and Ott Roos were friends from Indianapolis. Aunt Kate was Katherine Kniptash, sister of Wilhelm Kniptash. Daryl Glenister was a cousin who lived in Chicago. Clyde and Claire Annette Wolfe were the parents of Maude Wolfe.

25. John Peterson was reported as killed in action on October 9, 1918; he was eighteen. See John Peterson, Roll No. 23, "Perkins, Burl E.—Pringle, Herbert.," WWI SR.

Oct. 11, 1918   Still here, but "snow" has it that we leave this sector all together. Our Regiment has suffered quite a few casualties since we hit this place. "A" battery had one killed and six wounded and "B" and "D" batteries had a few. Don't know who the "A" Battery boys are. The communiqué last night read good. The French are still advancing and have now taken back the Chemin des Dames and are still going. — Pulled out last night at 8:30 and reached the eschelon at 10:20. We are going to take up positions in the sector to our left.

Oct. 12, 1918   Pulling out of here this morning at 10:30 A.M. — That "snow" about the 4th German Army surrendering was almost, but not quite true. The English captured Cambrai and 10,000 prisoners, but that wasn't the whole 4th Army. Have heard no more about Austria and Turkey dropping out. — Walked down to Peterson's grave. It's very pretty. Poor kid. I sure hate to think of it. Reached this town of Boulny at 2:30 P.M. and set up station. The Germans dug a network of tunnels underneath the entire town. It's an elaborate system. 60 ft. underground and must have represented years of work. This P.C. is going to be a whole lot healthier, both in regards to shell and sanitary conditions. There's plenty of dugouts and the place is cleaner. That other place gave me the diarrhea and I'm still affected with it. Went to bed a very sick man last night. Our guns start firing at 10:00 P.M. and, as yet, the telephone men haven't strung a line.[26] They'll have to hustle when they get here. The Colonel's raving.

Oct. 13, 1918   Am on duty now. 4 A.M. There's a big barrage taking place and quite a few shells coming this way. I think our doughs go over after them sometime this morning. — The chaplain just showed me the latest report from Div. H.Q. It read that Germany was ready to evacuate all Allied sick. That the government and people both are sincere in their desires for peace, and,

---

26. The artillery bombardment that opened on October 12 was a massive effort. One member of the Alabama regiment, on being taken to the hospital for treatment of a wound, told the Rainbow artillerymen: "Oh, boys, you all doan [sic] know how powerful you alls guns is." Sherwood, *Rainbow Hoosier*, 130. See also Ferrell, *Diary of Elmer Sherwood*, 92. Between October 14 and 15, the Rainbow artillery fired 23,000 rounds of 75 mm shells and 2,600 rounds of 155 mm shells. Cooke, *Rainbow Division*, 174.

as soon as the German Army has withdrawn from invaded territory, her commission will meet with the Allies' commission and
take preliminary measures towards establishing peace. It has a
true ring to it, even if it does come from that bunch of round-
heads. Sure hope something comes out of it. The telephone
detail ran out of wire, and we had to take over communication.
Had a little trouble, but managed to get our messages through.
Received six more letters today.

x---x

Oct. 14, 11 A.M.   On duty again. Another heavy barrage being
pulled off. The doughs go over at 5:30 this morning. This barrage started at 3:30. Two hours' artillery preparation is all our
doughs need. Suppose we'll move forward when Alabama gets
through. Quite a few shells lit around. — Our doughs advanced
from four kil. and then had to wait for the 32$^{\underline{nd}}$ Div. doughs on
our right to catch up. The casualties are heavy. — Our doughs
reached their objective, St. Juvien, while the 32$^{\underline{nd}}$ failed to reach
theirs.[27]

Oct. 15, 1918   We're putting up another barrage so that means
the doughs go over again. "Snow" says our 84$^{\underline{th}}$ Brig. was pretty
badly shot up. They're meeting all kind of resistance. "Beaucoup" shells hitting around the station, too. They're big babies.
A wounded German prisoner says the Bosche are fighting for
time to get their supplies away. Says the town of Meziers is one
large German supply base and they are working night and day
removing supplies from there. Wish we could get there before
they finished their job. — Whitaker blew two fingers off and
gashed his face caused by a hand grenade. It was accidental and
might have been a Bosche trap.[28] Went to Exermont for batteries. While there, I saw the Germans lay down a barrage on the
side of a big hill. It was pretty, but didn't help our side any. Our

27. German resistance to the mid-October offensive was initially exceedingly
stiff with German rear guard units fighting desperately as the Germans attempted
to evacuate their men and supplies. See Cooke, *Rainbow Division*, 174.

28. Edwin Whitaker was reported as seriously wounded in action on October
16, 1918. It is possible that Whitaker incurred the wound on October 15, as Kniptash wrote, but the wound was not documented officially until the next day. See
Edwin Whitaker, Roll No. 33, "Walling, Thomas D.—White, Alva Orse," WWI SR.

casualties are very heavy. The 167th Field Artillery in this town handled 1300 wounded men yesterday.[29] I saw a gritty bunch of soldiers. Some of them were in a bad way, but the biggest part were only slightly wounded. Was talking to a wounded Cpl. out of the New York Regiment. He said the Bosche are fighting like tigers up here. Said it's the worst that he's run up against yet. See where Germany's peace note falls through anyway. I guess it's fight to the finish. Well, if diplomats can't settle it, soldiers can.

Oct. 16, 1918   Have got our little dugout fixed up pretty cozy. Danny stole a stove and I could fight a wicked war here this winter. Have answered all but one of my letters. There were 21 altogether.

Oct. 17, 1918   The roads in this neck of the woods are jammed with artillery and tanks moving up to the front. Understand the country up here is one big, flat plain for some thirty miles so I guess we are going to take advantage of it. Heard that our doughs finally captured the hill that has been delaying the game.[30]

Oct. 18, 1918   Just one year ago today we left the States. I can still remember how the Statue of Liberty looked and made me feel as it slowly vanished out of sight. It's a feeling that I never want to experience again. — We are going to move up to Exermont today if nothing happens. The sun is out for a change and I think we pull a big party. — Moved to this place this afternoon. It is up here in [indecipherable] country. We're in a row of shacks about a kil. out of Exermont. We're ahead of A, B, C, and D batteries and aligned with E and F. There isn't a minute passes, but what you have a Bosche shell whining. They're doing counter-battery work and Lord knows they've sure got enough batteries on this

29. As the Rainbow Division moved from place to place, it enhanced its reputation as a fighting force. Asked by a Red Cross officer to name his unit, Elmer Sherwood responded, "Rainbow." "Well," said the Red Cross man, "here's where [the] hospital trade picks up." *Diary of a Rainbow Veteran*, 158. See also Ferrell, *Diary of Elmer Sherwood*, 85.

30. The hill to which Kniptash refers was Hill 288, taken by the Rainbows on October 12–13, and one of the key German defensive positions along the front. See Cooke, *Rainbow Division*, 168; James, *Years of MacArthur*, 1:223; Sherwood, *Rainbow Hoosier*, 126; Eisenhower, *Yanks*, 255–56.

side to fire at. Some of the closest shells lit about fifty yards from us. That's plenty close. I'm afraid the Col. has chosen a rather wicked P.C. In the last shack, there is a bunch of dead Bosche. Haven't had time to bury them. Over on the hill is one of four Bosche machines that were brought down today. — Captain [Frank] Kelly had the fun of capturing the pilot and observer.[31] The machines lit within fifty feet of his battery. The observer was shot through the lung. The hills and valleys carry sound something fierce and when the guns open up it sounds as if the world is coming to an end. This is sure a hot place, and I'll bet we are forced to move out of it. The big party didn't come off last night. — A couple of majors from Base #32 came up to pay the Col. a visit. Wanted to get a taste of the war. Don't know how long they intended to stay, but I know they left last night when the shells got too thick. They'll sure have something to tell the boys back in the S.O.S.

x--------------------------------x

Oct. 19, 1918   Very few shells come this way today, thank the Lord. The Col. spent all morning locating a dugout and finally found one near the 3ʳᵈ Bn. — Saw the most gruesome sight I've seen. I began running into dead German soldiers. Saw where one of our shells had scored a direct hit on one unfortunate and blew him into pieces. You could see parts of his body hanging from limbs of trees. An arm here, a leg there. It was terrible. The valleys and hills around here are strewn pretty thickly with dead Germans. — Night- Heinie has commenced his little hate party again.[32] Just shot over gas. They're lighting close on some places, but the majority of them are going over our heads. See where the Allies are in Ostend and Lille (Belgium). We're slowly, but surely taking Germany's submarine bases away from her. — Received some letters from Mumsey and Maude this evening. They think

31. There is no service record for a Captain Kelly (as Kniptash spells it), but there is one for Capt. Frank Kelley, listed as an officer with Battery E (whom we may reasonably assume is the individual named in the diary, here and later). See WWI SR, enlistment papers.

32. "Heinie," like "Fritzie," was a term used by Americans in reference to German troops. See Farwell, *Over There*, 303.

I've gone to some sort of instruction school due to the hazy let-ters I wrote them while at the last two day school in radio at St. Thiaubault [*sic*]. — Albert went back to the eschelon today, a very sick boy. He may have to go to the hospital.

Oct. 20, 1918   Nothing much today. Raining and miscrable out-side, but we're pretty comfy in our little shack. It's all right in the daytime, but at night the chills sort of "annoy a body." Went down and took a peek at a dud 77 that lit some 50 ft. from us. As long as they're duds, we're sitting pretty. — Received some more let-ters and one from Maude and that she'd received my black Bosche helmet. Said Mumsey had received hers, too. They still think that I'm at the blamed school. Probably know by now that I've been on the St. Mihiel drive. I know that will disappoint them, but it can't be helped now. — Found out that Albert has a bad case of Spanish Influenza. They sent him to the 168th field hospital. Sure hope it doesn't turn into pneumonia. Maude writes and says that there are several cases of it in the camps back in the States. I'm sure keeping watch on myself.[33] — Heinie just sent over eight more gas shells. They're litting in the same old place; down in the valley directly below us. Rather close, but an inch is as good as a mile. However, I'd just as leave he'd stop. Their whine sounds like they're coming in the front door. I'm glad he's shooting gas instead of H-E. Gas doesn't scare me, but H-E is wicked.

Oct. 21, 1918   They shelled around here pretty heavily last night. One gas shell lit within fifteen yards of this shack. Splashed dirt and rocks all over. Sounded like the roof was coming down. It was mustard gas. Don't know whether the boys got touched by it or

33. Kniptash had good reason for "keeping watch" on himself. More American troops died from influenza, often called the Spanish flu, than from wounds suffered in combat in World War I. The origins of the influenza epidemic are disputed. In his comprehensive study, John M. Barry argues that it began in Kansas in March 1918 and was transported to American military bases, then carried to soldiers aboard troopships and then to the western front; see Barry, *Great Influenza*, 169–71. See also Persico, *Eleventh Month*, 303–304. Others believe that the Spanish flu epidemic began in June 1918, in India and Great Britain, and then was transported to the west-ern front. American forces suffered 48,909 combat deaths in World War I but more than 62,000 deaths due to the flu. See Farwell, *Over There*, 233–34; Gilbert, *First World War*, 437; Keegan, *First World War*, 408; Marshall, *Memoirs*, 87.

not. Most of us put our gas masks on. You can still smell the gas when you're near the hole. We're some six feet lower in the hole, so we're not getting the full benefit. I feel itchy, but suppose it's because I haven't taken a bath for ages. The sector on our left is attacking and we're preparing our fire. Don't know when our little party comes off. — Night — Heinie is sending over his 15" shells again. One of them just hit fifty feet from this shack. It was H-E and a "spare part" therefore hit our little home a ton. The piece was as big as my hand. Oh, she's a rather rough war, boys, but she's better than no war at all.

Oct. 22, 1918   Well, I'll live to see another day. This place is getting worse than our own last stand on the Vesle. If a man can live through the night he won't be bothered during the day. Fritzie doesn't show around here in the daytime. He sends ten to fifteen over at 6:00 o'clock P.M. Same number at midnight, and about twenty come over at 4 A.M. It works every night to the second. Damn methodical squareheads. — All kinds of conflicting "snow" is flying around. It simmers down to this. One of the higher-ups, General Summerall I think, is disappointed that the 42$\underline{nd}$ Div. didn't reach its objectives on this front. He says that our objectives will be gained if the whole Div. has to be annihilated. Don't know whether the General asked for it, or whether Col. Tyndel was trying a little grandstand stuff, but, anyway, Colonel Tyndel offered some 450 men out of his Regt. to act as infantrymen in case our doughs failed to get anywhere. The order has already gone down to the batteries calling for 75 volunteers from each battery. The H.Q. Co. will supply 35. Don't know how the other batteries took it, but do know that every man in F battery volunteered his services. It seems to be just a 42nd Division order and it seems that the honor of this Division is at stake. It's just a case of having to break up the Bosche resistance and the General doesn't want any outside help. It sounds rather foolish to me to take artillery men, who require at least 3 months training, and shoot them up to the front line. They'd be next to helpless up there. However, if they call on me, I'll sure go. Understand P.C. is going to send 5 men, so I may be one. I'll do more harm than good. I know because I never shot a rifle in my life. Don't know whether anything will come to it or not. The big party may come off tonight.[34] Fritzie failed to shell at 6 o'clock this evening. Can't understand that. Maybe our batteries finally put the big smack on him.

Oct. 23, 1918   A fine day for aerial activity and both sides made use of it. I saw two or three cases where our aviators proved to be "par bon." The Bosche got three of our balloons, theirs remained untouched. When they shot down the third one, one of our patrols gave chase and just about had the Bosche where he wanted him. Then he suddenly gave us the chase and beat it for home. He sure could've finished his man if he'd kept after him. Don't know whether the machine gun went bad or whether he got a yellow streak. He sure let an easy victim get away from him. The boys were pretty well disgusted. — Fitz [Philip E. Fitzsimons], Danny, and I dug ourselves a "petit" dugout and Fitz and I are going to sleep in it tonight. I'm leery about these shacks. They look too much like targets to yours truly. We're sure in for a helluva shelling tonight. The Bosche got his eyes full today. It's a bright night tonight and the bombing planes are sailing hither and thither. Beautiful night for a murder. The place has got the Vesle looking like a picnic.

Oct. 24, 1918   The Bosche made bombing trips at half-hour intervals last night, shot machine guns and all that sort of stuff. The Bosche big guns shot shells over that the boys pleased to call G.I. Camped and hang around in the air for five minutes trying to find a suitable place to light. Sure are big babies. — I take back all my sarcastic remarks about yesterday's air fighting. Read the official American communiqué, and it said that the Bosche got six of our planes and three balloons, and we got fifteen planes and one balloon, so I guess our aviators didn't do so bad after all. We don't get to see all the fireworks up front and on the German side of the lines. I'll never knock our air service again. — Fitz and I slept in our little dugout last night, and I never enjoy it better than when I sleep. Wrote Dad a birthday letter this evening, first

34. The "big party" was a planned offensive, scheduled for November 1, although the troops in the field did not learn of the exact date until the very last moment. In the meantime, the Rainbow artillery lay exposed in position on the open fields, unable to respond to the periodic German shelling. Straub, *Sergeant's Diary*, 204–206.

letter I've written him. I know it will please him. Some big babies
were hitting pretty close while I wrote it. It was sure a war letter.
Oct. 25, 1918   Last night the American communiqué said that
thirty German divisions are facing the Americans on this front.
They sure mean to hold the ground. Our batteries are going to
move way up front Saturday night. There was thirty-five tanks
moved in yesterday. The big party is not very far off now, and it is
going to be so big that Mr. Bosche is going to be forced to retreat
even against his will. He's held this ground too long anyway. —
Was talking to Mooney today and he put out some wild "snow,"
said the Major of the 3rd tipped all the boys off as to the time and
nature of our coming party. He comes off Sunday morning. The
75s will follow on the heels of the dough boys at all times. The
155s will do the work the 75s ordinarily do. The 6-inch rifles will
handle the 155s['] job and so on back. Tomorrow night all our
batteries pull into position at a point just out of Sommehance
[*sic*]; it's within sniping distance of the Bosche. The 6-inch rifles
started pulling out of their old post positions tonight. They will
take over our positions when we move out. In case the doughs
meet too much resistance, all the artillery men that can be
spared will go up to help them out. We're going to bust them or
know the reason why. The terrain [is] sprinkled heavily with batteries. It's going to be a second Champagne. This is all "snow"
now, but I believe it's pretty straight stuff. We'll find out Sunday
morning. It will be a nice way to spend the Sabbath. — Heinie is
filling our little valley with gas tonight. A few H.E.'s now and then
for good measure but mostly gas. Gas don't worry me half as
much as the old H.E. Lord, how I hate the "crump" of an H.E.
Oct. 26, Sat. night   Our batteries are on the road to their forward
positions now, don't know for sure whether the party starts
tomorrow morning or not, but it surely will. They wouldn't haul
six-inch Howitzers within one kilometer of the front and let
them stand idle for very long. I think that as soon as they pull into
position, they'll start firing. Don't believe the Germans are wise
to a thing. — A Bosche airman dropped a tub full of propaganda
this afternoon. I read one of the sheets, the content was pretty
poorly gotten up. They must take us for a bunch of eggs to have
the nerve to think that it would make an impression. The boys

all laughed and said, "We'll send you back our answer tomorrow." Meaning the party. — Heinie pulled off his little hate party as per schedule again tonight.

Oct. 27, 1918   Well, the party didn't come off this morning so now I haven't got any idea when it'll come off. Don Trent just came back from Sommerhance, and he said he has never seen artillery packed as thickly as it is up here. Says six-inch and eight-inch rifles are in position along side of 75s. Lord if Heinie just doesn't get wise! It's a clear sunshiny day, and there is "beaucoup" aerial activity. I'm afraid some Bosche airman will get a glimpse and then we'll be in for a hot old reception. Sure hope the party takes place within the next 24 hours so that if the Germans had found us out they won't get a chance to do much damage. The Germans adjusted by airplane on a road about a hundred yards from our shack. We were in the line of fire and got the benefit of the shorts. Two of them fell short and fell too close for comfort. This is sure a wicked front. I feel pretty safe in my little dugout. I kind of get the willies when I'm on the set, though.

x---------------------x

Oct. 28, 1918   I came on the set at 7:00 A.M., and Olsen asked me if I knew about Danny getting hurt. He said a shell came over, bursted at the corner of the shack and a fragment got Danny in the hip. It happened at 4:15 this morning. I was down in my dugout sleeping peacefully, and no one woke me up. They carried Danny to Exermont on a litter. The boys all chipped in and we gave him money so he won't be broke when he's at the base. The wound is not serious; it's the kind I hope I'll get. One of these kind give you much rest in the hospital; clean clothes, baths and a nurse to wait on you. Then, finally a wound stripe. I sure would have liked to have seen Danny before he was taken away. Went up to see the shell hole and it was <u>too close</u> to the shack. It hit about six feet away from Danny. He sure got off lucky. Lord, I hate to see him go. I feel like I've lost a brother. He was one of the best friends I've made. They're talking of sending Ted Corbin in here to take Danny's place.[35] We're short on operators now. — The

35. Ted Corbin was a friend of Vernon Kniptash's who came from Worthington, Indiana. Sgt. Fred Daniels, "Danny," participated in the fighting at Lorraine,

first Bn. had eight men wounded yesterday. Last night we had to sit from 8:00 to 8:30 with our gas masks on . . . highly concentrated sneeze gas. First real gas attack I've been in. This front is getting me down. The boys' morale is dropping every day. If the party would only come off! — Sonny, Olsen, [William] Seward, and [Riley] Hicks tell some funny stories of what they did on the spur of the moment just after the shell hit. Seward and Hicks sat straight up in bed and stared at each other. Sonny crawled over to the stove. Olsen, who was on the set, slammed the receiver down and threw himself under the table. All of them thought that the shell hit in the next room, said it rained dirt and fragments for a full minute after the burst. I know of several rocks as big as a man's head on the roof this morning. The shell, judging from the size of the whole, was about a 105. Lieut. [John] Speed put me in charge of the station until Danny gets back. I guess I can handle the work O.K. — 6:00 P.M. Heinie threw over eight 150s and the first one got a direct hit on the end shack of this row. We had our station in there the first two days we were up here. That's the second lucky move the wireless detail has made. The other one was made in Champagne. It's funny to see how the boys' nerves are cracking and how their morale is going down. As for myself, I jump and duck every time I hear a shell whine. Getting jumpy and nervous: this offensive has just about ruined the 42nd Div. Nine months at the front without more than a week's rest at any one time is enough to get anybody down. We have the "rep" of being a crack division, but it's turning out to be a cracked division. The boys are all going to pieces, and if relief don't come soon, something is going to bust. [Leo A.] Biddle came back from A battery suffering with hysterics. He wasn't shell shocked, just a plain nervous breakdown.[36] That's the kind of strain the whole

---

Champagne-Marne, Saint-Mihiel, and along the Verdun front. He was severely wounded in action on October 28, 1918, and his overseas service ended on February 11, 1919. He was honorably discharged on April 24, with a 25 percent disability. See Fred Daniels, Roll No. 6, "Crose, Hohn O.—Dulin, Hale M.," WWI SR.

36. Kniptash was not entirely clear on the status of Biddle. The service record for Biddle reveals that he was severely wounded in combat on July 28, 1918, and then wounded again on October 27 (wound undetermined). See Leo A. Biddle, Roll No. 2, "Baker, Ollie—Blake, Kenneth B.," WWI SR.

Div. is working under. Now they got all the big guns up toward where they have to keep quiet until the party comes off. If they fire, they give themselves away. There's about five guns back here that are answering the fire of the Germans. If they keep that party off much longer, the Germans will get wise and there will be Hell to pay. I was never as sick of this war as I am right now. Got to keep a grip on myself to keep from going to pieces all together. It's only the fact that the Bosche are suffering even a worse fate that keeps us going. Paper said that Ludendorf[f] resigned.[37] They're losing their big moguls one by one. — Bosche airplane dropped some more propaganda today. It rings a whole lot truer than the other one, but it still doesn't make an impression.

x----------------------x

Oct. 29, 1918   Still no party, I'd like to know what's holding it up. We're all set for it, and every day we put it off gives the Germans a better chance to meet it. Benny says the attack will take in a front of some 12 kil. I think they're waiting for the French to finish their doings, and then we'll open up. That's the way General Foch seems to be working it. The English are resting now after their attack. Just as soon as they stopped, the French took it up on their front. Then we take it up. Just won't let the Bosche rest for a minute. The Italians are hitting on their front making things very unpleasant for the Austrians. This front here is what holds the Germans on either side of Verdun together. If we can break through here things will be pretty serious for Heinie. We are massing new artillery every day. I believe they have every idle gun in France up here. It looks as if we intend to literally wipe the Germans off of this section of France. The P.C. moved back to Exermont this afternoon. This burg is shelled as bad as the place

37. The reference here is to General Erich von Ludendorff, the head of Germany's military high command. Ludendorff's resignation occurred at the end of a terrible two months for the German army in France. On September 28, unable to stem the Allied advance, Ludendorff confessed to his nominal superior, Paul von Hindenburg, that the Germans could not win the war and must seek an armistice. The Allied victories in October only accelerated the need for the Germans to negotiate an end to the conflict. See Gilbert, *First World War*, 483; Keegan, *First World War*, 412. Ludendorff submitted his resignation on October 26. See Eisenhower, *Yanks*, 277–78.

we just left. We set up our station in Ted Corbin's old dugout. She's a deep one, and we'll turn a good sized shell. It's a relief to sit down here and laugh at them as they come over. It's wet and miserable down here, but it's safe and worlds better than the place we just left. The rest of the P.C. is having a hard time finding a place for their horses, etc. Maybe we'll move again tomorrow. Not if I can help it though. It feels good to feel safe again.

Oct. 30, 1918   Still no party. Heinie laid across us a few big ones last night and this morning. Between 9:30 and 10 o'clock this morning he put over some 40 odd. They hit close and the concussion from one of the nearest ones put our candle out. We sat down here and laughed at 'em. Down in a deep dugout is the best way to fight those H-E's and I know from experience. It may not be D.S.C. stuff, but you stand a better chance of going home when the old "guerre" ends.[38] Something I ate made me feel pretty sick this evening. Was a sick headache. Been a long time since I've had to put up with one. I soon get relief.

Oct. 31, 1918   One year ago today our ship bumped into France. One year ago today we saw land for the first time in two weeks. Today we are seeing what H-E shells can do to that same land. Lord, what the things that have happened in that year! Three months of it in a training camp learning how to fight the Bosche and the remaining nine months putting our training into practice. We've sure done our share of practicing. Put on our two service stripes today. — Understand that the 42nd will not follow up this drive. It will stay in until our guns are out of range and then we pull out. That's the "snow" Captain [Samuel A.] Peck was putting out. He didn't say where we would go to. Hope we go down to the Baccarat sector for the winter. Talking to some of the boys out of the 82nd and 36th Divisions and they said that they heard that the 42nd would be taken off the front altogether this winter. That would sure be the fair thing to do. I don't know of any division that has earned a rest any more than we. — The New York *Herald* gave the 42nd a nice little write-up. — It also came out in big headlines and said that Austria sued for a separate peace. We sure

38. "D.S.C." refers to the American military award the Distinguished Service Cross.

got the Entente where we want 'em.[39] Overheard the Col. [Tyn-dall] say that the party opened up tomorrow morning at 3:30. There is to be a nine-hour bombardment. He said he had a hunch that the Bosche pulled out last night. They haven't fired a shot at us since yesterday afternoon. He thinks the Germans are wise to our party and the biggest portion of those have dropped back, leaving a few sacrifice machine gunners and artillery men. I think that's the case or else it's the other extreme. They may think that we were satisfied to give ourselves a mental rest. We'll see in the morning. As soon as the bombardment ceases, our Division pulls out and goes into position again in the sector to our left. There's no rest in sight for the 42$^{\underline{nd}}$. Our doughboys were relieved last night. I guess our Artillery is supporting the Marines. That's the way it goes. Keeps our doughboys in the line for three weeks, holding it and then when a chance comes to add further honors on to their already long string, they pull 'em out and give the much-talked-about Marines the honor of opening up the party. The papers and magazines were chock full of their battle in Belleau Wood way back in July. Where have they been since that battle? From that write-up one would think it's the only battle the war has had. They're coming to the line now as fresh as daisies, while our poor doughs are all in. Half of 'em were sent to the hospital marked physically exhausted. I can't help but believe that the 42nd is getting a raw deal somewhere. Maybe not, though. I can't see why they should want to ruin a scrappy Division and I guess they have no intention of doing so, but they'll sure do it if they don't give us a rest pretty soon.

Nov. 1, 1918   The bombardment started at 3:30 A.M. It's now 11:00 A.M. and the guns are still at it. Was talking to Artie Bryan and he said he knew two official reports. Once was that the Marines were meeting little or no resistance and were ahead of the tanks and the other was that we're already past our third

39. Austria-Hungary asked for an armistice on October 27, 1918. As in some other parts of the diary, Kniptash displays some inaccuracy in describing the warring countries. Germany and Austria-Hungary belonged to the Triple Alliance, later the Central powers, and not the Triple Entente. See Gilbert, *First World War*, 487. Portions of Kniptash's diary entry of October 31, 1918, were published in Ferrell, *Diary of Elmer Sherwood*, 177n9.

objective. It seems that Heinie got wise to our attack, even to the zero hour. He withdrew most of his troops and we are capturing the men he left behind as sacrifice troops. He dropped a little barrage early this morning, but after it fizzled out, he hasn't sent a shell this way. The party is progressing nicely. Don't know when we move, but the 3$^{\underline{rd}}$ Bn. was rolling packs a few minutes ago. Heard that our party is turning out to be one huge glorious success. We've captured "beaucoup" artillery. Also heard that a battalion of our doughs that were being held back in reserve got it up among themselves to beat the Marines. They decided the Marines weren't going to get all the credit for this drive so when the time came they went over the top of the "First to fight" boys and have been leading them ever since. They did not let their officers know a thing about it and went over with a Sergeant in charge of the battalion. Suppose when the battle comes to a stop this battalion will catch Hell. It was the Alabama boys. Alabama hasn't got a whole lot of love for the Marines so when the time came they said to Hell with the Marines. We're not going to hold this line for twenty days and then let them come up here and go over. We're going over and they sure did.[40] — The battle has shifted over to our left now. Prisoners have been coming in steadily all day long. Must have been close to 2,000 altogether.[41] They all said that the war was lost and they jeered when somebody mentioned the Kaiser. They were all in. Guess our Artillery didn't give 'em much rest. Understand the Marines and our doughs have reached the outskirts of Buzancy. That means

40. Other accounts of the massive Allied offensive on November 1, 1918, may be found in Farwell, *Over There*, 233–34; Sherwood, *Rainbow Hoosier*, 134; and Straub, *Sergeant's Diary*, 209. Straub also wrote: "There was practically no retaliation fire from the Germans" to the American artillery barrage" (209). The soldiers in the Alabama unit were particularly fierce fighters. Upon learning that the "Alabams" unsheathed their Bowie knives and used them in hand-to-hand combat with the Germans, Elmer Sherwood wrote that "they are a wild bunch, not knowing what fear is"; *Diary of a Rainbow Veteran*, 22.

41. The attitude of German POWs was quite remarkable. Many of the Germans captured by American forces inquired if they were going to be transferred to America. As Pete Straub wrote: "All of these [German] prisoners ask but one question when they came in and that was 'Do we go to America?' they sure all wanted to go." *Sergeant's Diary*, 210. See also Sherwood, *Diary of a Rainbow Veteran*, 205.

they've advanced some 9 kil., quite a little ground for a bad sector like this one. Said the Bosche were offering very little resistance. A doughboy came back dragging a German Colonel along with him. He was one of these aloof, cocky sort of ducks, but the doughboy made him step. When he finally reached the bullpen, he isolated himself from the rest of the prisoners and put on an offended look as if he was being sadly mistreated. I'd have given a million dollars to have been allowed to punch his nose just once, bet I'd have taken some of those high toned airs out of him. Damn Prussian square head. — The midnight American communiqué said that an attack 20 kil. wide was made this morning. The 4th French Army was on our left. We took the towns of St. Georges, Landres, St. Juvien, Imecourt, Landrevilles [Landeville], Chennoy, Bayonnville, Remonville, and Andevanne. Captured 2,602 prisoners, of whom 151 are officers. That's a pretty good day's work. Wonder what tomorrow will net us.

x---------------------x

Nov. 2, 1918   The P.C. was going to move to St. Juvien this noon, but something came up and we stay here till further orders now. Front is pretty quiet. It's just as Fitz says, two days before the drive a fellow can't find room to pitch a pup tent and a day after the drive is over a fellow can't find anybody to talk to. — Found out that we're being held in reserve. We're sure in the S.O.S. Must be 15 kil. from the front line. Barely hear the Artillery.

Nov. 3, 1918   Made the most disagreeable hike I've ever taken as far today. Left Exermont at 4 o'clock this afternoon, and hit the town of Champigneulle at 3 o'clock the next morning. Was some 8 kil. in traffic blocked the whole distance. Rained all the way and then turned cold. Mud up to my ankles. Sat by a fire the rest of the night and almost got the chill out of my bones by morning.

Nov. 4, 1918   The Chaplain came up here this morning and put out some very good news. Said that Austria would be out of the war officially either today or tomorrow. Said peace negotiations with Germany are under way right now. Said he'd be some surprised if this old "guerre" wouldn't be over in 2 or 3 weeks. Said that the Germans are retreating up here so fast that our doughs can't keep up with them. Our doughs are going after them in trucks. It's the best retreat the Bosche has made yet. He's taking everything with him. There is none of his material lying around this burg. From the rumors I've heard, the Germans are no longer in France around this sector. They've withdrawn to their border. The English have started up again, taking the town of Ghent yesterday. Poor old Bosche! They don't give him a chance to catch his breath. — We're going to move again this morning. The P.C. is going to be 12 kil. up farther front. Left Champigneulle at 10 o'clock in the morning. Passed thru <u>Bar</u>, <u>Buzancy</u>, and when we reached a crossroads a kil. out of Buzancy the M.P. shot us out the wrong road. It was 7:00 P.M. then, and Lieut. Speed pulled off the road and made camp. Decided to stay right where we were rather than meander all over France looking for Autrouche. We had only one meal yesterday and one today. We raided a cabbage patch planted by the Bosche and made raw cabbage stew for one meal. Lord, but how cold, hungry, and miserable we were. I didn't even pitch a pup tent. Threw my blankets out on the wet ground and slept away.

Nov. 5, 1918   Went down and bummed a breakfast off the 117th H.Q. Lord, but it went good. The dew was so heavy last night that we thought we'd slept through a rain. Started out for Autrouche and there being no traffic jam good time was made. Yesterday was terrible. Took us all day to go ten kil. The Bosche bombed pretty heavily, too. Don't know where the forest is at the present running, but I think we've finally caught up with the war. The town is intact. They didn't hang around here very long.

Nov. 6, 1918   Going to move again this afternoon to a town some 15 kil. from <u>Sedan</u>. This town of Sedan is our final objective. We are still in reserve. We took a road yesterday that the Bosche used to carry 40% of his communication supplies and troops over. In other words, we've cut off one of his two paths of retreat out of France. — Austria dropped out of the fight at 3:00 P.M. Nov. 4, 1918. — All the Germans facing the French forces are in full retreat. It's only a question of days before every German will be out of France and Belgium. — All orders affecting the 42nd Div. were cancelled and every outfit will stay where they are now billeted. We're billeted in a house and have things pretty nifty. Big fireplace, etc. Don't know how long we stay here, but I think we'll go up front before long.

Nov. 7, 1918   Still here and nobody knows a thing about moving. English communiqué said that the Germans sent a commission of four men (two Generals and two Admirals) over the line to talk armistice with the Allies. General Foch formally received them today. Can't help but feel that these men will accept all the terms laid down by Gen. Foch. They can hardly do otherwise now. Heard the "snow" that General [Edmund] Allenby's Army is coming thru Austria to make another front on the border between Germany and Austria.[42] It's a cinch Germany can't take any men off this front to defend her border down there. I think she's reached the end of her rope and that we can expect peace any day now. Lord, how I'd like to eat my Xmas dinner at home this year. The Germans are still retreating on the whole front from Verdun north to the sea. The retreat is still orderly, but the pressure is beginning to tell. Would like to see them surrender at <u>Sedan</u> as the French did back in 1870.

Nov. 8, 1918   Copied a Paris note today at 12 o'clock. First time Paris has sent at that time. It was from the German commission at Paris to the German command at <u>Spa</u>, Belgium. Gen. Foch gives them 72 hours to accept or decline the terms of the armistice. The Germans asked for all fighting to stop during this time, but Foch told 'em nothing doing. They are communicating by courier and wireless. — English communiqué said that the German retreat has turned into a race for safety. — The American communiqué mentioned the Rainbow Division for the first time today. Said the Rainbow troops were the first to enter Sedan.[43] Our sector was gradually shifted to the left and I

42. By this time, Allenby had been reassigned to command British troops that were fighting in Palestine. Kniptash appeared to be confused about the identity of this officer and his assignment. See Strachan, *First World War*, 283, 284.

43. Kniptash's reference to the taking of Sedan by the Rainbow Division is inaccurate and indicative of the faulty communication that existed within the various units of the AEF as the fighting came closer to a conclusion in early November 1918. Pershing nearly precipitated a major clash with the French military leadership when he authorized American forces, including the 42nd Division, to mount an offensive designed to capture Sedan. Sedan, of course, had been the scene of two major French defeats at the hands of the Germans, first in 1870 in the final battle of the Franco-Prussian War and again in 1914 during the first weeks of World War I. The French deserved the honor of retaking Sedan and avenging the

honestly believe that this honor was intentionally given to us. Part of our Division is fighting and part of us are from 40 to 50 kil. from the battle. We're back here because they have all the 6" stuff they need up there. The 75's are doing the same. Don't care if the war ends while we're here. Don't care if I never hear another shell whine. I've heard all the whining I care to.

Nov. 9   The 42nd was officially relieved today and all the outfits are pulling back this way. Heard that we move tomorrow.[44] I understand that this town is out of the Divisional area. Sure will hate to leave this big fireplace. — All sorts of important messages coming via wireless. The German general in Paris sent a message to his H.Q. telling them to arrest some Bosche captain who was destroying the bridges on the laCappele road as he retreated. This road is to be used by the couriers and this Captain was slowing things by his work. — Copied an English communiqué which said that Prince Max of Baden resigned and told about his farewell speech to the German people.[45] He said that it was only a question of hours before the Armistice would be signed now. Said the German Army could not do the impossible and hold off the whole Allied Army by itself. Said that, although Germany lost, she won one big battle. That was the one in which she found out that right, and not might, will win in the long run. — It was plain, outspoken admission that Germany had been in the wrong all the time.[46] — The people in Germany are clamoring

---

earlier, crushing defeats. Although the AEF pulled back from its offensive around Sedan, in deference to the French, the Armistice went into effect before Sedan was completely retaken by Allied forces. See Farwell, *Over There*, 214–44; James, *Years of MacArthur*, 1:229–36; Smythe, *Pershing*, 227–30; Vandiver, *Black Jack*, 2:983–85.

44. As of November 8, the Rainbow Division's position in the sector was slated for takeover by General Henri Gouraud's 4th Army. The Rainbows were soon to be formed into the Army of Occupation under the command of the American general Joseph Dickman. See Cooke, *Rainbow Division*, 201–202.

45. Prince Max of Baden was the German chancellor who helped negotiate the eventual Armistice between the warring countries. He resigned on November 9, and the leader of Germany's Social Democratic Party, Friedrich Ebert, became the chancellor. See Gilbert, *First World War*, 498; Fleming, *Illusion of Victory*, 301.

46. Useful accounts of the German decision to seek an end to the fighting may be found in Farwell, *Over There*, 257; Freidel, *Over There*, 215–17; Gilbert, *First World War*, 494–96; Keegan, *First World War*, 418–19; and Marshall, *Memoirs*, 200–201.

for peace, and the higher-ups are pleading with them not to start internal troubles now that bloodshed is about to cease on the front. They increased the bread allowance to appease the crowds. — The Frenchies are running around, hog wild, yelling, "Finis la guerre tout de suite." They are crazy with joy. I am saving my outburst until Monday morning at 11:00 o'clock. Want to know for sure before I cut loose. There's a remote possibility of the Germans not signing the armistice, but it's <u>some</u> remote. Would like to know what the terms are. Bet they don't leave Germany very much. — Wild "snow" has it that the 1st, 2nd, 26th, and 42nd are going south for the winter, and will not see another front before the spring drive.[47] This is in case peace is not declared before spring. Also, the 150th will be motorized and will turn their horses over to the 75th regiment. I'm not much interested in motors. What I'm looking forward to is big ships; big ships to take a fellow from a certain French port to New York City, then a train from there to Indpls. If the war should end, wonder how soon the 42nd will get to leave. We certainly deserve anything good they give us. Oh! but how I'd like to spend Xmas at home.

Nov. 10, 1918   Copied the English last night. It was the Prime Minister's speech to the House of Commons. One line said that the Kaiser and Crown Prince had abdicated. Boy, oh boy, those Germans will just have to accept those terms. We're slated to move this afternoon and suppose we'll be on the road when the big news is flashed. — Started moving at 2:30, just in time to hear the French communiqué. Hiked to Haracourt and are sleeping in pup tents. Heard some wild "snow" that the 1st, 26th, and 42nd Div. were entraining for a base port.

x-----x

Nov. 11, 1918   There was an intense barrage up 'til 10:55 this morning. Then all guns ceased. This was the hour set for all firing to stop. The French and Americans certainly used up what ammunition they had on hand. Everything is quiet now. Copied the communiqué today, and it said that the Armistice had been signed. The end of the war didn't turn out as I thought it would.

---

47. Cooke, *Rainbow Division*, 202.

The boys did very little carrying on. Just took it as a matter of course. Paper said that Paris celebrated elaborately. Wonder how long it'll take before peace is finally declared. Capt. Hofmann, Kelly, and Major Miller put on a little party last night and I was invited. They got gloriously drunk, but I didn't touch a thing. Hofmann said we'd hike to <u>Grand Pre</u> tomorrow or day after and get brand new equipment all around. Can't savvy that. <u>Grand Pre</u> is a railhead so I suppose we'll entrain from there.

x----------------------x

Figure 1. The Kniptash family of Indianapolis (*left to right*): Vernon's father, Wilhelm Kniptash; his brother, Robert; his mother, Ollie Cottom Kniptash; and Vernon.

ENLISTMENT RECORD.

Gw A

Indianapolis Ind

Name: *Vernon E Kniptash*   Grade: *Corporal*

Enlisted, or Inducted, *April 23* 1917, at *Indianapolis Ind*

Serving in *First* enlistment period at date of discharge.

Prior service: * *None*

Noncommissioned officer: *Corporal from Private S.O 240 Nov. 28-1918*

Marksmanship, gunner qualification or rating: † *not qualified*

Horsemanship: *not mounted*

Battles, engagements, skirmishes, expeditions: *Luneville Sector 2/23/18~ 3/22/18 Baccarat Sector 3/30/18 to 6/20/18" Champagne-Marne Offensive 7/15/18 to 7/18/18. Aisne Marne offensive 7/23/18 to 8/11/18. St Mihiel Offensive 9/12/18 to 9/16/18" minor operations in Woevre 9/11/18 9/13/18 mean Argonne off 9/30/18 to 11/11/18 Army of Occupation 11/17/18 to 3/23/19*

Knowledge of any vocation: *Draughman*

Wounds received in service: *None*

Physical condition when discharged: *good*

Typhoid prophylaxis completed *August 3 — 1917*

Paratyphoid prophylaxis completed *August 30 1917*

Married or single: *Single*

Character: *Excellent*

Remarks: *Last assigned Hg Company 150 Field Artillery*

Signature of soldier: *Vernon E. Kniptash*

Geo W B—

* Give company and regiment or corps or department, with inclusive dates of service in each enlistment.
† Give date of qualification or rating and number, date, and source of order announcing same.

Figure 2. Vernon Kniptash's enlistment record in the Indiana National Guard.

Figure 3. The two red, cloth-covered diary books that contained Vernon Kniptash's recollections of his service in World War I.

Figure 4. The inside front cover of the first book of the Kniptash diaries. Vernon Kniptash was a skilled artist, and this diagram depicts the Rainbow Division, its campaigns, the state of Indiana, and the 150th Field Artillery designation, set against the background of the French countryside. Kniptash also included two German stamps on this page.

119

Figure 5. The second inside page of Kniptash's first volume contained pieces of German currency and a drawing of a German airplane.

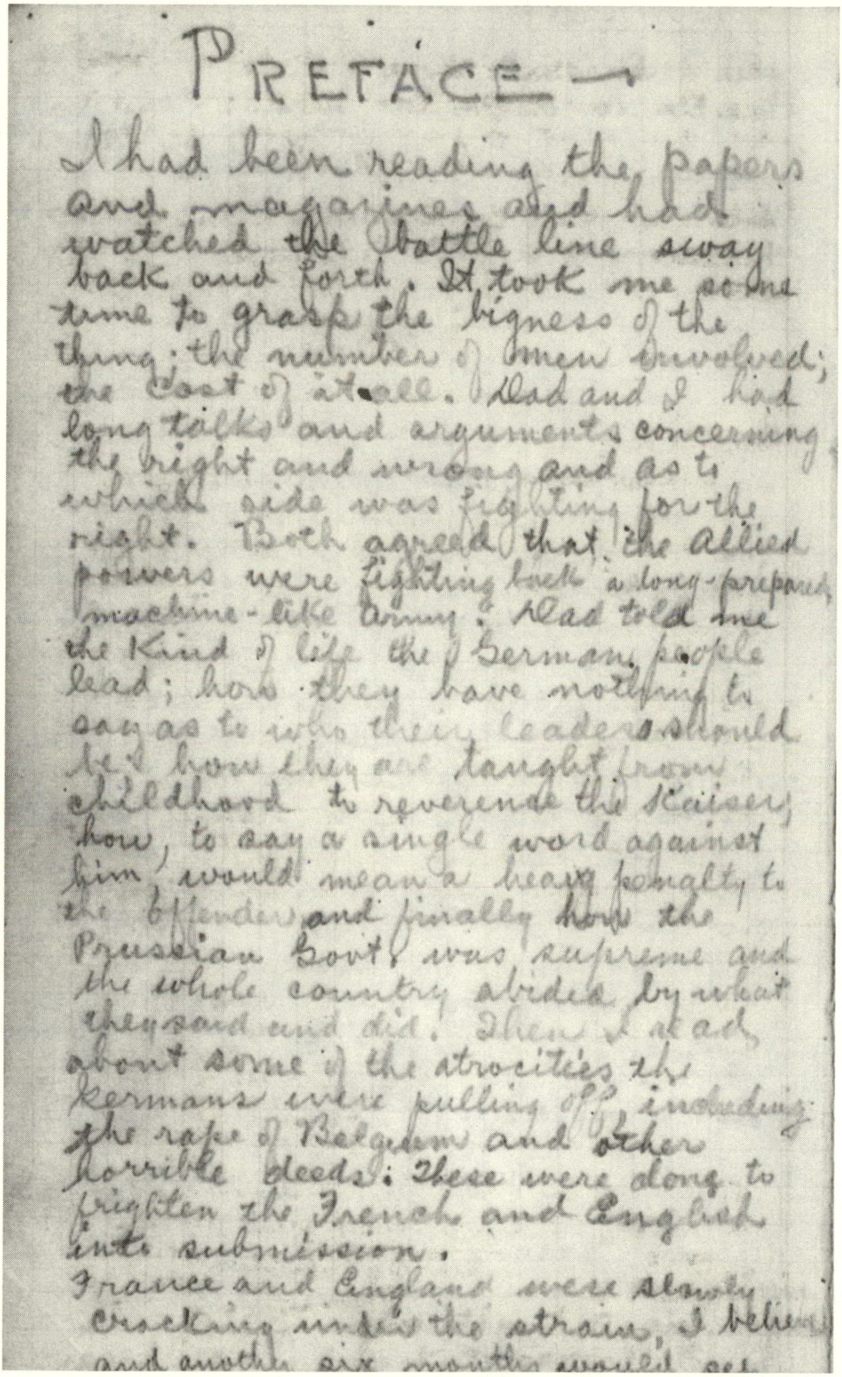

PREFACE

I had been reading the papers and magazines and had watched the battle line sway back and forth. It took me some time to grasp the bigness of the thing; the number of men involved; the cost of it all. Dad and I had long talks and arguments concerning the right and wrong and as to which side was fighting for the right. Both agreed that the Allied powers were fighting back a long-prepared machine-like army. Dad told me the kind of life the German people lead; how they have nothing to say as to who their leaders should be; how they are taught from childhood to reverence the Kaiser; how, to say a single word against him would mean a heavy penalty to the offender and finally how the Prussian Govt was supreme and the whole country abided by what they said and did. Then I read about some of the atrocities the Germans were pulling off, including the rape of Belgium and other horrible deeds. These were done to frighten the French and English into submission.

France and England were slowly cracking under the strain, I believe and another six months would see

Figure 6. Kniptash began his diary entries with a preface, shown here.

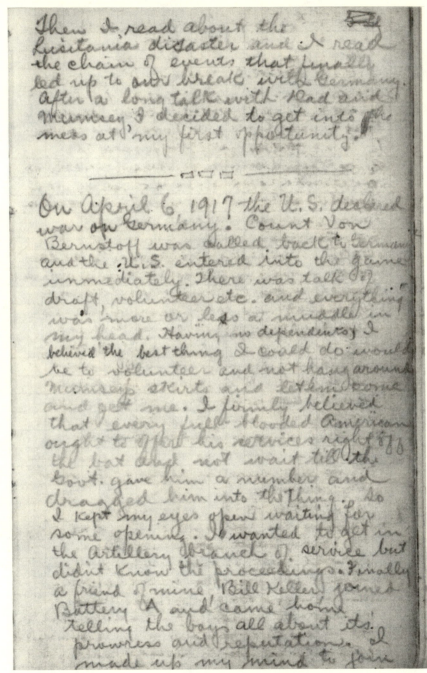

Then I read about the
Lusitania disaster and I read
the chain of events that finally
led up to our break with Germany.
After a long talk with Dad and
McInsey I decided to get into the
mess at my first opportunity.

On April 6, 1917 the U.S. declared
war on Germany. Count Von
Bernstoff was called back to Germany
and the U.S. entered into the game
immediately. There was talk of
draft, volunteer etc. and everything
was more or less at muddle in
my head. Having no dependents, I
believed the best thing I could do would
be to volunteer and not hang around
McInsey's skirts and let time come
and get me. I firmly believed
that every full blooded American
ought to offer his services right off
the bat and not wait till the
Govt. gave him a number and
dragged him into the thing. So
I kept my eyes open waiting for
some opening. I wanted to get in
the Artillery branch of service but
didn't know the proceedings. Finally
a friend of mine Bill Keller joined
Battery A and came home
telling the boys all about its
prowess and reputation. I
made up my mind to join

Figure 7. In this diary entry, following the preface, Kniptash explains how
he reached his decision to enlist in the Indiana National Guard.

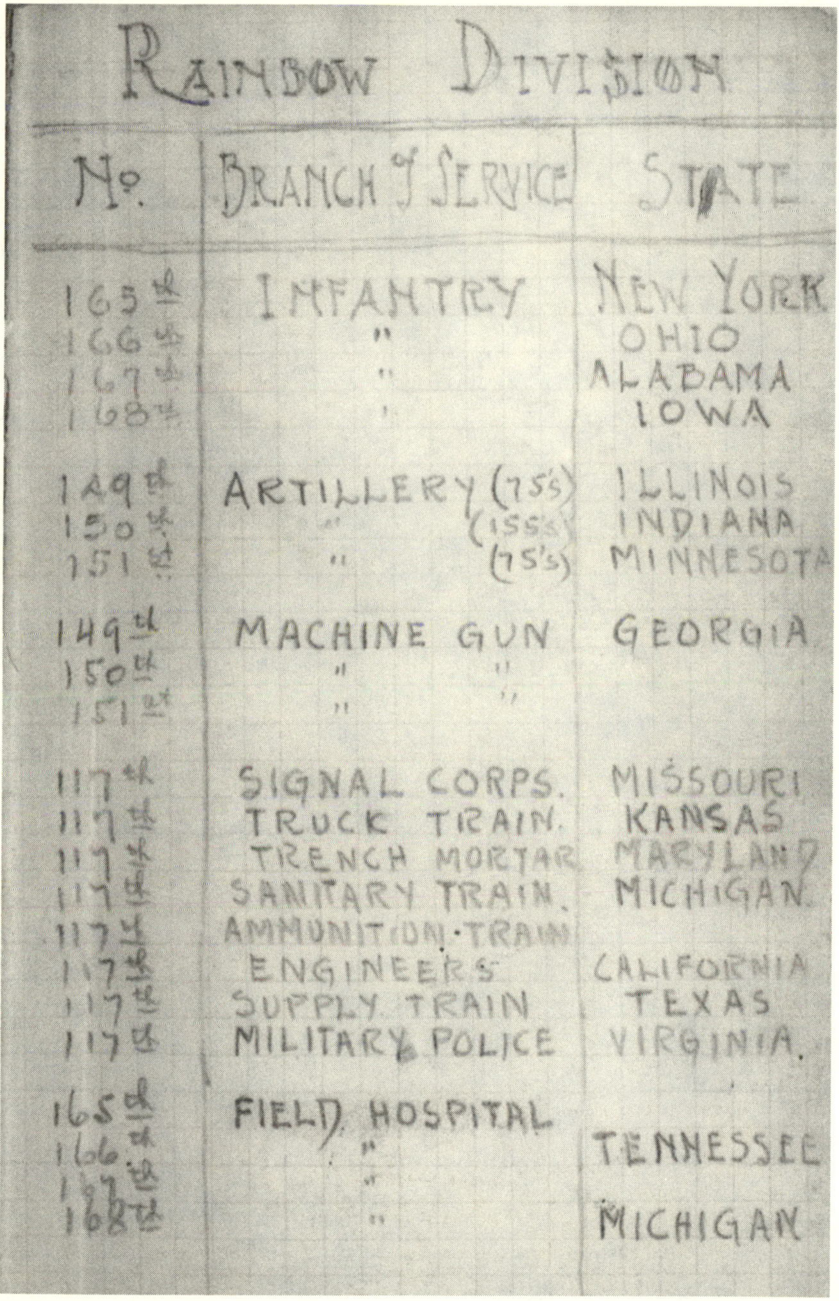

No.	BRANCH of SERVICE	STATE
165th	INFANTRY	NEW YORK
166th	"	OHIO
167th	"	ALABAMA
168th	'	IOWA
149th	ARTILLERY (75's)	ILLINOIS
150th	" (155's)	INDIANA
151st	" (75's)	MINNESOTA
149th	MACHINE GUN	GEORGIA
150th	" "	
151st	" "	
117th	SIGNAL CORPS.	MISSOURI
117th	TRUCK TRAIN.	KANSAS
117th	TRENCH MORTAR	MARYLAND
117th	SANITARY TRAIN.	MICHIGAN.
117th	AMMUNITION·TRAIN	
117th	ENGINEERS	CALIFORNIA
117th	SUPPLY TRAIN	TEXAS
117th	MILITARY POLICE	VIRGINIA.
165th	FIELD HOSPITAL	
166th	"	TENNESSEE
167th	"	
168th	"	MICHIGAN

Figure 8. On the outside back page of the first volume of the Kniptash diaries, Vernon wrote a diagram that listed many of the state National Guard units that comprised the Rainbow division.

Figure 9. The poster prepared to commemorate the service of Battery A (mostly soldiers from Indianapolis) of the 150th Field Artillery. The artist of the poster is Dan Smith; the sponsor is not identified. The names of the soldiers who are listed on the poster are included in the appendix. The poster was in the possession of Harry Norman Bryan, who, like Kniptash, left for Europe as a member of Battery A of the 150th Field Artillery. Illustration courtesy C. Thomas Bryan.

Figure 10. This photo was taken of Kniptash at an unknown location in France.

Figure 11. This photo was taken of Kniptash with his horse, May. As Kniptash recorded in his diary between September 27 and October 1, 1918, May ran away from the unit and never returned.

Headquarters, 42nd Division,
AMERICAN EXPEDITIONARY FORCES, FRANCE
August 13th, 1918.

TO THE OFFICERS AND MEN OF THE 42ND DIVISION:

A year has elapsed since the formation of your organization. It is, therefore, fitting to consider what you have accomplished as a combat division and what you should prepare to accomplish in the future.

Your first elements entered the trenches in Lorraine on February 21st. You served on that front for 110 days. You were the first American division to hold a divisional sector and when you left the sector June 21st, you had served continuously as a division in the trenches for a longer time than any other American division. Although you entered the sector without experience in actual warfare, you so conducted yourselves as to win the respect and affection of the French veterans with whom you fought. Under gas and bombardment, in raids, in patrols, in the heat of hand to hand combat and in the long dull hours of trench routine so trying to a soldier's spirit, you bore yourselves in a manner worthy of the traditions of our country.

You were withdrawn from Lorraine and moved immediately to the Champagne front where during the critical days from July 14th to July 18th, you had the honor of being the only American division to fight in General Gouraud's Army which so gloriously obeyed his order, "We will stand or die", and by its iron defense crushed the German assault and made possible the offensive of July 18th to the west of Reims.

From Champagne you were called to take part in exploiting the success north of the Marne. Fresh from the battle front before Chalons, you were thrown against the picked troops of Germany. For eight consecutive days, you attacked skillfully prepared positions. You captured great stores of arms and munitions. You forced the crossings of the Ourcq. You took Hill 212, Sergy, Meurcy Ferme and Seringes by assault. You drove the enemy, including an Imperial Guard Division, before you for a depth of fifteen kilometers. When your infantry was relieved, it was in full pursuit of the retreating Germans, and your artillery continued to progress and support another American division in the advance to the Vesle.

For your services in Lorraine, your division was formally commended in General Orders by the French Army Corps under which you served. For your services in Champagne, your assembled officers received the personal thanks and commendation of General Gouraud himself. For your services on the Ourcq, your division was officially complimented in a letter from the Commanding General, 1st Army Corps, of July 28th, 1918.

To your success, all ranks and all services have contributed, and I desire to express to every man in the command my appreciation of his devoted and courageous effort.

However, our position places a burden of responsibility upon us which we must strive to bear steadily forward without faltering. To our comrades who have fallen, we owe the sacred obligation of maintaining the reputation which they died to establish. The influence of our performance on our allies and our enemies cannot be over-estimated for we were one of the first divisions sent from our country to France to show the world that Americans can fight.

Hard battles and long campaigns lie before us. Only by ceaseless vigilance and tireless preparation can we fit ourselves for them. I urge you, therefore, to approach the future with confidence but above all with firm determination that so far as it is in your power you will spare no effort whether in training or in combat to maintain the record of our division and the honor of our country.

CHARLES T. MENOHER,
Major General, U. S. Army.

Figure 12. The officers and men of the Rainbow Division received a letter of commendation from their commanding officer, Major General Charles T. Menoher, on August 13, 1918, for their service to that point in the conflict.

oct. 7

The German People Offers Peace.

The new German democratic government has this programme:

"The will of the people is the highest law."

The German people wants quickly to end the slaughter.

The new German popular government therefore has offered an

Armistice

and has declared itself ready for

Peace

on the basis of justice and reconciliation of nations.

It is the will of the German people that it should live in peace with all peoples, honestly and loyally.

What has the new German popular government done so far to put into practice the will of the people and to prove its good and upright intentions?

a) The new German government has appealed to President Wilson to bring about peace.

It has recognized and accepted all the principles which President Wilson proclaimed as a basis for a general lasting peace of justice among the nations.

b) The new German government has so emnly declared its readiness to evacuate Belgium and to restore it.

c) The new German government is ready to come to an honest understanding with France about.

Alsace-Lorraine.

č) The new German government has restricted the U-boat War.

No passengers steamers not carrying troops or war material will be attacked in future.

e) The new German government has declared that it will withdraw all German troops back over the German frontier.

f) — The new German government has asked the Allied Governments to name commissioners to agree upon, the practical measures of the evacuation of Belgium and France.

These are the deeds of the new German popular government. Can these be called mere words, or bluff, or propaganda?

Who is to blame, if an armistice is not called now?

Who is to blame if daily thousands of brave soldiers needlessly have to shed their blood and die?

Who is to blame, if the hitherto undestroyed towns and villages of France and Belgium sink in ashes?

Who is to blame, if hundreds of thousands of unhappy women and children are driven from their homes to hunger and freeze?

The German people offers its hand for peace.

Figure 13. Kniptash kept this broadsheet of German propaganda. In his diary entry of October 26, 1918, he mentions that a German "airman dropped a tub full of propaganda this afternoon." Another diary entry on October 28 also mentions a drop of German propaganda.

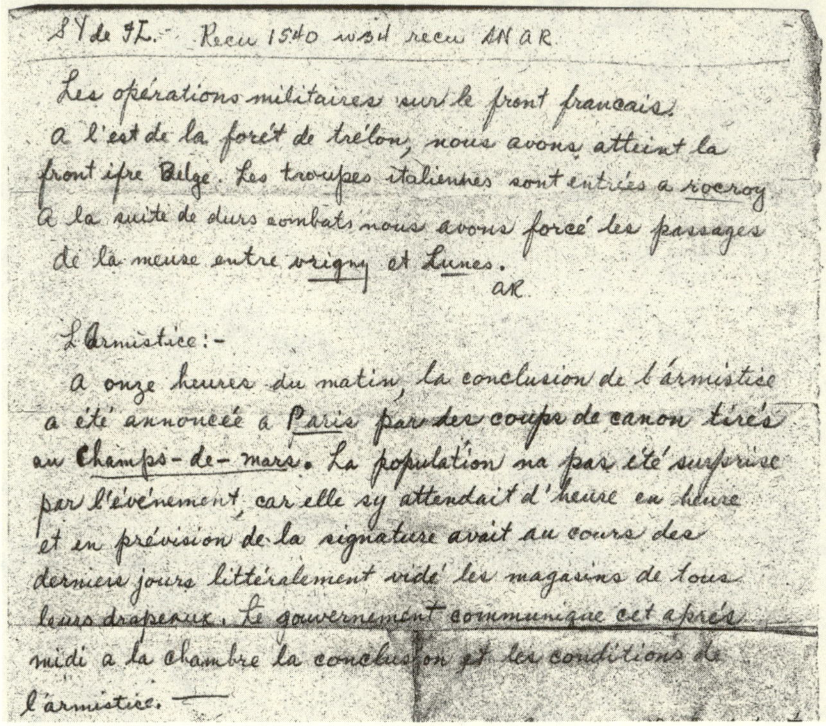

S Y de FL.- Recu 1540 w.s.d recu AN AR

Les opérations militaires sur le front français.
A l'est de la forêt de trélon, nous avons atteint la
frontifre Belge. Les troupes italiennes sont entrées a rocroy
A la suite de durs combats nous avons forcé les passages
de la meuse entre vrigny et Lunes.

AR

L'Armistice:-

a onze heures du matin, la conclusion de l'ármistice
a été annoncée a Paris par des coups de canon tirés
au Champs-de-mars. La population na pas été surprise
par l'événement, car elle sy attendait d'heure en heure
et en prévision de la signature avait au cours des
derniers jours littéralement vidé les magasins de tous
leurs drapeaux. Le gouvernement communique cet après
midi a la chambre la conclusion et les conditions de
l'armistice. ——

Figure 14. A communiqué Kniptash received on November 11, 1918, that confirmed the Armistice.

> Military operations on the French front. To the east of the Trélon forest, we have reached the Belgian frontier. The Italian troops have entered Rocroy. Following hard fighting we have forced [open] the crossings of the Meuse [river] between Vrigny and Lunes.
>
> AR
>
> The Armistice: —
>
> At eleven o'clock in the morning, the agreement of the armistice was announced in Paris by cannon fire at the Champs-de-Mars. The population was not surprised by the event for it was waiting for this [development] hour by hour and in expectation of the signature had during the preceding days literally emptied stores of all their flags. The government will communicate this afternoon to the Chamber [of Deputies] the agreement and conditions of the armistice. ———

Translated from the French by Christopher S. Thompson.

G. H. Q.
AMERICAN EXPEDITIONARY FORCES,

GENERAL ORDERS}
No. 38-A. }

FRANCE, *February 28, 1919.*

MY FELLOW SOLDIERS:

Now that your service with the American Expeditionary Forces is about to terminate, I can not let you go without a personal word. At the call to arms, the patriotic young manhood of America eagerly responded and became the formidable army whose decisive victories testify to its efficiency and its valor. With the support of the nation firmly united to defend the cause of liberty, our army has executed the will of the people with resolute purpose. Our democracy has been tested, and the forces of autocracy have been defeated. To the glory of the citizen-soldier, our troops have faithfully fulfilled their trust, and in a succession of brilliant offensives have overcome the menace to our civilization.

As an individual, your part in the world war has been an important one in the sum total of our achievements. Whether keeping lonely vigil in the trenches, or gallantly storming the enemy's stronghold; whether enduring monotonous drudgery at the rear, or sustaining the fighting line at the front, each has bravely and efficiently played his part. By willing sacrifice of personal rights; by cheerful endurance of hardship and privation; by vigor, strength and indomitable will, made effective by thorough organization and cordial co-operation, you inspired the war-worn Allies with new life and turned the tide of threatened defeat into overwhelming victory.

With a consecrated devotion to duty and a will to conquer, you have loyally served your country. By your exemplary conduct a standard has been established and maintained never before attained by any army. With mind and body as clean and strong as the decisive blows you delivered against the foe, you are soon to return to the pursuits of peace. In leaving the scenes of your victories, may I ask that you carry home your high ideals and continue to live as you have served—an honor to the principles for which you have fought and to the fallen comrades you leave behind.

It is with pride in our success that I extend to you my sincere thanks for your splendid service to the army and to the nation.

Faithfully,

John J. Pershing

Commander in Chief.

OFFICIAL:
ROBERT C. DAVIS,
Adjutant General.

Copy furnished to *Corp Vernon Kniptash*

Capt U.S.A. 150 F.A.

Commanding.

Figure 15. Following the armistice, each soldier in the American Expeditionary Forces received a letter, dated February 28, 1919, from General John J. Pershing, commander-in-chief of the AEF. As Kniptash recorded in his diaries, Pershing reviewed the 150th Field Artillery on March 16, 1919, in Germany.

Figure 16. This photo was taken of Kniptash in the spring of 1919, during the occupation of Germany.

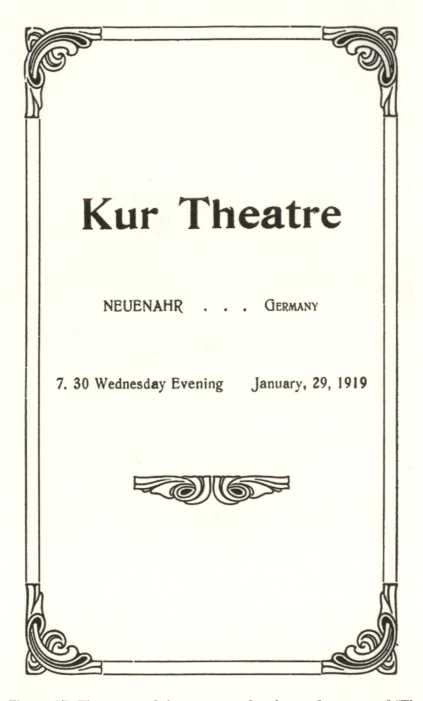

Kur Theatre

NEUENAHR . . . GERMANY

7. 30 Wednesday Evening   January, 29, 1919

Figure 17. The cover of the program for the performance of "The Hoosier Follies," on January 29, 1919, in Neuenahr, Germany.

REGINALD A. BRINKLOW
Presents
150th. FIELD ARTILLERY BAND & BUGLE CORPS
in
HOOSIER FOLLIES
A whirlwind farce furor by
Cal B. Clifford
A. Merry Musical Melee in Two Parts.

CAST

System	Mr. Rust
Singer	Mr. Vance
Iveries	Mr. Wells
Gouard	Mr. Skinner
Singer	Mr. Conkle
Uke	Mr. Kniptasch
Madolene	Mr. Hall
Singer	Mr. Jenkins
Jo	Mr. Donovan
Orpheus	Mr. Neff
Morpheus	Mr. Von Berg
The Judge	Mr. Bowers
Attorney Smart . . .	Mr. Rust
Attorney Baun	Mr. Woodward
Salvation Harry . . .	Mr. R. Bucher
Pete	Mr. E. Bucher
Tim	Mr. McMullen
Annie	Mr. Wilson
O. Limburger	Mr. Purdue
Mrs. Suff	Mr Morrow
Puss Foot	Mr. E. Gaddis
Fatima	Mr. Webb

SYNOPSIS
(ON LEAVE) ACT I PLACE, BRITTANY LEAVE AREA
ST. MALO, FRANCE. Time . . . Present
(THE HOOSIER COURT) ACT II PLACE, 45 Minutes
From Indianapolis.
TIME . . . 1908

MUSICAL NUMBERS
Orchestra Under Direction of Bandmaster
Reginald A. Brinklow

OVERTURE

Prelude	System
Opening Chorus	Vance and Chorus
Some Jazz	Jazz-Time Four
Howdy	Rust and Bucher Bros
Quartette from „Rigoletto"	Novelty Four
You're in Style	Jenkins and Chorus
Musical Melee	Saxophone Sextette
There's A Lump of Sugar .	Conkle and Chorus
Finale	Entire Company

INTERMISSION . . . . Entre Act . . . . . . Orchestra

Opening Chorus Act 2 . .	Entire Company
Dance of the Cigarette . .	Fatima
Grand Finale	Entire Company

Ladies and Gentlemen of the Chorus

Danacher-Philly-Wilson-Zeikiel-Randolph-Armstrong
Woodward-Wheelan-Stricklin-Webb-Borsch-E. Bucher
Tomlinson-Loway-Rankin-Ray-Harrington Mahle
R. Bucher-DeVilbus-Morrow-Purdue-Hall-Donovan

Novelty Four	(Bowers
	(Owen
	(Bucher
	(Toole

Staff for Mr. Brinklow

Cal. B. Clifford	Manager & Producer
Lloyd Rust	Treasure
Donald Wilson	Carpenter
J. H. Fink	Electrican
Sam Purdue	Master of Properties
Eugene H. Gaddis . . .	Scenic Artist
Earl C. Bucher	Advertising
Lee M. Bowers	Costumes

Figure 18. This program shows the various acts, and the soldiers who performed the entertainment, for "The Hoosier Follies."

Figure 19. This is the record of leave granted to Kniptash to take a boat trip on the Rhine river to Cologne on February 1, 1919. On this trip, Kniptash hoped to meet up with some of his relatives who lived in Germany.

Figure 20. Kniptash took this photo in Germany in the spring of 1919. In the background is a train with some "40 and 8" boxcars prepared to transport American soldiers from Germany to France for their eventual return to the United States.

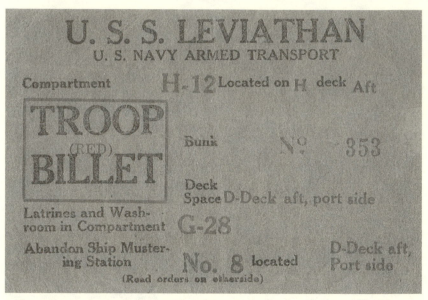

Figure 21. Kniptash received this document as a boarding pass for the USS *Leviathan* and the return voyage to the United States.

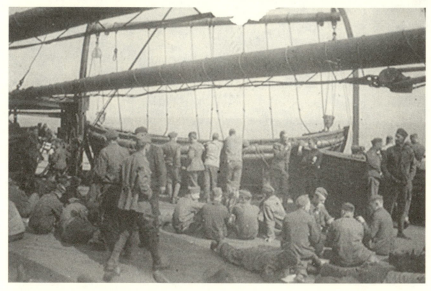

Figure 22. Kniptash took this photo of groups of troops assembled on the deck of the USS *Leviathan* as they made their Atlantic crossing in April 1919.

Honorable Discharge from The United States Army

TO ALL WHOM IT MAY CONCERN:

This is to Certify, That* _Vernon E Kniptash_

†144974 Cpl. Unassigned Last assigned Hq Co 150 39

THE UNITED STATES ARMY, as a Testimonial of Honest and Faithful

Service, is hereby Honorably Discharged from the military service of the

United States by reason of ‡ Par 1 S.O. 128 Hq 3d Sy mbry 8-19

Convenience of the Government

Said _Vernon E Kniptash_ was born

in _Terre Haute_, in the State of _Indiana_

When enlisted he was 20½ years of age and by occupation a _Draughtsman_

He had Brown eyes, Brown hair, Fair complexion, and

was 6 feet 0 inches in height.

Given under my hand at Camp Zachary Taylor Ky this

9th day of May, one thousand nine hundred and Nineteen

Bonus of Sixty Dollars "$60.00"
paid Soldier at Camp F. L. St Claire
QMC Camp Zachary Taylor, Ky.

W.E. Smith

MAY 9 1919

R. Smith, 1st Lieut Inf. US

Orville B. Kilmer,
Lieut Col Inf USA
Commanding.

Figure 23. Vernon Kniptash's honorable discharge from the United States Army, stamped May 9, 1919.

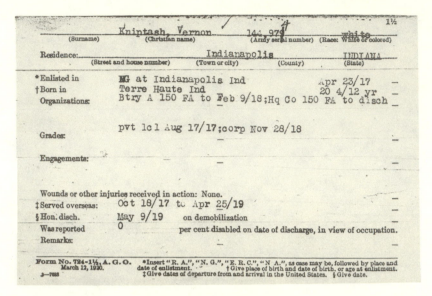

| (Surname) Kniptash, Vernon | (Christian name) | 144,979 (Army serial number) | (Race: White or colored) white | 1½ |

Residence:_____ Indianapolis _____ INDIANA __
(Street and house number)   (Town or city)   (County)   (State)

* Enlisted in   **NG** at Indianapolis Ind   Apr 23/17 —
† Born in   Terre Haute Ind   20 4/12 yr —
Organizations: Btry A 150 FA to Feb 9/18;Hq Co 150 FA to disch _

Grades: pvt lc l Aug 17/17;corp Nov 28/18   _

Engagements: —   _

Wounds or other injuries received in action: None.   _
‡ Served overseas: Oct 18/17 to Apr 25/19   _
§ Hon. disch.   May 9/19   on demobilization
Was reported   0   per cent disabled on date of discharge, in view of occupation.
Remarks:

Form No. 724-1½, A. G. O.   *Insert "R. A.", "N. G.", "E. R. C.", "N A.", as case may be, followed by place and
   March 12, 1920.   date of enlistment.   † Give place of birth and date of birth, or age at enlistment.
   3—7683   ‡ Give dates of departure from and arrival in the United States.   § Give date.

Figure 24. The service record for Vernon Kniptash, detailing his date of enlistment, service overseas, length of service, and other information. Courtesy Indiana State Archives, Commission on Public Records.

Figure 25. William R. Kniptash, in the photograph, discovered the diaries of his father, Vernon Kniptash, after his father passed away in 1987. Until that time, Bill Kniptash was unaware of the existence of the diaries and the other materials, including photos, propaganda, and letters, that Vernon Kniptash brought back with him after World War I.

CHAPTER 4

The March to the Rhine and the Occupation of Germany, November 12, 1918–April 1, 1919

No human enterprise goes flat so instantly as an Army training camp when war ends. Everything that sustains morale—peril to the country, imminent combat, zeal for victory, [and] sense of importance—disappears. The only thing that counts for a citizen soldier is his date of discharge.

From Dwight D. Eisenhower, *At Ease*

SPEAKING OF CONDITIONS AFTER WORLD WAR I, General Eisenhower could have been referring to the attitudes of the Rainbow Division, indeed the entire American Expeditionary Forces, after the Armistice was signed on November 11, 1918. In the minds of the American troops, the war was over and their paramount concern centered on a prompt, speedy departure for the United States.

The conclusion to World War I was a complicated undertaking, however, a fact that Vernon Kniptash and his fellow soldiers quickly discovered. For the Rainbow Division, as well as for tens of thousands of other American troops, the return home was a ways distant. On November 8, 1918, three days before the actual cessation of hostilities, the 42nd Division was reconstituted (along with several other divisions) into the American Third Army under the command of Major General Joseph Dickman. This combined force subsequently became the American Army of Occupation and, by November 15, had received its orders to prepare for an extensive march to Germany, where it would take up positions to support the

Epigraph. Eisenhower, *At Ease*, 152.

enforcement of the Armistice.[1] While the occupation of Germany remained in effect, the negotiations to end the war began at Versailles in January 1919. For their part, Germans began the process of establishing a new civilian government after the collapse of the kaiser's regime.

By mid-November Kniptash and his fellow Rainbows set out on their celebrated "March to the Rhine" as the first U.S. military force to occupy the territory of an enemy in Europe. The Rainbows marched through war-torn France, receiving a hero's welcome in the French villages along the way. A similar situation repeated itself in Belgium as throngs of Belgians came out to embrace the American soldiers, thankful for their role in defeating the German oppressors.

When the troops marched into Luxembourg, the Americans received a more subdued response from a people whose loyalties had been somewhat divided during the conflict. Finally, on December 2–3, the Rainbows marched into Germany proper with their final destination being the town of Coblenz, along the Rhine. The divisional headquarters was established in the neighboring city of Bad Neuenahr, and Kniptash arrived there on December 16, 1918.

From mid-December 1918 to the first week of April 1919, Kniptash and his fellow Rainbows carried out their duties as members of the Army of Occupation. Their daily existence was curious, however, especially since many of the troops were assigned to live in the homes of German families, at least temporarily. Though lacking the discipline required of a force that was constantly preparing for combat, the Army of Occupation nevertheless found a variety of activities to keep itself busy. In addition to the normal routine of drill and training, and frequent "Pass(es) in Review," the Army developed a wide range of recreational pursuits, including baseball contests and football games that were played between various units.

Vernon Kniptash and several of his friends chose a different pursuit to occupy their leisure. Along with three other Indiana soldiers: Lloyd Skinner, Hank Wells, and Bill Hall, Kniptash formed a string

1. The 3rd Army, the Army of Occupation (or "A of O"), also included the 1st, 2nd, 3rd, and 32nd Divisions of the AEF. See Cooke, *Rainbow Division*, 202; Farwell, *Over There*, 267; Marshall, *Memoirs*, 204.

jazz quartet that put on a series of musical performances billed as "The Hoosier Follies" for the benefit of the units of the Rainbow Division during the winter of 1918–19. So successful was this group that it played weekly throughout much of January and February 1919.

For most of that winter, Kniptash's thoughts centered on the time of departure from Europe. Rumors about the intended departure were frequent. In the weeks immediately after the Armistice, the Rainbows thought they would be leaving as early as January 10, 1919. Once January 10 passed with no orders to leave, the soldiers picked up a rumor that their departure was to commence around February 12. Once again, no orders came to confirm the rumor. Then a rumor surfaced that the troops were scheduled to leave Germany on March 15—but again, no confirmation. Finally, on February 26, 1919, Kniptash read in the army newspaper *Stars and Stripes* that the 150th Field Artillery was scheduled to depart the first week of April 1919. The end was clearly in sight.

During January, February, and March 1919, the monotony and tedium of military life, without combat and conflict, took its toll in terms of anxiety and restlessness within the Army of Occupation. Kniptash wrote openly of tensions between soldiers and their officers, between units in the field and their divisional headquarters, between National Guard units and the Regular Army, and between West Point—trained soldiers and the "citizen" soldiers. As the occupation wore on, the military also became disenchanted with the work of the YMCA in the field and the chilly treatment that they frequently received from the Y's personnel.

As Kniptash describes the months in Germany, his moods seem to alternate uncertainty and confusion, on the one hand, as in the days immediately following the Armistice when the future looked unclear, and anticipation and expectation, on the other, as Kniptash and his fellow soldiers awaited news about their impending departure to America and their discharge from the service. Along with this expectancy came the occasional frustrations and bouts of homesickness that inevitably accompanied the seemingly endless wait. The soldiers also experienced curiosity and amazement resulting from their extensive travels throughout Belgium and Germany. Travel in Germany was especially poignant for Kniptash, who

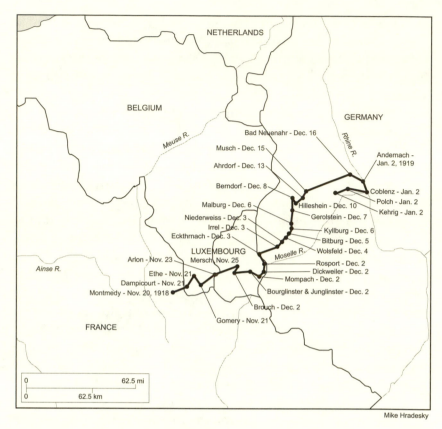

Map 1. The March to the Rhine, November 20, 1918–January 2, 1919.
This map shows the route that Kniptash took with the Army of Occupation to take up positions in Germany after the Armistice. Map by Michael
Hradesky.

140

desired to visit Cologne, his family's ancestral homeland. Finally, there was the sense of relief, combined with a tinge of sadness, with which the troops met the news of their departure for America. All told, the period of the occupation, like the periods of training and combat that preceded it, makes for a fascinating element of Kniptash's World War I experience.

Nov. 12   Pay day today. Drew 165 francs. Am going to salt it. Latest "snow" has it that we go to occupy Strasbourg. Have heard part of the terms of the Armistice. 1) They (the Germans) are given 35 days to declare peace, 2) They must give up all their submarines and part of their Navy, 3) They lose all their colonies and Alsace-Lorraine and Belgium, 4) They return all Allied prisoners and we hold on to all German prisoners until the 35 days are up. There's a whole lot more and the grand total doesn't leave Germany much to start up another war with.[2]

Nov. 13, 1918   Hung around all day and smoked myself at our bon-fire. Probably move tomorrow.

Nov. 14, 1918   Move today and are camping in pup tents "encore" just outside of Imecourt. Heard that somebody killed the Crown Prince. That was too easy a death for that dude. Hope they catch the old man (the Kaiser).[3] — If everything works smoothly, I'll be among the first eleven to get passes. We're supposed to leave on the 16th, but lots of things can happen in two days.

Nov. 15, 1918   Hanging around freezing to death. This bivouacking in wintertime isn't what it's cracked up to be. — All orders

2. Kniptash's recitation of the terms of the Armistice is accurate. He apparently had not learned that the Allies were scheduled to occupy all of western Germany up to the left bank of the Rhine River and also hold three bridgeheads across the Rhine at Mainz, Coblenz, and Cologne. According to the terms of the Armistice, the German army surrendered 5,000 heavy guns and artillery pieces, 25,000 machine guns, 3,000 trench mortars, and 17,000 aircraft. See Gilbert, *First World War*, 500.

3. Kaiser Wilhelm II abdicated the German monarchy on November 10, 1918; he sought, and was granted, asylum in the Netherlands. He lived the rest of his life in exile until his death in 1941. See Fleming, *Illusion of Victory*, 485. Crown Prince Wilhelm, his son and heir, went into exile with Wilhelm II but returned to Germany in 1923, with the permission of the Weimar government. He lived in Germany until his death in 1951.

affecting the 42$\underline{nd}$ were cancelled. All passes were cancelled. Guess this Div. doesn't rank a pass. Don't know what's in the air, but I do know that I'm getting tired of living out in the middle of big, windy fields.[4]

Nov. 16, 1918   We move today. Don't know whether it's toward Germany or away from it. Move due east and are camping "encore" in a big field outside of Aincerviller. Hear we move out again tomorrow. The general "snow" has it that we hike to Coblenz, some 300 kilometers. Said it would take us 30 days to get there. Sure hope this isn't true. If H.Q.'s can't get us, exposure will.

Nov. 17, 1918   Move again today. Supposed to start at 11:45, but it's 12:15 now, late as always. Never pulled out on time since I've been in the Army. Boys say the hike covers 22 kil. Suppose we've got a nice, big, open field waiting for us when we get there. This march to the Rhine may be historical, but it's damn strenuous. Passed through Dun Haumont etc and reached this burg of Brekeville. We're billeted in a big church for a change. There was mail waiting for us, and I drew 12 letters. War isn't so bad after all.

Nov. 18   Have seen groups of Russian soldiers straggling in the whole day. The most of them have been prisoners for four years. They look fairly healthy, everything considered. — Was issued a leather jerkin today.[5] Wool gloves and socks tomorrow. Need to keep us warm on this hike, I guess. We'll need 'em. Snowed a little this afternoon. Rumor has it that our hike is called off. Say the horses won't be able to make the grade so they are going to hike to the closest railhead and entrain. Lord, hope this is true.

Nov. 19, 1918   Saw in the Daily Mail a long article on the occupation of German territory. They call us the Third American Army

4. Kniptash's entry on November 15, 1918, reveals the ignorance of the troops regarding their future assignment. In *Rainbow Hoosier*, Elmer Sherwood recorded sentiments similar to Kniptash's: "We don't know where we're going but we're on our way. . . . We did not know definitely whether we were going home or to Germany. Both had their advantage in our estimation." *Rainbow Hoosier*, 150. See also Ferrell, *Diary of Elmer Sherwood*, 101–104.

5. A leather jerkin was a vestlike garment that provided additional warmth. See Ferrell, ed., *Diary of Elmer Sherwood*, 103.

and is composed of all veteran divisions. They are the 1st, 2nd, 3rd, 4th, 5th, 26th, 32nd, 42nd, 89th, and 90th. About 250,000 men in all. We keep on moving steadily from now on. The 42nd is just about re-equipped now and will probably move on tomorrow. Probably due for a long hike. Well, I've got plenty of warm clothes now, so I won't freeze to death anyhow.

x-----------------------x

Nov. 20, 1918   Got up at 5:30 AM and on the road at 7:00 AM. Passed thru <u>Lissey</u>, <u>Jarnetz</u>, and finally reached the town of <u>Montmiedy</u> [Montmedy].We are billeted on the outskirts of the town. Reached here at 3:00 P.M. Steady marching for 8 hours. — Walked down town this eve and it's a sight for tired eyes. All houses and buildings flying the French tri-color or Belgian and American flags. Five or six shops selling German-made merchandise to the boys. The people crying, singing, and happy as kids; electric lights blazing away, civilization once more. Caught myself walking in the street and cement sidewalks on both sides of me! I've sure dropped back to the stone age. Heard that our program calls for 100 kil. a week and we're supposed to be in Coblenz the 12th of December. Then we get relieved on the 13th. That sounds curious to me. Can't figure this hiking 200 miles to a town, and no sooner we reach it, turn around and hike back! However, they can do anything in this Army. — See in the papers where they start mustering out the boys in the steam heated barracks back home. Says they will be mustered out at the rate of 30,000 a day. Each man gets an extra month's pay as a bonus. That's all very fine, but it doesn't give the 42nd any relief. I wouldn't change places with them at that. This trip to the Rhine is more of a privilege than a grind. We're in country now that hasn't seen much bombarding and is quite an agreeable change from places we have been in. We'll sure see some wonderful sights before we get back. The president of France was delivering a speech to the people when we came through.[6] This town was the permanent Headquarters of the Crown Prince.

6. The passage through Montmedy was a historic day for the Rainbows. Not only were the jubilant French crowds enthusiastic in welcoming the troops, but also M. Henri Poincaré, the president of France, visited the city that day to congratulate its liberated citizens. See Sherwood, *Rainbow Hoosier*, 153.

Nov. 21, 1918   Started hiking once more at 10:30 in the morning. At 12:30 we crossed the border. In a few minutes, we're passing thru Dampicourt, our first Belgian town.[7] Passed thru Virton. It's a big place. Several Germans were left there. They were Red Cross men. The Germans had a big Base Hospital there, and I suppose they had some wounded that couldn't be moved. Passed thru Ethe and stopped in this town of Gomery, 2 and ½ kil. out of Ethe. The hike covered 23 kil. My feet are all in. — Belgian towns are a whole lot cleaner than French towns. The people are about the same and speak French. They were very enthusiastic and all the towns were decorated up to a million. "Snow" has it that we hike 25 kil. tomorrow. Supposed to take us to Luxembourg. I'm afraid I'll never make it with my feet in this condition. Sure give it a try, though.

Nov. 22, 1918   Started hiking at 8:00 A.M. and reached the farm at 3:00 P.M. Another 30 kil. closer to the Rhine. My feet are dead. Passed through <u>Arlon</u>. It's a very large town and boasts one of the prettiest churches I've seen since I've been over here. We were extended a cordial welcome everywhere. At the entrance of every town, the people had erected an archway of cedars and pines decorated with the flags of all the Allied countries. This little town is 6 kil. out of <u>Arlon</u>, and isn't named on the map. The people had the road leading to our billets decorated for ½ kil. It was the prettiest thing I've seen in a long time. The Germans left here about 4 days ago. The 2<u>nd</u> Division is the one that's on their heels. They are keeping in constant contact with the rear guards. At present, we are 1 kil. from the Duchy of Luxembourg. We cover an "encore" of 25 kil. tomorrow. That will take us very near the town of Luxembourg. The chaplain says that the people are very hostile to the Americans. Close up all the watering places and put guards on the woodpiles. Well, that will never slow the Yankees. We are not above stealing. If they are that way in Luxembourg, I wonder how they'll be in Germany proper. Don't suppose we'll get much of a welcome there. These Belgian folks

7. The Alabama regiment led the 42nd Division into Belgium. The Rainbows entered Belgium to the sounds of "Dixie," played by the marching band of the Alabama unit. See Cooke, *Rainbow Division*, 204; Freidel, *Over There*, 224.

tell the boys that if it wasn't for the Americans, they would have starved to death during their four years' imprisonment.[8] Several of the boys stopped in cafés along the road, and the owners couldn't do enough for them. Little kids lined up along the road. Sang out "Vive l'Amerique." It was all very wonderful. Although the hike is a grind, still I wouldn't miss it for anything. Only hope I don't have to fall out before we get to the destination.

Nov. 23, 1918   Left the cheering and decorations at 9:20 this morning. At that time, we crossed the border and started out thru Luxembourg. This hike covered 15 kil. and landed us in the town of Sauel. The people are cold and distant, but not too cold.[9] They speak German, of course, but a great many of them speak fluent French. They accept French money, but prefer Marks to Francs. The town is neat and very clean. We are sleeping in a room directly connected to a café. The boys are buying his stock as fast as he passes it across the counter.

Nov. 24   Sunday. On guard last night. First time in a long time. Sure was cold. But a big bon-fire helped matters considerably. — Haven't seen the paper for ages, but the boys say they saw a Daily Mail yesterday, and it said that Gen. [Peyton] March has asked General Pershing to have the Rainbow Division come home with the first of them. Said owing to our composition and our brilliant record, we will parade the streets of Washington, D.C. on our return. It seems as though Mrs. [Edith] Wilson is the mother of this Division and she gave it its name. Suppose she has quite a bit

8. Once in Belgium, the Americans heard frequent stories of the brutality the Germans inflicted on the Belgian civilians during the wartime occupation. As Sherwood wrote: "The inhabitants told us how the Germans had swept across the country in 1914 and how the Belgians were forced at the point of bayonets to choose between Germany and Belgium. A woman told me how she had been thrown out of her home naked and holding her half-year old baby in her arms." *Rainbow Hoosier*, 155.

9. During the war, the Duchy of Luxembourg had maintained neutrality, although the sympathies of the population were more pro-German than pro-Allied. In describing the people of Luxembourg as "cold and distant," Kniptash shared a sentiment common to other American soldiers who also felt uncomfortable by comparison with the reception they received from the Belgians. See Cooke, *Rainbow Division*, 209, 211. After the initial chilly reception, however, the Americans were well treated in Luxembourg. See Sherwood, *Rainbow Hoosier*, 157, 159.

of suction with Woody.[10] — We are now about 150 kil. from Coblenz. We probably stay in this town a couple more days. Heard a hot old drill schedule is coming down in a couple days. Boy Scout stuff again. — Also hear that 12 hour passes to Luxembourg will be given to part of the boys tomorrow. Hope I get one. I'm craving some grub that's not cooked in an Army Field Kitchen.

Nov. 25, 1918   Our passes came down at 8:00 A.M., but we didn't get started until 9:00. Started hiking and hopping trucks, and we reached Marsch at 10:00 A.M. It is 17 kil. from Marsch to Luxembourg and we didn't care to hike it, so we hung around looking for a truck. We were still hanging at 12:00 and went into a restaurant and had an excellent dinner. Went out to find a truck encore and 2:30 P.M. rolled around before we knew it. We gave up the trip to Luxembourg. I hated it because I sure wanted to see that place. — This town is strong for the Americans. They built a huge archway out of cedars and had a big sign "Welcome our Deliverers". The people charge fairly reasonable. Candy is high, though. I bought a small sack of it that would have cost 5 cents in the States. It cost me 5 marks here. That's better than a dollar in American money. Our dinner cost us 6 marks, but it wouldn't have made any difference if it had cost 27 marks. It was the best meal I've had since last Thanksgiving. Mashed potatoes, steak, gravy, sauer kraut, apple butter, and coffee with sugar. We furnished our own bread. Stole a couple of loaves off a Q.M. [quartermaster] truck. Sure was a relief from Army cooking. — Hung around and ordered a supper. Left the place with a very full stomach. Caught a truck and was back home by 6:30 P.M. Some of the boys were lucky enough to make Luxembourg, but most of them fared the way I did.

Nov. 26, 1918   Was down at stables this morning and Capt. Hofmann called me over and told me he was going to make me corporal. Told Sgt. Ringold to shoot the order thru "tout de suite" so I guess I'll be sporting two stripes in a couple of days. Every

10. Edith Bolling Wilson did not give the 42nd Division its name, although rumors persisted to that effect. Likewise, the Rainbows did not march in Washington after their return to America. General Peyton March was the Army Chief of Staff during World War I.

member of the old club who joined this Regiment is a non-com. Pete is a sgt., and Keller, Al Brunner, and I are cpls. Mine came late, but better late, than never. We had to set up the station and are keeping 24 hour service. It gets us out of drill, and that's what we want. It's some stiff drill schedule, too. — See where most all of the censorship restrictions have been lifted. A fellow can write anything home now, but criticism. We are not allowed to air our views about some officers—yet. — Charlie went in to Marsch and brought chickens, etc. for our Thanksgiving feed. Don't think this feed will be as elaborate as last year's.

Nov. 27, 1918   Not much but rain today. Things are all set for Thanksgiving tomorrow.

Nov. 28, 1918   Thanksgiving Day. Second one I've spent away from home. Had an excellent dinner. Chicken, pie, mashed potatoes and gravy, cheese, slaw, doughnuts, bread and butter, coffee with cream and sugar. Wasn't quite as elaborate as last year's, but it was a very good dinner at that. Then the order giving a list of promotions for the H.Q. Co. was posted today and my name was among the ones made corporals. My old friend [Edward] Mooney was also made. We came over together from A Battery and both of us suffered the same fate. Mooney should have been made a cpl. at the 3rd Bn. way last March. I should have been made as soon as Stratton left us at Chateau-Thierry. I've been in charge of the detail ever since that time, and only a private, first class. However, I got it finally so we'll forget the rest of it. The best part about it is that I earned it and didn't run around with a quill in my mouth like I've seen others do. Ted Corbin was promoted from corporal to sergeant and will take Danny's place. Poor little Danny has been dropped. He'll be going back to the States before long. Got a letter from him. Said he'd just gone through two operations, and it left him very weak. [Burl] Johnson the telephone man who was gassed on the Vesle is in Danny's ward. It was mustard gas and he was burned terribly. Danny's case must be more serious than it looked. Sure wish I had got to see him before they carried him away. He was one of the best friends I've ever made.

Nov. 29, 1918   Same old story. Hanging around and the only thing to worry us is to wonder what we're going to have for mess. It's a gay life in these small burgs. The noise at Crown Hill will scare me after having lived in those dead towns.[11] Sure hope we move from here soon. I'm getting restless. Hiking's going to be disagreeable from now on in. The raining season has started and it hasn't missed a day for the past week. We'll enter Germany rainingly. — See where President Wilson is in France. Came over to start peace negotiations. Said he'd be here for six weeks.[12] Our gang of crepe-hangers [pessimists] in this Regt. said we'd be over here long enough to sew on another service stripe. Somebody's always taking the joy out of life. Lieutenant Speed said he heard the latest "snow." Said we were going to <u>Coblenz</u> alright, but he was willing to bet money that we'd be relieved to go home within six weeks after we hit the place. That's the kind of "snow" I like to believe. Only like to kid myself that we'll be going home "tout de suite."

Nov. 30, 1918   We move tomorrow. The officers threw a little party this evening, and Bill Hall, [Lloyd] Skinner, and myself put on a little string music. I was rather warm. — Find that we have to set up station at the end of each hike. That makes it nice. Hike all day and set up all night.

Dec. 1, 1918   We covered 18 kil. today. I finished fresh as a daisy. The hike was thru the most monotonous country I've seen yet. In one case we had to go about five kil. to reach a spot two kil. away. Had to go around a mountain. The horses and mules were all in. We set up station, but our sending set got its back up and refused to work. Guess Brigade will think that we didn't set up station. I'm going to get a hold of Stratton and have him fathom the difficulty. It's sure got me whipped. — The name of this town is <u>Blascheid</u>. Spent the biggest part of the evening talking to the Herr and Frau of this house. Was tickled to find that I could make myself understood. We had quite a chat and talked of everything from the high cost of shoes to wireless telegraphy. — Tomorrow we take a man-killing hike. Said to cover 40 kil. and will land us at the German border. This old man tells me that

---

11. Kniptash's reference here is to the Crown Hill Cemetery in Indianapolis.
12. Actually, President Wilson did not arrive in France until December 13. See Fleming, *Illusion of Victory*, 317–18.

there were three Americans killed up here last Monday. It was the work of some narrow-minded sniper. We carry our pistols at all times from now on in. — After this hike tomorrow we'll have 80 or 90 kil. left and we'll have 10 days to do it in. If I can live through this hike, I'll sure manage to make the grade the rest of the way.

Dec. 2, 1918   Well, we did it, and we're here, all of us, sore feet and all. The hike easily covered 40 kil. and it was up and down hill all the way. They call this little strip of country we just passed thru "Little Switzerland." Suppose it's because of its mountainous terrain. If the Alps are any worse than these hills then I don't want to get anywhere near them. I think we climbed a thousand hills today, and I don't remember any of them having an "other side." Don't remember going down a hill, it was always up. We must be a million miles above sea level. We start at 7:30 A.M. and reach this town of Rosport at 5:00 P.M. It was steady going all the time. Rested for a half hour at noon to eat a corn willy sandwich and rested about 5 minutes every 10 kilometers. We passed thru the towns of Bourglinster, Junglinster, Giedweider, Brouch, Beirbourg, Mompach, Dickweiler, and then stopped in Rosport. We are now within a 5 minute walk of Germany. All the people here speak German. No French spoken at all. Saw several Bosche soldiers. They were stragglers lost from their organizations. Brigade H.Q.'s is in this town, so we don't have to set up station. That sure helps our side. — Had five hours sleep last night, and than made the big hike. Guess I won't knock off a few licks of sleep tonight. Understand we have a short march scheduled tomorrow. Sure hope it's a damn short one.

Dec. 3, 1918   Start at 7:30 AM. and hiked to Eckternach. There we crossed the river Seur, and it landed us in Germany. 10:45 A.M. The German kids are wearing the rest cap of the German soldiers. The first German town we passed thru was Irrel. We are stopping in <u>Niederweiss</u>. We're due for a rest tomorrow, but I hear that we move "encore."[13] — "Dusty" Rhodes was pinched

13. A rainbow appeared in the once-rainy skies when the 42nd Division entered Germany. See Cooke, *Rainbow Division*, 211. A portion of Kniptash's diary entry of December 2, 1918, was published in Ferrell, *Diary of Elmer Sherwood*, 178n6.

today. He stole 4000 marks yesterday from a Luxembourgor, and they caught him today. It's hard labor at Ft. Leavenworth for him. "Dusty" always did look crooked to me.[14] — The boys are dropping out one by one. The grind is telling on them. The different Germans around here have just been discharged from the Army. They have been civilians two and three days now. Don't seem to hate it either. — Ted Corbin came in today and took charge of the wireless.

Dec. 4, 1918   Started hiking at 9:00 A.M. in a drizzling rain. It was only a 12 kil. hike. Passed through the towns of <u>Alsdorf</u> and <u>Wolsfeld</u> and stopped in this town of <u>Messerich</u>. Slept in a feather bed last night and will sleep in one tonight. "Some hard war," I claim. German roads so far have proved to be poorer than any I have seen in France, Belgium, or Luxembourg. They are cut up worse. This is probably due to the steel tires on all of their automobiles and trucks. The country isn't near as pretty either. I thought the towns would be cleaner than French towns, but it proved just the opposite. — An old German told me that all the soldiers living on this side of the Rhine were discharged from the Army and sent to their homes. They looked a whole lot more harmless in their "civvies" than they did in their gray. All of them are busy around the house and farm, making up for lost time. They treat us fairly hospitable and are not anywhere near as hostile as some of the boys thought they would be. We may run into a fanatic or two before we reach <u>Coblenz</u>, but I doubt it.[15]

14. It was not possible to confirm the accuracy of this entry since Kniptash refers to this individual only by his nickname. A review of the service records of soldiers in the 150th Field Artillery reveals that there were two men in the unit with the last name of Rhodes: Oscar Rhodes, Battery B; and Ralph C. Rhodes, Headquarters Company. Both individuals returned to the United States on April 25, 1919. Oscar Rhodes was discharged, honorably, on May 10, 1919; Ralph C. Rhodes was discharged, honorably, on May 9, 1919. See Service Record, Oscar Rhodes, and Service Record, Ralph C. Rhodes, both in Roll No. 24, "Pringle, Herbert—Rice, Carl F.," WWI SR.

15. Pete Straub also recounted how war-weary German soldiers had returned to their homes shortly after the signing of the Armistice. As Straub described his conversation with one former German soldier: "He told us about how the German soldiers after the Armistice threw down their arms and threw away their heavy helmets and started for home." *Sergeant's Diary*, 234. Likewise, the German reception to the Allied occupation was hardly hostile. As Donald Smythe wrote: "German

Dec. 5, 1918   Started hiking at 7:00 A.M. We were supposed to
rest yesterday. But I heard that we made that small hike in order
to shorten this long one we have today. We passed thru Bitburg.
It's a fairly good sized town, and the streets are full of discharged
soldiers and officers. Lord, how those officers glared at us. They
wanted to chew our ears off.[16] The soldiers usually greeted us
with a smile or a wave of the hand. The commanding German
General of the 3rd Army had his H.Q. in Bitburg. All road signs
read "Cologne," out of this town. Haven't seen any place where
Coblenz was mentioned. Maybe we'll go to Cologne after all.
Sure hope so. Maybe I'll get to see some of the Knips if we do. —
Reached this town of Sefferveich at 12:30 P.M. About an 18 kil.
hike. Find that the people around this vicinity are more or less
afraid of the Americans. Several of the boys went around and
ordered suppers, and when time came to settle up the people
wouldn't take the money. The boys had to force it on them.
Some of them got their supper for 5 marks. It would have cost
double that much in France. They act like Americans are out for
blood; can't quite savvy it all. Suppose the farther inland we get
the worse it will be. An old German told me that we are about 100
kil. from <u>Coblenz</u> now. We don't seem to get any nearer than 100
kil. to that town no matter how many 20 kil. hikes we take. They
say that after this hike tomorrow the road branches off and
makes a bee-line for <u>Coblenz</u>. It's about time. Don't think much
of this idea of getting there by walking away from it. Tomorrow
is my second birthday away from home. We'll make this entry the
last one for this book, and start the new book off on my birthday.
[Editor's Note: The entry for December 5, 1918, was the final
entry in the first book of Kniptash's diary. The entry for December 6 began his second book.]

---

reaction to the American occupation was generally friendly. Field hands went out
of their way to put American troops on the right road; housewives lent their cooking utensils. . . . People were kindly, helpful, courteous." *Pershing*, 245. See also
Freidel, *Over There*, 224–26; James, *Years of MacArthur*, 1:245; Keegan, *First World
War*, 420.
    16. As Martin Gilbert wrote, the officers in the German army felt betrayed by
the Armistice, especially since the war ended with German "troops still under
arms, their trenches manned, [and] their soldiers everywhere still on French and
Belgian soil." *First World War*, 503.

Dec. 6, 1918   My birthday and we celebrate by taking an "encore" hike. Bet I wouldn't be hiking if I happened to be in Indianapolis on this date. Started hiking at 9:00 o'clock. Passed through Kyllburg and Malburg. Both of these towns were fairly large and very beautiful. Managed to buy some postcards of the different buildings. We reached this town of Murlenbach at 3:00 P.M. Hiked around 22 kilometers. Was talking to a young German who had managed to live thru two years of infantry exposure. He said this town had 24 men killed, 16 taken prisoner, and three missing for their share of the war. The town only boasts 900 people. — Found out that Coblenz is now 83 kil. away, and we're practically on a straight shoot to it now. The Brigade boys say we will take over a town about 10 kil. out of Coblenz. It couldn't possibly be our luck to anchor in the big city. — This is our sixth day of steady hiking. Hear we got another 20 kil. ahead of us tomorrow. We sure put "beaucoup" kil. between us and the Savel. The roads are in poor condition and have changed from white to a brownish red. Saw a French train pulling American box cars steam down a German railroad. Was headed for a point somewhere ahead of us, loaded to the eaves with supplies, porridge, and rations. Hope they get enough of these trains together to haul us away from Coblenz when we finish our job there. It'd be just like them to hike us back to France. Guess if the ocean had a bridge across it, they'd have us hiking across it. The Rainbow boys are sure merry little hikers.

Dec. 7, 1918   Slept on about 18 ft. of good hay last night and sure slept sound. Got up this morning and washed wagons. Had breakfast with a good German family. The people are treating the boys like kings, and the boys can't understand it.[17] Dickered

17. One of the peculiarities of the Rainbow Division's occupation of Germany involved the fact that the American troops were often assigned to lodging quarters (and sometimes meals) with German families. Despite strict instructions against "fraternization" with German civilians, the Americans and Germans soon forged generally amicable relationships. The Americans enjoyed the surprising friendliness of the Germans, and the Germans appreciated the cordial attitude of the Americans. As one German confided to Elmer Sherwood, "The Yanks treated them (the Germans) much better than their own soldiers [did]"; *Rainbow Hoosier*, 162. See also Cooke, *Rainbow Division*, 212; Farwell, *Over There*, 268–69. Carl Hixon had

with some of the men for souvenirs and bought some belt buck-
les. Am going to try for an Iron Cross and an officer's helmet
before we get back. This hike today is supposed to cover 12 kil.
We pulled out at 11:30, passed <u>Lissengen</u> and stopped at this
town <u>Gerolstein</u>. It's a good-sized town: brick streets, cement
sidewalks, plate glass windows, and everything. The shops are
exhibiting Xmas toys! Sure makes me homesick. — We are billeted in a big house that was used by railroad men. There are six
beds in each room and ticks and pillows, electric lights thru out.
Best barracks we've had in a long time. Ted Corbin, Slim Car-
penter, Charlie Oliver, and myself planted our feet under a table-
clothed table and enjoyed an excellent meal. The white cloth
made us nervous. "Slim" knocked over a glass of wine immediately after we sit down. Then we dripped brown gravy, spilled
sauerkraut, etc. until it wasn't long until that snow-white [table
cloth] took on an olive, drab hue. We are sure cave men alright.
We used honest-to-goodness silver too. It's going to take me
some time to get used to civilization again. The daintiness of the
dining room this evening actually frightened me. The Army has
sure ruined me socially. Was told that we are now only 104 kil.
from Coblenz. This morning before the hike we were 83. The
day's hike covered 16 kil. Subtracting 16 from 83 we get 104.
That's getting to <u>Coblenz</u> fast. I guess they intend to hike us thru
China first. The dope is that we don't go to Coblenz but to a town
a few kil. this side of it. Hope we are getting closer to that town
anyway. I don't care to go sight seeing on foot. We'll hike again
tomorrow according to dope. No more rests, I guess, until we hit
the Rhine. This town is a well-known summer resort noted for its
fresh air and mineral water baths. Every other building here is a
hotel. Wouldn't mind paying it a visit under different conditions
than the present. — German roads so far have been as bad as the
French roads that passed through No Man's Land. They sure surprise me. Suppose they just couldn't spare the men to keep them
in condition. The French had Chinese at their disposal and

---

a similar memory, as he recalled: "When we were in [the] Army of Occupation in
Neuenahr, I became very friendly with Germans (I am half-German) since I could
speak a little German." Military Survey, U.S. Army Military History Institute, 9.

made good use of them. — A fellow can get almost anything he wants from this country for a few bars of soap. These people absolutely are "finis" on soap. They speak to you in terms of soap value. It's as good as gold, over here.[18]

Dec. 8, 1918   Another hike to our credit. Pulled stakes at 8:30 A.M. and made the 19 kil. by 2:00 P.M. I'm stopping in the town of <u>Berndorf</u>. Sleeping on the floor tonight. Don't know how I'll get along with all of those feather beds and hay lofts I've been used to. We are now 70 kil. from Coblenz according to the gentleman of this house. Heard that the 2nd Div. is now in that town. Also heard that we turn in all our rolling stock between the 15th and 25th of December. That looks like home to me.

x--------------x

Dec. 9, 1918   The old man of this house brought us hay to sleep on. Talk about hospitality! The 2nd Bn. had a Review today. It was held in drizzling rain and was a ridiculous affair from start to finish. Col. Bob will have a tough time making an impression on the German people by showing them a bunch of soldiers. They're sick and tired of soldiers. They enjoyed the music of the band, but paid no attention to the soldiers. It's Bob's speed, though. — Had a big supper again this evening and paid for it with ten bars of soap that we stole. Got to examine a bar of German soap. It's far from the real article and a very poor substitute. Weighs a ton. Saw their substitute for coffee too. It's nothing but burned wheat. They're sure in a bad way for these two articles. Also their bread is rotten. This town has plenty of potatoes but absolutely no meat. Sugar is scarce here while in other towns the people have all of it they need. The small towns have enough to eat, but the large towns are up against it. These people say that Berlin is worse off than any. — Every German I've talked to hates the Kaiser, the Crown Prince, Ludendorf[f] and [Admiral Alfred] von Tripitz [*sic*]. They are all strong for old man [General Paul von] Hindenburg, though. He was the only one of the big guns

18. Like other American soldiers, Kniptash discovered that the Germans placed a premium on American soap. The trading value of soap was higher than just about any other American item. See Cooke, *Rainbow Division*, 217. Elmer Sherwood explained: "[The German] housefraus prided themselves before the war on their white clothes [and thus] soap was priceless." *Rainbow Hoosier*, 162.

that did not desert the German Army when the Army needed men of his caliber to lead them. They say that Ludendorf[f] and von Tripitz have gone to Denmark, and the Kaiser and his long-nosed son have hid themselves in Holland.[19] This pair had better stay away from this neck of the woods.

x--------------x

Dec. 10, 1918   Took a walk over to <u>Hilleshein</u> to see Stratton, but he had moved. Brigade is now up 29 kil. That'll make it nice for batteries. Going to eat another supper with this family this evening. Bought two chickens. Then there will be potatoes, gravy, slaw, applesauce, bread, and coffee. And this Frau can sure cook. Managed to get two letters a piece home to Mumsey and Maude. First time in 10 days. They won't accept anymore mail now until we move up and stop again.

Dec. 11, 1918   Our wireless station did "beaucoup" business today, was receiving and sending messages from 7:00 this morning till 9:00 tonight. Never was quite so busy. Received a message from General Gatley that said we would not move tomorrow.[20] It saved [Franklin] Heinzman a 27 kil. ride over and back. — Had another big supper tonight. This is sure a game war here. Got the Baccarat war beat a million ways.

Dec. 12, 1918   Copied another order from the General saying that we will not move tomorrow. Didn't seem to please the skipper very much. Eddie wants to be on his way. This dead burg has got him slowed. A divisional order tells us not to fraternize with the German people. Says not to act nasty or not to get friendly, just split the difference. Make them keep their distance. It's going to be a job after the way they've been treating us. It's hard to believe that these are the same people who committed all the crimes I've read about and in a few cases seen. It's a shame the poor, misguided soldiers didn't tell some of their officers to go to Hell. They sure hate them now and wouldn't hesitate a minute

19. General Erich von Ludendorff went into exile in Sweden, briefly, after the war. Admiral Alfred von Tirpitz, chief of the Imperial Navy, remained in Germany, however. (Kniptash misspells the name of von Tirpitz in his diary.)

20. The reference here is to Brigadier General George Gatley, who assumed the command of the 67th Artillery Brigade during the Occupation period.

to tell them a few things about militarism and what it's cost them. — Heard that President Wilson is supposed to land on this side today. Thought he'd been over here for a month. Wish I could get my hands on a newspaper to find out what's going on. This idea of being exiled from the whole world is getting to be serious. Haven't heard any outside news for better than two weeks.

Dec. 13, 1918   Drizzling rain all day today. The landscape is a sea of beautiful, squashy mud, a sight to cheer any man. Gives a fellow the willies. We move tomorrow. Heard the name of the town is <u>Ahrdorf</u>. Don't know where it's located, but I guess it's a good long hike from here. — Had another supper at this home. We've had one every night since we've been here. Kinda hate to leave this place. Only hope we fare this good the rest of the trip. These German people think that we are going to <u>Coblenz</u> and then to Japan to fight the Japs. Their propaganda has got them believing that America and Japan are at the point of war and are going to settle it while American troops are over here. It's pitiful the way the German government has lied to the people.

Dec. 14, 1918   Moved today 12 kilometers. The old Frau of the house was at the point of crying when we left. We were sure ace high with that lady. Stopping in this town of <u>Ahrdorf</u>. We are now some 30 kil. from the Rhine and about 50 from Coblenz. — Had a big, glorious mail day. Netted me 21 letters. Mumsey, Maude, Babe, Peggy, Louis, and Dad. A long, breezy letter from Dad. It was the best bunch of letters I've ever received. Will have to wait until we reach our destination before I can answer them. That letter from Dad was a peach. Never thought it of him. Bet it cost him many an hour's work. — The people back home heard that the Armistice was signed on November 7 and they celebrated up to a million. Then the next day they found out that such wasn't the case, and everybody's day was spoiled. When the news came officially that it had been signed officially on Nov. 11, they had it all to do all over again. Would sure have liked to have been there to see it all. They sure put on more ceremony than the boys did at the front. Outside of an occasional shout now and then and some rockets, there wasn't much carrying on. The things we did to celebrate would sound curious to the folks back home. One was to build huge bon-fires (more to keep warm than celebrate).

And the other was when a big, yellow moon came out on the night of Nov. 11, to say, "What a wonderful moon." During the war a full moon was the soldier's enemy because it meant planes and bombs. Never saw it to fail. And if there is anything worse than the drone of a Bosche motor and the crump of exploding bombs, I've yet to hear it. Ever since that experience I had in Champagne, I never want to hear an airplane again. — We move again tomorrow at 8:45 A.M. The hike covers 27 kil. We either reach our destination tomorrow or the day after tomorrow. Then "snow" has it that we'll be here only a short while before we'll be relieved. Says we'll turn our equipment over to the 6th Div. and highball for home. It sounds reasonable but, "you never know."

Dec. 15, 1918   Started hiking at 8:45 A.M. Reread all my letters again. This 27 kil. will be easy after reading that bunch of joy. Passed through Musch, etc. and stopped in Druck. Slept on ticks on the floor. This old German family treated us royally. The old Frau made us cookies, and we had supper with them. They had a big German police dog that some soldier had given them. It had been used as a Red Cross dog in the German army. Name is Lux. The boys bought him for 200 marks. Captain Hofmann said he'll see that it got on the ship O.K. He's sure a darb.

x--------------x

Dec. 16, 1918   Started hiking at 9:00 A.M. on our final hike. Passed thru several towns that were used as summer resorts. Beautiful places. Looked very American. After 20 kil. of heavy hiking we reached this town of <u>Bad</u> <u>Neuenahr</u>. It's like Wonderland. The buildings are gay; the people are gay; everything is gay. Every other building is a hotel. Large hotels too. It's a summer resort for English, French and all countries. That is, it was before the war. We are quartered in a big hotel and have set up station. Feather beds, running water, electric lights, and in fact, all modern conveniences. It's too much. I just naturally yelled when I saw what we would have to put up with. After sleeping in hog pens, gutters, etc. for a year and then finally be billeted in a place like this. Again I say, it's too much.[21] And there's only 5 candy stores

21. The quarters for the Rainbow Division at Bad Neuenahr were fabulous. As Elmer Sherwood wrote: "The hotels and villas which had in the past housed the

in town! Sure as Hell I bought 25 marks worth of candy before I laid my pack down. The people speak English due to the English patronage they had before the war. There is one bathhouse in town that's a marvel. It's so spic and span and beautiful that it will be a shame to dirty the water with our bodies. This town is sure worth coming over 300 kil. to see. Hope we "occupy" this place for a month. Got a hunch I can get rid of these cooties if I stay here long enough. Sure am going to take a bath tomorrow. The Rhine is only 10 kil. from here. I'm going to see that river if I have to go A.W.O.L. Wish I could get a pass to Cologne. It's only about 40 kil. from here. Paid my respects to the Knip family. Our antenna is running parallel to some high tension wires some place. Our set sounds like a boiler works. We'll hope to run it tomorrow and there's a remote chance that we may have to move our station to some other location. I'd rather lose a lung than lose this room. Lord, how that mahogany furniture shines and those beds!!!

The country we've just passed thru and that surrounds us now cannot be described. I saw scenes that took my breath away. I certainly enjoyed the last 90 kil. of this hike. Somebody counted up the hikes we've taken since we left Camp Coetquidan, and he said it totaled 60. Today's hike is the 60th. That's quite a few, and the grand total covers quite a few kilometers of Europe. — Just came back from strolling around town. Wanted to hear my heels click on cement sidewalks and pussy foot across asphalt streets. All the wine rooms boast pianos, and the Yankees are hammering away at most of them. You can't beat a Yank. They're at home anywhere at any time. Ted and I are going to hit the hay early tonight. We feel that the bed is going to waste. Ted is now readying his undershirt, and I am going to do likewise. No cooties sleep with me tonight. — I'm going to catch up with my mail tomorrow.

x--------------x

Dec. 17, 1918   Ted and I took a bath today. Hot sulfur baths and in a bldg. that came pretty close to my idea of a palace. Were

---

rich health seekers of Germany became the billets of healthy Yankee fighting men." *Rainbow Hoosier*, 164.

given a towel bigger than a blanket and rough as a file. I sure was a brand new soldier when I came out of that place. Handed my dirty clothes over to a German laundry man. Oh! It's a cruel war. Think I'll take another bath tomorrow. — We have a mess hall now. Was used as a dining room by one of the big hotels before the war. Very beautiful. This cruel war is going to get me down.

Dec. 18, 1918   Colder than Hell today. First winter day we've had. — Wrote letters all day long. I'm catching up on my correspondence. — Heard that Capt. [Frank] Kelly of E Battery is under arrest. Seems as though he knocked a mere West Point major down. Oh! Those West Pointers. Talk about Prussianism. It's miles compared to the tactics those birds use. Hope Cap[t]. Kelly gets out of it lightly.[22]

Dec. 19, 1918   Lieutenant Speed is putting out the latest "snow." Says he read it in the paper. Secretary of War Baker announces that the veterans' divisions will be the last to go home. They will stay here until peace is signed, and President Wilson says there will not be peace until the Germans have established their new government. That may be good for another service stripe or two. Lord, I hope not. I'd like about another week of this life, and then leave for home. Just be our luck though. We've always played in that sort of luck.

Dec. 20   Went to bed last night at 5:00. Was feeling rotten. Touch of the "grippe," I guess. Fever and chills. Spent a miserable night. Woke up this morning still feeling rotten and stayed in bed till noon. Went over to the medics then and got some dope. It hasn't relieved me yet, but I think a good night's sleep will get me straight again.[23]

22. Captain Kelly was arrested for "fighting," as Colonel Tyndall wrote in his diary on December 17, 1918. Disciplinary action against Kelly continued into January 1919. See Tyndall diary, December 19, 21, 23, and 26, 1918, and January 9 and 10, 1919, RHTC. Kelly received an automatic discharge after the war.

23. Like thousands of other American soldiers, Kniptash came down with influenza in December 1918. The latest surge of the flu epidemic started in late November and lasted well into January 1919. Between January and March 1919, about 31,500 troops were admitted to military hospitals in the occupied territory. Over one-third of those admitted were treated for influenza. *Grippe* is the French word that was used to describe influenza. See Cooke, *Rainbow Division*, 221.

Dec. 21, 1918   Went to bed early again last night. But woke up feeling as rotten as ever. It's all in my head now and sure pains. Have got rid of the fever, however. "Bus" Cottingham is down with the same ailment. Is contagious, I guess, because I know several of the boys are down on their backs with it. Sure hope it leaves me by Xmas. H.Q. Co. is pulling off a big feed and entertainment Xmas day. Bill Hall, Skinner, and I are going to practice tomorrow. — Was in bed when the boys came back from the Y. The Y threw a big show to a crowded house, and between the two of the acts Chaplain [Norman R.] Nash got up and said, "We will be on our way home by January 10, 1919. This is 'snow,' but it comes from the Colonel. You can take it or leave it as you wish." That's a damn good "snow," and there must be something to it or the Chaplain wouldn't spout off to a packed house that way. Chaplain Nash's "snow" is pretty reliable, I've found. I laid awake half the night thinking about it. It sounds too good to be true. Only 20 more days. I'm going to see the Chaplain and hear it from his own lips.

Dec. 22   Feeling O.K. once more. Sure was low. Skinner, Bill Hall, Hank Wells, and I knocked off a few songs this evening. Rather warm. By an oversight we will not play in the H.Q.'s show. Don't make me mad. I'd rather be a spectator this time. We are billed to show before A Battery Christmas night. "C" Battery is giving their entertainment Xmas night too, and they asked us to play for them too. Couldn't be at both places same time, so I had to turn them down.

Dec. 23, 1918   Today is the first of a series of "Pass in Reviews" that are going to take place now until we're mustered out, I guess. It's Bob's speed. By the way, Bob [Tyndall] is wearing a "Croix de Guerre" very nonchalantly now.[24] We earned it for him in Champagne, and instead of every boy wearing the green card on their shoulder, Bob sports the Croix for all of us. Nice of him. It rained too hard for the Review, and everything was called off. Hooray.

Dec. 24   Went over to the dentist with Ted to do interpreter's work. Ted is having all is teeth overhauled, and I think I'll follow

24. Colonel Tyndall was notified that he had received the Croix de Guerre in a letter in mid-December 1918; see letter, Acting Division Adjutant, 42nd Division to Colonel Robert H. Tyndall, December 16, 1918, Box 2, Folder 8, RHTC.

suit. A German dentist and he's sure a whole lot more painstaking than these Army dentists. — Xmas Eve. The band thru a show for the Regt. at the big theatre across the river. Had several outside acts, and the program taken as a whole was excellent. The theatre was as good as any we've got at home and seated 200 people. Hardwood floors too. First time my feet's been on a hardwood floor since I left home.[25] Am gradually becoming civilized again. Show let out at 10:00, and I came home and crawled beneath the blankets. The boys are all broke, and so there won't be much celebrating. We've Oct. and Nov. pay coming to us. Couple more days, and they'll owe us for December too. There will sure be Hell in this town when pay day does come. Heard we're going to have one swell feed tomorrow. Pie and cake and everything. Had our first "Pass in Review" today. Got through it without a hitch.

Dec. 25, 1918   My second Christmas away from home. Woke up and found an inch of snow had fallen during the night. Very beautiful. Then dinner. Time came and it was some dinner. Baked chicken, dressing, mashed potatoes, asparagus, cabbage slaw, fruit, pickles, lemon cake, cream pie, whipped cream, candy, cigars and cigarettes, coffee, light wine and beer. Some menu.[26] Then the H.Q. Co. gave a show in the afternoon that was a hummer. Bill Hall, Skinner, Hank Wells and I ate with "A" Battery in the evening. Then we put on our little string jazz. I added

---

25. The "Hoosier Follies" must have made an impression on the units where Kniptash and his friends performed. Pete Straub recalled: "After we had our baker-shop meal some of us went over to the Kurhaus Theatre and saw the Hoosier Follies put on by the One Hundred and Fiftieth Band, and it was very good." *Sergeant's Diary*, 264.

26. The Christmas meal for the troops in Germany in 1918 was truly bountiful. In a veritable banquet setting at one of Bad Neuenahr's great dining rooms, the troops enjoyed a sumptuous meal. As James Cooke wrote: "Every effort was made to see that Yuletide in Germany was as pleasant as possible. The Germans celebrated Christmas in a festive mood, and 1918 was especially joyous after four years of war. Due to the state of food preservation and shipment, the main Christmas meal reflected a great many locally purchased items." *Rainbow Division*, 216. So sumptuous was the meal that Pete Straub commented, "Every man was supplied with a plate of food; we had chicken, duck, potatoes, gravy, slaw, butter, bread, coffee, sugar, milk, apple sauce, puddings, pies, and fruits." *Sergeant's Diary*, 247.

to the parody I wrote last year, and the boys seemed to like the results. Then we went over to "C" Battery and put on the sketch. Returned to "A" Battery and raised Hell till 10 P.M. Captain Hofmann and Major Miller had enough in them by this time to be funny. And we all decided on a party in their rooms. The saxophone sextet and the four of us went ahead and met the officers at the bridge. Held a Burlesque "Pass in Review" with the sextet jazzing a march. It was the funniest thing I've ever seen. Major Miller was drum major. Captain Hofmann was reviewing officer. No one was on the streets but the M.P.s who stared, saucer eyed, at the actions of the officers. We finally got down the street towards the room, waking up every household along the way. The party broke up at 12:00 P.M. with everybody pretty tanked. I drank a couple glasses of champagne, but no more. There's another big party framed up for New Year's Eve.

Dec. 26   Pay day today. 330 franks. Am going to salt $35.00 of it. Received my Xmas box today. Camera was broken. Finder. Can use Shorty's finder when I need it. Mean to take 80 good pictures with those ten films. Pretty low today. Too much Christmas yesterday.

Dec. 27, 1918   The Regiment is beginning to play war again sending reconnaissance parties up the Rhine to pick out gun positions, o.p.s [observation posts] etc. Ted had to go, and he's cussed everybody from the Col. on down. Sure glad they missed me.

Dec. 28, 1918   Sent $35.00 home to Mumsey. Number of order is 616112. The folks received that $30.00 I sent them from Essey so there should be no trouble with this order. — The four of us practiced again tonight.

Dec. 29   Practiced again tonight. Have learned the Indiana Blues. They're hot. We're booked for the Y.M.C.A. tomorrow night and play before the D Battery New Year's afternoon. Captain Glassburn asked for us. It's swell to be popular. Walked around town with Ted and took some pictures. Found out that Dad's birthplace is just 30 kil. from here. It's in neutral territory.

Dec. 30, 1918   Lieutenant Speed said that the Division is going to have a maneuver near Coblenz January 2 and 3. We have to go and set up station. Lord, I wish they'd can that stuff. I don't want to soldier anymore. I wish they'd realize the war's over.

Dec. 31, 1918   Well we finally checked the old year off, and bring on 1919. I guess 1918 will go down in history as the one big year. I'm sure I'll never forget it as long as I live. Tonight the non-coms are throwing a party, and everyone will get drunk. Don't know but what I may slip. The four of us are going to make the rounds and end up at the party. We're in for a Hell of a time. — 'Twas the wildest night I've ever taken part in. Got in bed at 12:30, however, and none the worse for the part.

Jan. 1, 1919   Played for "D" battery this afternoon. Had a feed afterwards. Went to bed early. Too much night before.

Jan. 2, 1919   Got all our stuff packed and loaded in trucks, ready to go to the "battle ground." Pulled out at 10:00 A.M. Passed thru <u>Andernach</u>, and then stopped for a hot dinner at the Y.M.C.A. in Coblenz. Took some snaps of the Rhine and the Moselle. Sure is beautiful country and Coblenz is <u>some</u> town. — Got underway again. Passed thru <u>Polch</u> and stopped in <u>Kehrig</u>. We sleep here tonight. Hayloft. Quite a comedown from mahogany beds. Soldiering again. We start the maneuver tomorrow morning. It is supposed to end tomorrow noon. I'm satisfied now that I visited <u>Coblenz</u> and the <u>Rhine</u>. Sure wanted to see them both.

Jan. 3, 1919   The maneuver, so far as I was concerned, was a glorious failure. Did nothing but stand around in the rain and cold and wondering when they were going to call it off. The "war" ended at 1:30 P.M. Then we hopped on the trucks and highballed those 70 kil. Home in 4 hours. Sure was glad to get back. "Snow" says that the 117th Trench Mortars have left for parts unknown. Left yesterday. "Snow" is sure flying thick, but I can't believe any of it. Heard a good one today. A 79th Div.'s drafted boy asked Sonny what the yellow stripe in the Rainbow chevron on his shoulder stood for. Sonny told him it stood for the drafted replacements our Division got. The drafted boy made himself scarce.

Jan. 4, 1919   All wireless stations will close up temporarily. That means stables and drill for me. Sure hope it won't be for long. The "snow" is wild all over the Division. Everybody thinks we're going home this month. I refuse to bite. — Went over to our movie house and saw David Copperfield.

Jan. 5, 1919   Started in on duty today. Answered reveille and stables. Everything by the count.

Jan. 6, 1919   Was corporal of the guard tonight. It was my first experience at posting relief, but everything ran smoothly. Had to sleep down in the stable though and caught another mess of cooties. I had just got rid of them, too. The German mark has gone down to 142.80 again. It was as high as 166. When we were in Luxembourg the mark was worth 1¼ francs. It's been going down ever since. Now it's about right. — From the looks of things we'll be lucky to pull out of here a year from this month. We are building a big stable on the house for the kitchen, and yesterday 150 head of new horses came in. Can't understand this getting new horses when we've sent a detail down to southern France to get tractors and trucks. We are going to be motorized, and yet they bring in new "tigers." It's a curious army.

Jan. 7, 1919   There was a big inspection and a Review for a new Major General today. I missed them both, thank the Lord. Being on guard last night let me out of it. We get a new General every time the wind blows. First we had Menoher commanding the division. Then McArthur [sic] and now this new bird just fresh from the States. Don't know his name. The 67th brigade started out with Gen. Somerall, then McInstry, and now Gatley.[27] "The old division ain't what she used to be." — I took a long walk out in the country while the Review was going on and got lost. Took me an hour to get my bearings again. Had to walk thru a German baron's hunting ground and front yard to get on the road

27. General Charles P. Summerall (not *Somerall*, as Kniptash wrote) was the first commanding officer of the 67th Field Artillery. When Summerall left the brigade to command the artillery of the 1st Infantry Division, Pershing appointed Major General Charles H. McKinstry as his successor. Pershing reassigned McKinstry shortly before the German summer offensive of July 1918, whereupon Brigadier General George Gatley took command of the 67th. See Cooke, *Rainbow Division*, 21, 84. With respect to the command of the 42nd Division, Maj. Gen. Charles T. Menoher commanded the division during most of its time in France although Maj. Gen. Charles T. Rhodes was initially assigned to succeed Menoher but never took command of the division. Brig. Gen. Douglas MacArthur commanded the Rainbows November 10–22, 1918. MacArthur was succeeded by General Clement F. Flagler. Flagler commanded the division during the occupation. It is difficult to know who Kniptash thought was the "new bird just fresh from the States" because both Rhodes and Flagler saw extensive service in France prior to association with the Rainbows. See also James, *Years of MacArthur*, 1:239–50; Manchester, *American Caesar*, 110–11; Cooke, *Rainbow Division*, 203.

again. Every dog in the radius of 5 miles barked at me while on his private grounds. But the baron didn't come out to find out the reason. I took some good snaps. — Went out with the Company in the afternoon to exercise the horses bareback. Like to kill me, but I stuck it out. — Gathered around the stove after supper and twiddled our thumbs. Everybody's broke, and there's no place to go. Everybody had the Blues. Another year over here, and I'll be nuts.[28]

Jan. 8, 1919   Ate half of a big apple pie. First I tasted since I left Camp Coetquidan. Had to do it on the sly, because the Germans are not allowed to sell anything that is connected with flour. Took in the Band Concert at night. "Brink" puts one on twice a week at the theatre.[29] Our string quartet is billed for an act next Sunday. "Brink" refuses to play for Y.M.C.A. entertainments. All of us are down on the Y and are bucking it every chance we get. This old Division will sure show up the Y.M.C.A. when we get back. It's been a joke.[30]

Jan. 9, 1919   On camp police today. We got things fixed in good order and passed the Colonel's inspection O.K. Mr. Boison (the secretary for the Y.M.C.A.) came up to our rooms to feel out the boys. Wanted to find out just what we thought of the Y. We were not a bit backward in telling him. He hemmed and hawed and exited. He's about as popular in the company as the Colonel.

Jan. 10, 1919   The four of us practiced tonight. We're on at the Kur Theatre Sunday night. Another big Review and Inspection

28. Kniptash's frustration with being a "peacetime soldier" was widely shared in the ranks. In January 1919 the social scientist Raymond B. Fosdick, chairman of the Commission on Training Camp Activities, reported that the morale of U.S. troops was "little short of desperate. Everybody had a bellyful of the damn Army." See Smythe, *Pershing*, 249–50; see also Farwell, *Over There*, 270; James, *Years of MacArthur*, 1:251.

29. "Brink" was Reginald Brinklow, the director of musical programs and entertainment for the 150th Field Artillery. Brinklow's service record may be found in Indiana State Archives, Commission on Public Records, ING, 32–4-8, Box 36, "Brinker, Donald W.—Brock, Wilber W." Brinklow was born in Britain and was a student at Indiana University when he was drafted on August 5, 1917.

30. James Cooke writes extensively of the tension between the troops and YMCA personnel during the Occupation. See *Rainbow Division*, 225–26. For a more positive view of the YMCA's role, see Farwell, *Over There*, 137, 139; and Freidel, *Over There*, 183–84.

tomorrow morning. Think it's Gen. Gatley this time. Reveille at 5 A.M. Makes me tired. Lord, I wish we were on our way home. I hate [being] a peace-time soldier. — This was the day the "snow" said we were going home. Sure was bum "snow."

Jan. 11, 1919   Had a hurry up call to go to Ahrweiler and play for the Red Cross. Went over and came back in a truck. Had choco-late cakes, doughnuts and cigarettes and got to talk to honest-to-goodness American women. Got invitation to come again. — Now we're sitting around the fire twiddling our thumbs. Hell of a fine way to spend Saturday night.

Jan. 12, 1919   I hate to see Sunday come around. It gives me the willies. Sit around and look at each other. It's a relief to answer stables for the simple reason that it occupies a fellow's mind. — These German people are sure doing their damnedest to get the Americans to split with the English and French. It's propaganda pure and simple, and they are so plain spoken that it's laugh-able. Europe is sure a curious country. I know for a fact that the French despise the English. Everybody hates each other. They're never satisfied unless they are quarreling. Sure will be glad when I get back in God's country. — The entertainment was post-poned till tomorrow night. The German civil population is hold-ing a meeting at the Theatre. It's the first step towards an election. Next week they elect a delegate to represent them in the new German government. The old gent that owns this hotel was made a precinct committeeman, and he's beaming all over. His old sister is still a Kaiser-lover, and the two of them had a heated argument when they got back from the meeting. He hates the Kaiser like poison. — Had supper with "F" battery's top sergeant. They're sure living like kings. Had pumpkin pie as a chaser. Played for them awhile and then came home to meet a fellow from Div. H.Q. who plays Hell out of a banjo. He came all the way from Ahrweiler to see us. We played till 10:00 P.M., and then the party broke up.

Jan. 13, 1919   At the non-coms school this evening Capt. Hof-mann said that if any of us cared to be officers in the next war, he'd recommend us. We would sign up for 5 trs. in the reserve corps. If a new war broke out in those 5 years, we would enter it as officers. In case no war came up, we wouldn't be called for any duties. It all sounded very interesting until he said sign up for 5 years and queered it all. I signed my name once, and that's enough. — Put on our act at the Kur Theatre tonight. The place was jammed. We went thru without a hitch. I wasn't a bit nervous. Big crowds don't worry me like they used to. We got a big hand, even if I do say it. Had to put on our "encore" to quiet them.

Jan. 14, 1919   The Rainbow Club put on our entertainment tonight and it was a clever show all the way thru. The Club is made up of talent from every Regiment in the Division. There is a rumor that the Saxophone Sextet and our quartette will be taken in the club and made permanent entertainers from now on in. Sure hope this is so. It'll be a snap.

Jan. 15, 1919   Went over to the Red Cross in Ahrweiler and put on our sketch again. Heard that a regular set of entertainers is going to be formed, and the circuit will cover all the territory occupied by the Army of Occupation. Don't suppose our act rates a place in this. Would sure like to take a crack at it, though.

Jan. 16, 1919   For the past three days we've been posing for photographs. One day a picture of the whole Regiment. The next day a picture of the H.Q. Co. It's getting tiresome. Hope they get one to suit them. Guess Bob [Tyndall] wants to have something new to show the folks when he gets back. "Me and my regiment." I'm corporal of the guard tonight. Kitchen guard. It's a great old Army. — Our quartette plays for the Masons tomorrow night, and for the 117th Engineers Saturday night. We leave in a truck at 1:00 P.M., have supper at the Sergeant's Mess, put on our act, and then return in the truck. They are sure keeping the four of us on the jump.[31]

Jan. 17, 1919   Got a big hand at the Masonic party and also got to enjoy one of the best meals I've had since I've been over here. Dessert was ice cream and cake. Sure hope they throw another party.

Jan. 18, 1919   Paid the 117th Engineers a visit this afternoon. They're billeted in a small burg called Mayschoss. Out in the sticks. The boys were hungry for entertainment, and it was a

---

31. Portions of Kniptash's diary entries of January 16 and 18 were published in Ferrell, *Diary of Elmer Sherwood*, 179nn2–3.

pleasure to play for them. I know just how they feel living in barns and so forth. This Regiment sure hit lucky when we drew the town. We're living better than Divisional H.Q. The higher-ups didn't know at the time they were assigning us towns, just what sort of place Neuenahr was or we'd have never got within a hundred miles of it. I'm still afraid they'll rank us out. — Left the 117th at 9:00 P.M., and played for the officers till 12:00. Then the feathers.

Jan. 19, 1919   Four wonderful letters from home today. Sure relieved my mind.

Jan. 20, 1919   About 1000 Canadians, men and officers, came down from Bonn today to see the boxing matches between the 2nd Canadian Division and the 42nd American Division. We entertained them all day. They're sure a bunch of good scouts. I slipped in to see the fights. The Americans won them all but the last one. Three knockouts were scored. It was my first time to see a prizefight and they sure are exciting. Lots of action.[32] — Some "snow" that we get paid tomorrow.

Jan. 21, 1919   Took a trip up the Rhine today. Went up to Remagen. Beautiful country. Took some snaps, but I don't think they'll be any good as there was no sun. Am stiff and sore tonight. Feathers for me. We get paid tomorrow. Am going to send $10.00 home. That will make my savings up to $400.00. I hope to have $500.00 saved up by the time I head home. That, and the little girl's "hope" box ought to get along nicely.

Jan. 22, 1919   Payday today. Paid in marks. Drew 274 marks. "Hank" is going to Bonn today, and he is going to buy me 10 rolls of film. Those German films fit my camera nicely. Four of the wireless boys are going to Coblenz Feb. 2 and take a week's course in radio work. I'm included. Also our quartette is billed in Hoosier Follies, a show gotten up by the Band. It plays its first performance sometime next week. Hope it doesn't conflict with the Coblenz affair. Don't think I can spare the $10.00 home this month. — Several of the boys got passes to Bonn yesterday. They

32. Pete Straub also avidly followed the boxing matches between the Americans and the Canadians, as well as the wrestling matches between the Americans and the English. See *Sergeant's Diary*, 258–59.

caught the electric there, and went A.W.O.L. to Cologne. They say it's some town, and they tell some wild stories of the time they had. Sure hope I rate to pass. I want to see that Cologne Cathedral.

Jan. 23, 1919   "Hank" got in Bonn too late to buy the films. Saw our new tractors yesterday. They're powerful little devils and will make more speed than a horse. Our trucks will be coming in about two weeks. Doesn't interest me much now. The Hell with being motorized after the war was over with. Only one consolation. We get rid of the goats. However, that will mean just that much more time for squads east and west. They've got you going and coming. In a letter from Mumsey she said that she wrote out a check for the government for $30.00. It seems she was receiving my allotment at the same time I was. This went on for three months. So that makes me 30 dollars minus.

Jan. 24, 1919   Got my pictures today that I took in Remagen. They were all good. I've got quite a collection, and I hope to get 200 pictures of this country and France before we leave. There is a Grand Opera at the Kur Theatre tonight given by a German troop. Doesn't interest me in the least. — Germany's coming along quite nicely with their new government according to the paper. [Friedrich] Ebert and [Philip] Scheid[e]mann seem to be the leaders.[33] Well, they can't make it too soon for me. It only means we'll go home that much faster. — We have had reviews, parades, and presentations of the flag for the past four days now. Getting ready for the States, I guess.

Jan. 25, 1919   [Rollin] "Monk" Reed came back today. Went down to a town just out of Paris to get officers' baggage. Managed to spend 5 days in Paris. Every detail we've sent so far managed to "get into that town." I'm never in on anything. — The 2nd Canadian division is giving a show at the Kur Theatre tonight, but I haven't got enough ambition to go over. The Hoosier Follies plays next Wednesday and our quartette is in it. [See figs. 17–18.] We

---

33. Friedrich Ebert and Philip Scheidemann were members of Germany's Social Democratic Party. Both men were leaders in the newly formed German Republic, which came into existence in 1919. See Gilbert, *First World War*, 498; Keegan, *First World War*, 417–19.

haven't done a thing towards getting new songs. Suppose we'll be a failure that night. There is talking of making this town a divisional leave area. If such a thing should happen, we'll probably lose our happy home. Hope they change their minds. — The Stars and Stripes have devoted all its energies toward writing up the 42nd this week. Told about our work on the Ourcq, and in another column is wrote up this town of Neuenahr, and mentioned our regiment in the 117th Sanitary Train. Said we were sittin' pretty, and they weren't very far wrong.

Jan. 26, 1919   Another long old Sunday. Was corporal of the guard tonight. Staid [*sic*] up till 1:00 o'clock to post my 3rd relief. Wrote Mumsey and Maude a letter. Had the Blues bad. Lord, I never longed for home so bad in my life.

Jan. 27, 1919   Snow and zero weather today. Quite a disagreeable change after what we have been having. Capt. Eddie was in a good humor this afternoon. Out playing football with the boys. Told me he'd buy Newman's banjo for Bill. We need it in our business. Rehearsals all day tomorrow. — Lot of "snow" about going home February 12. Pretty thick.

Jan. 28, 1919   Rehearsed this morning and afternoon. Believe the show is going big. Got a lot of good stuff. — Went over to hear the minstrel put on by the 165th Infantry. Had some wonderful singers and every song was new. Like to know when they got hold of their new songs. It's a cinch none of them are coming our way.

Jan. 29, 1919   Rehearsed this morning and afternoon. The show comes off tonight. Sure hope everything works O.K. [Carl] Slim Graham just caused a panic. Said Hecquist was on the set and overheard a conversation between Col. Johnson and Col. Tyndal. Col. Johnson said that he'd just come back from Coblenz (3rd Army H.Q.), and he saw the sailing orders for the Rainbow division. Said we will embark 6 weeks after date of memo, and this memo is three days old now. Col. Tyndal said he guessed that meant we move out of here within the next two weeks. Col. Johnson said "Yes, we follow the 26th Division, and the 32nd follows us." Slim says it's straight stuff, and I'm almost tempted to believe him. Good Lord, it sounds too good to be true! The "snow" is awful thick all over the division. Got that Jan. 10th "snow" beat 40 ways for Sunday. It can't be possible that we'll be home and in civvies somewhere around April 1. — Later — The show was a huge success from start to finish. No stage fright anywhere. The boys put it over like old-timers.

Jan. 30, 1919   The higher-ups have asked that the Hoosier Follies be put on again February 4. Don't know how I'm going to be there and in Coblenz at the same time. Today's intelligence reports say that we're leaving shortly. This "snow" is getting me down. I'll be the disappointed boy if it doesn't come true.

Jan. 31, 1919   Was off my feet today. Believe I had a touch of the Flu. "E" battery had 51 men on sick call this morning, and all but one were marked quarters. Lord, I hope it isn't a Flu epidemic. — The boys assigned to the truck, tractors, touring cars, etc. are learning the ropes quickly. They fool around with them everyday. — Our string jazz is going to play for the K[nights] of C[olumbus] banquet tomorrow night. Plenty of eats. The Y.M.C.A. is throwing a boat ride on the Rhine, and I'm one of the lucky ones to go. We leave at 7:00 o'clock tomorrow morning.

Feb. 1, 1919   The Y.M.C.A. threw a boat ride on the Rhine for the boys, and I rated a ticket. Went up as far as Cologne. Beautiful scenery, and that Cologne Cathedral is all that it's said to be. Took some snaps, but there was no sun. Got back just in time to play for the K of C banquet. Some eats.

Feb. 2, 1919   Loaded in a truck at 9:00 A.M. and high-balled for Coblenz, reaching here at 11:00. Sure was a cold ride. Are billeted in an old fort that overlooks the town. The drill schedule is going to be a pipe. The aviators are going to give a series of lectures and show us how the planes work. Passes to Coblenz are given out every night. This week is going to pass quickly. — The "snow" about leaving shortly is getting thicker and thicker. Believe it's the straight stuff this time.

Feb. 3, 1919   First day of school, and it was a snap. About two hours of lectures this morning and an hour this afternoon. Went over to the hangers and looked over the planes. There's quite a few Bosche planes there, too. The last of the week the aviators are going to take our officers and a few of the enlisted men up with them. I'm sure going to try for a ride. — Went down to the big city this evening and bought films and postcards. Came back to the Y. — Yesterday I got knocked a curve. Was sitting in the Y writing a letter to Maude and looked up to see a Y lady that was an exact double of her: actions, manners, everything. She was with a couple of officers, so I didn't get to talk to her. I cried the Blues the rest of the night. I never saw such a close resemblance before in all my life.

Feb. 4, 1919   Had talks on ground and air liaison this morning and then went over to the field. The weather was fine for flying, and several of our officers went up. The Captain in charge of the squadron got in a little quad, and did some tricks for us. He's sure a merry cuss. He wears the Croix de Guerre and the D.S.C. According to the number of Iron Crosses he has painted on the hat band of Uncle Sam's hat, he has 7 Bosche machines to his credit. I took some pictures of the planes, but there was no sun again so I doubt whether a single picture in this whole roll will be any good. — This school is a regular vacation. First real rest I've had since I left home. Paid Coblenz another visit tonight. Like to mix with crowds. Coblenz is a leave area, and there were soldiers from every division on the streets. The old town is bone dry so far as soldiers are concerned. William Hagenbach's circus is in town, and the boys are taking it in.[34] It's a pretty good town for a leave area at that.

Feb. 5, 1919   The aviators took several boys up today. Corporal Breeze of Brigade H.Q. went up with a lieut. that he went to school with in civil life. The lieut. wanted to find out if Breeze had guts or not and looped the loop. Breeze said it's some sensation. Feels like you're leaving everything behind. Said the dips were the worst. Lord, I hope I'm lucky enough to rate a ride.

Feb. 6, 1919   School this morning and passes to the football game between our Division and the 4th Div. They beat us 7 to 0. We were outweighed 20 pounds to the man. It was a good game at that. Had dinner at the Y in Coblenz and came home. I'm tired of Coblenz. Nothing there.

---

34. The correct spelling is Hagenbeck; William Hagenbeck was involved in the Hagenbeck-Wallace circus that was based in Peru, Indiana. The article may also be found on the internet at http://www.circushalloffame.com. For a brief account of this company, see Nancy Newman, "It All Began When Ben Wallace Bought a Circus," *Peru Daily Tribune*, July 15, 1986, Circus Edition.

Feb. 7, 1919   Had a maneuver this morning, and that ended the school. Now we hang around waiting for Sunday to come so we can go home. Took some pictures this afternoon. Also saw an accident at the field. One of the mechanics was turning the propeller over, and the engine started before he had a chance to get away. The blade hit him in the knee, breaking his leg and knocking him out. The propeller snapped in two. — Paid Coblenz another visit and brought home some more film. We got all day off tomorrow, and I don't know what's going on.

Feb. 8, 1919   Slept till 11:20 A.M. and spent the afternoon at the "Y". Some war.

Feb. 9, 1919   Left in trucks this morn, and highballed back to Neuenahr. Col. Bob is on a 14 day leave, and some West Point Lieut. Col. is in charge.[35] He's another one of those discipline babies. He's fixed up a schedule that keeps a fellow busy from 6 A.M. to 6 P.M. Wrote letters this evening.

Feb. 10, 1919   Letters from Mumsey and Maude today. They received the letters I wrote way back in Gerolstein. Maude hasn't been receiving her mail right. Only got one letter when she should have received as many as Mumsey. Sure hope they didn't get lost. The "snow" about our Division leaving is getting deeper and deeper. I really believe it this time and think we'll be on the ocean by the middle of March. — "E" and "F" batteries turned over their horses today. H.Q. Co. turned theirs over sometime this week. Significant. — Our Jazz Band practiced tonight. Some dope about putting on the Hoosier Follies at Coblenz soon. Payday yesterday. Guess I'll send some of it home.

Feb. 11, 1919   Received seven letters and my box of cigs and candy today. Sure made me happy. I'm Corporal of the Guard tonight and answered all my letters so I'm caught up again. Capt. Eddie told some of the boys that we'd be here till July and that this town would be a leave area. We'll have to move to some

---

35. On his leave, Tyndall did some traveling throughout Italy, Monaco, and France. When he returned, however, he was feeling very ill and was admitted to the hospital with a diagnosis of pneumonia. See Tyndall's diary entries for February 6, 7, 14, and 15, 1919, RHTC. In his diary entry of February 15, Tyndall wrote that he had "taken sick in [the] evening"; RHTC.

one-horse town to make room. Don't know whether he's trying to hang a crepe or just put a quietus on this "snow" about our early leave for the States. Guess he doesn't want the boys to run their hopes up too high on going home.

Feb. 12, 1919   Put on the Hoosier Follies at Remagen for the 165th Infantry this evening. Was feeling rotten all day long but bucked up towards night. The show went big. Doughboys make a good audience. Capt. Hofmann told the Sgts. that we were leaving within the next two weeks. Said there was no doubt connected with it. Whenever Eddie says so, it's usually right.

Feb. 13, 1919   Snap, snap, snap everything was snap today. The Div. got news that General Pershing is coming to review the entire Division somewhere between Feb. 15 and 18. Our drill schedule was changed three times today. We squads east and west all morning, and cleaned personal equipment all afternoon. Military discipline and courtesy has become a passion. Everyone is hog wild. Must do this, and must do that. Like to run me raggedy today. It sure looks more and more like home. Whenever the C in C comes to look you over, there must be something more to it than a casual visit. Sure don't mind all the "snap" if it will bring us nearer to the going away time. — The Hoosier Follies made another trip up to the Rhine to play for the Alabama boys. Our string jazz stalled out of it. Can't stand the late hours. Too much drill during the day. The soldiers can't "bake 'em" like the Band can. It's me for the feathers.

Feb. 14, 1919   "Snow" getting deeper again. See the sailing orders are down, and we'll be in New York by Mar. 15. I'm sitting tight and holding my breath. The drill schedule is the stiffest I've ever bucked up against.[36] On your toes from 6 to 6. This town is a leave area for the Division. Run on the same plans as the Coblenz business. — Went over to buy some jewelry for the folks and Maude. I'm sure green when it comes to this. I'm afraid these Germans will skin me. Didn't price any of the stuff, but suppose

36. The military regimen continued at Bad Neuenahr, even though the opportunities for relaxation increased. Pete Straub's diary entry for February 15, 1919, reveals that the soldiers were busy throughout the day feeding the horses and maintaining their trucks and tractors. *Sergeant's Diary*, 269.

it doesn't cost any more than American-made stuff. Don't believe this jewelry is as good as America's. — Colonel Bob got back today. Suppose he had a good trip, and suppose the drill schedule will remain the same. I hate that Lieut. Col. worse every day. When I get out of the Army, I believe I'll get up the gang and mob him. Damn West Point and everybody connected with it.

Feb. 15, 1919   Saturday and just like any other day. According to the old schedule, we're supposed to rest this afternoon, but according to the new one, we're not. Drill "toujours." Went to the theatre tonight to see moving pictures of the 42nd Div. in action. The pictures were good. Everything from some lousy soldier readying his shirt up to ruined villages. It's a funny sensation to be reminded of things you went thru by pictures. They sure were vivid. Scenes of every front except the last one, the Argonne-Meuse. — "Snow" says that the sailing orders are down. I believe all this stuff is bunk, and the only hope I have is Capt. Hofmann's statement to the sergeants that we'd be home in April. Whenever he comes out with a statement that bold, it comes pretty straight. — Tomorrow is Sunday, and from the looks of things it will be like any other weekday. I will be glad when Black Jack gets here and gets it over with. A General's a Hell of a lot of bother.[37]

Feb. 16, 1919   Sunday over, thank the Lord. Mac just came in and said that the Review is postponed for two weeks. I thought it would be something like that. Kinda looks bad for this going home "snow." — Our Jazz Band practiced tonight.

Feb. 17, 1919   Spring today. Worked up a sweat. We're back to the old schedule again, and it makes things easier. — Mac just came in and said we leave within two weeks or less. He's been to division H.Q. to see about getting up the paperwork.

A Captain from the G.H.Q. told all present that the Rainbow Div. was Homeward bound "toot sweet." My morale is hitting a 100 again.

---

37. Black Jack was the well-known nickname of General John J. Pershing. The moniker was applied to him by his critics who referred to his command of African American troops on the U.S. western frontier in the 1880s and 1890s. See Smythe, *Pershing*, 2; Farwell, *Over There*, 148.

Feb. 18, 1919   Been out buying presents for the folks. Bought Maude a beaded purse. Babe a knife. Mr. Kahlo a cigarette case. Am going to buy Mumsey a cameo and Parker a paper knife. The Jazz Band practiced this evening. — Heard we turn over the horses tomorrow or the next day.

Feb. 19   Am Corporal of the Guard tonight. Received 7 letters today and spent the night answering them. Capt. Hofmann said that we get rid of the horses tomorrow. Hope it's straight stuff this time. The stables are as bad as they were at Coetquidan, mud knee deep and with the drill schedule we've got, a fellow doesn't get a chance to clean up. I've sure got my fill of horses. Heard today that Colonel Bob is in the hospital with pneumonia and is pretty low.[38] Bought Dad a pipe. Will soon have my box ready to send.

Feb. 20, 1919   Nothing much today. Slept till dinnertime. An order has come down to stop all of this talk about going home. Says it's bad on our morale. Don't suppose we'll leave until the last dog dies. I'm lucky enough to get to go to another school at Coblenz. Another week of baking.

Feb. 21, 1919   Went to Sinzig tonight and put on the Hoosier Follies for the Alabama bunch. Went big.

Feb. 22, 1919   Washington's Birthday and the higher-ups are giving us a few hours to ourselves. Sent my box home today. It left me broke but happy. Sure hope it doesn't get lost. — Heard Colonel Bob has been out of his head for three days: pneumonia and a bad case at that.[39]

I hope he pulls thru. Am going to Coblenz tomorrow for another week of baking. Anything to get away from these horses and drill schedule. The folks back home think all we're doing is laying around and taking things easy, but they don't know. They'll find out a few things about this Army when we get back. — The

---

38. Following his return to the unit, Tyndall was hospitalized at Base Hospital 26 with pneumonia. Tyndall diary, February 17, 1919, RHTC.

39. In a letter to his wife, Dean Tyndall, Colonel Tyndall explained that "the doctors and nurses have been telling me of the things I said and did the first three days here and they must have thought they had a 'nutty case.'" March 3, 1919, Correspondence, March 1919, Box 2, Folder 10, RHTC.

"snow" about us going home has died down to zero. Don't suppose we'll ever get home.

Feb. 23, 1919   Climbed in a Quad and came to Coblenz again. Major in command of this squadron was killed last Friday. Was up in a Bosche machine and lost control of it. He was buried today. Ten machines circled and dipped around the funeral procession. It was very impressive. — See in the paper where service chevrons and divisional insignia are taboo in the States. Causes friction between overseas and stay-at-home soldiers. It's laughable. As far as I'm concerned, they can strip me naked and send me home in a barrel. To Hell with decorations and all this hero stuff. I'll be all the hero I want to be with the folks and Maude. All I ask is to get out of this man's Army now. I didn't join it to be a soldier. Poor browbeaten soldiers. I hope they leave it up to us to vote on Universal Training. I'm afraid the bill would never pass. I'm just living from one day to another. Each day brings me nearer to the discharge time. It's a great life. I wouldn't be a peacetime soldier for any amount of money. I figure that all this time from November 11, 1918 till I'm discharged is wasted. Just a blank so far as getting anywhere is concerned. I'm sure full up to the neck with the Army.

Feb. 24, 1919   First day of school, and it's identical to the other one I had. A few new lecturers that weren't here before, but otherwise no change. One Lt. who spoke was a prisoner in Germany from the beginning of the last drive till a week or so after the Armistice was signed. I talked to him after class, and his experiences read like a novel. He started in about the same time we did and was on every front we were. He was an observer but did strafing work as a sideline. He was strafing Bosche troops when he was shot down. His pilot was killed instantly, and he suffered a fractured knee. The German soldiers wanted to kill him, but a Prussian soldier said, "no." He was sent to a hospital near Munich, but received no medical attention. Said he wasn't brutally manhandled, and the only reason he could account for was because the Bosche knew they were beaten then. He got to some of the 12th Engineers that were captured at Cambrai a year ago and they told him tales of cruelty at the hands of the Germans. One act was to make them stay outside all night absolutely naked and three inches of snow on the ground. He said if it wasn't for the Red Cross, he'd have never made the grade. As it is, his stomach is on the bum from lack of nourishment. He looks bad: no color and a slight limp when he walks. When the Armistice was signed, he was told that he was free, and was then left to his own resources. He walked and stole rides until he reached Switzerland, and from then on he was sitting pretty. Said he left Munich in a hurry because the Bolsheviki were getting restless.[40] Said he wouldn't give anything for his experience now, but it wasn't any fun then. — Was just thinking of how that "snow" about us going home died down, nary a whisper now, and a week ago that's all you heard. I'm surprised to find that I'm not near as disappointed as I thought I'd be. Guess I didn't believe it as much as I thought I did after all. It sounded too good to be true. — That kid brother of mine worked himself into a corporal's job in the Cadets at Manual. Hate to see him take soldiering the way he does, but since it won't lead into anything worse, I guess it's alright. I'll see to it that he doesn't get into the [National] Guard or even think about getting into it, and if another war breaks out, and he's eligible to go he won't enlist either. He'll take his chances on the draft. I volunteered, and that will do for the whole Kniptash family. I'm not sorry that I enlisted. I got in the best division in the world by doing so. It isn't that. It's the Army that makes it bad. The Regular Army officers are trying their best to make things unbearable for the National Guard. They tried it in the States, and now that they've got us over here, and we're almost helpless to fight back, they're getting away with it. They're playing Hell with our Regiment. They got rid of Major Miller some time ago. Just because Major [William] Taylor, Captain [Frank] Buschman[n] and Captain [Paul] Fechtman stood up for Captain Kelly, they got rid of them too. We've got two West Point majors and a W.P. Lt. Col. They are all three slave drivers, and I hate their guts. If Col. Tyndal doesn't get better, they'll be

40. By the end of the war, Germany was nearly plunged into a Bolshevik-style revolution. In fact, unrest and the threat of revolution at home played a major role in the decision by Germany's political rulers to seek an armistice. See Fleming, *Illusion of Victory*, 299–300.

easing in a West Point Col. to take his place, and then we will be sore. Sure will be glad when I get out of the whole affair. I'm sick of O.D., and I hate soldiers.[41] If I thought, as in the case of the Regulars, that I had from 2 to 5 years more of this Army ahead of me, I'd go plumb nuts. I'm about there now, but 2 additional years would put me in a padded cell. — This is the fourth time in succession that the victrola has played "I Ain't Got Nobody Much." The guy that's putting that record on must have the Blues as bad as I have. I'm going to bed.

Feb. 25, 1919   Went down to Coblenz this evening with Ted, and we got lost. Got to meandering along the Rhine, and after an hour of dark streets and alleys, we finally got our bearings. "Lost in a big city or how Lizzy got her start." Bought some more films. Had supper at a "Y," and got back in time to see the last two acts of the show the 148th put on for the boys. It was the best comedy I've seen for a long time. Plenty of action, something the Hoosier Follies lacks.

Feb. 26, 1919   The New York Herald put out its <u>best</u> paper today. A column devoted to getting the different Divisions home, and the old Rainbow leaves in March or April. I let out a yell when I saw it. No more "snow" to it. It's a settled fact now. Oh! Boy. My morale is batting a 1000. Going home for sure. It's too good to be true. I just feel like busting. Never so happy in my life. Home and in civvies by the 1st of May. Boy! Oh! Boy! Just want to get on top of the world, and tell everybody the good news. Wonder if the folks know. They surely must. I'm going to write them right now, and let them know I know. I'm going to enjoy a good night's sleep this night.

Feb. 27, 1919   School this morning and passes to the football game between the 4th and 89th Divisions. It was the game to decide the championship of the 3rd Army. The 89th won 14 to 0. Was a wonderful game. There were three bands, a drum corps, a bunch of clowns, and airplanes came over and performed a bunch of tricks before the game. There was a big parade afterwards. The 89th will now represent the 3rd Army when the game for the championship of the A.E.F. is played. They've got a

41. "O.D." is a military abbreviation meaning orders of the day.

snappy team, and can be depended upon to put up a battle. —
Meandered around town this evening. Nothing down there, so
came home and went to bed.

Feb. 28, 1919   Last day of February, and also the last day of school.
Hung around the "Y" all afternoon and night. Saw moving pictures of the "Salt of the Earth." Was coming back to the billets
happy and on good terms with the whole world when I passed
the officer's quarters, and then things changed. The officers and
nurses and Y.M.C.A. women and things were having a dance. I
looked in the window, and the "scenery" gave me the Blues so
bad I had to leave. Hall was beautifully decorated, and a big Jazz
Band and these birds trotting around having a glorious time. It
hurt. However, these American women over here are officer's
meat, and their meat only. We've been fighting for Democracy
for a year and yet it's a court martial for the enlisted men caught
talking to one of these dear things. I used to think it was an honorable thing for a woman to come over here and do war work,
but I've found out lots of things since then. The old Sam
Brown[e] belt can work wonders.[42] I know lots and lots of officers
that are men, but I know a whole lot more that are pricks. Well,
in a couple of months things are going to even up a bit. It's going
to take more than a Sam Browne to get by. Heard a good story
this eve. A couple of enlisted men were walking down the street
and crossed the paths of a couple of nurses. The nurses said,
"Hello boys." One of the men turned around and said, "I beg
your pardon miss, but you must be mistaken, we're not officers."
It sure took a fall out of the old girl. She exited like a clam. Lord,
I'll be glad when the day comes that I can tell some of these birds
to go to Hell. They might as well be overbearing while they can

---

42. Kniptash's mention of the Sam Browne belt refers to a belt with an over-the-
shoulder strap worn by officers of the AEF that was designed by a British officer by
that name. The belt was a source of controversy and friction as it set apart the officers from the rest of the troops. Pershing insisted, against some opposition from
the Army General Staff in Washington, that the officers wear the belt. See Smythe,
Pershing, 92–93; Farwell, *Over There*, 140, 304. Kniptash's experience also under-
scored the bad blood that existed between regular soldiers and the YMCA regarding the Y's entertainment of officers and women assigned to the military districts.
Kniptash's diary entry for February 28, 1919, was also published in Ferrell, *Diary
of Elmer Sherwood*, 181n7.

because it won't work in civvies. — We go back to our home tomorrow. Not going to wait till Sunday like we did the last time we were here. Heard they got rid of the horses while we were here. Sure hope this is true. I don't want to see a horse again so long as I live. — Just been reading over all that I've written tonight, and it sounds like jealousy on my part. It isn't jealousy. It's the unfairness of everything to the enlisted men. He hasn't got a chance.

Mar. 1, 1919   Left in trucks this morning and got back in Neuenahr in time for dinner. Hear we got rid of all our horses but 37. These were the ones that were condemned and will be sold to the German people around here. I'm sure glad that the goats have left us. They were the worry of my young life. Found a gang of letters waiting for me too. The missy sent me some snap shots of herself, Babe and Dad that made me crazier than ever to get home. So near and yet so far. Capt. Hofmann said that Pershing is going to review the Rainbow Division March 9–10. Sure hope he comes this time and gets it off his mind. — The clocks were set up an hour today. Cuts us out of an hour sleep in the morning. The M.P.s made a raid on our "hangout" to see if "Mother" was selling champagne.[43] They didn't find out anything. The M.P.s are as bad as the Germans.

Mar. 2, 1919   Another long old Sunday just about finished. Am Corporal of the Guard tonight, and am staying up to post my third relief. Then it's me for the feathers. Caught up with my mail finally. — Heard the H.Q. Co. has quite a few more noncoms than the table of organization calls for. It means that some of us will be busted, and I'll probably be one of them. Then again, I heard that there are just enough corporals, but too many sergeants. In that case, I won't lose my stripes. Don't care if I do now that we're so near the going home time. The corporal doesn't mean anything at all in the H.Q. Co. He just does as much work as the privates and has added responsibility. No, they won't break my heart by taking my stripes away.

43. Most likely, "Mother" was a German woman who befriended some American soldiers and occasionally supplied them with food, and perhaps in this instance, some alcohol.

Mar. 3, 1919   Capt. Hofmann told me today that he'd rec'd a letter from his mother dated February 5 saying that she was sending him a uke and banjo for us. It was mighty nice of him, and we ought to be getting them in a couple of days. — Ted Corbin wants me to put this down in my diary. We'll be in the States not later than April 20. He seems confident, but I don't believe him.

Mar. 4, 1919   An advanced school in architecture and other professions will open up in a town near Paris shortly. It will be run by the A.E.F., and there will be a little of the military connected with it. Got to talking with Lt. Hadley about it, and he talked me into going. He's going. I handed in my name, but I don't know whether I'll be lucky or not. If I do get to go, the courses will probably be over my head. I had a chance to go to an elementary school, but I'm afraid it would be a waste of time to go there. Afraid they'd spend too much time on the stuff I already know. I think this advanced course will spend a little time at the start with elementary principles. From then on I think I can ease myself thru. Now that I got to thinking about it, I really look forward to it. My old job at V + B is open for me when I get back, and a month or two of schooling at this time will come in very handy. We will be notified when the Division is ready to move, and we can come back in time to leave with it. The school is scheduled to last three months, and I figure on taking at best two months of the course. That will help. Sure hope I rate.

Mar. 5, 1919   Captain Hofmann O.K.'d my request to attend school, and it was sent to the higher-ups of Div. H.Q. Co. If they decide in my favor, I'll be leaving these parts shortly, and I sure won't hate to leave either. The drill schedule is so stiff and the routine so monotonous that it gives a fellow the willies. "Doc" Hadley told me lots of things about our West Point boys that I didn't know before. I'd like to meet Spence and Curitan down in some dark alley when I get out of this mess.[44] Damn slave drivers. — Will know tomorrow whether or not I get to go to school.

44. At the time, Major William Spence was the commanding officer of the 2nd Battalion and Major William Cureton (not *Curitan*, as Kniptash spelled it) commanded the 3rd Battalion of the 150th Field Artillery. See Tompkins, *Story of the Rainbow Division*, 243.

Pershing is supposed to review us around the tenth. Hope I miss that. Hell with Pershing. He's caused us enough trouble already. I'm getting so I hate everything and everybody that has or had anything to do with West Point.

Mar. 6, 1919   Haven't found out yet whether I get to go to that school. The boys that asked to go to the other one left this morning. Will learn our fate in a day or two. — Received seven letters from home today. One from Mumsey, from Dad, Maude, Mrs. Kahlo, Ronnie and Danny. Also received another from Albert. He's trying to get back to the Co. again. Hope he makes the grade. — Mooney went to the hospital yesterday with the Flu. Today they punctured his side and drew out two quarts of puss that was pressing against his lungs. He's feeling chipper. Tomorrow we have a Regt'l Review. Getting ready for Pershing. We wear helmets and carry haversacks. Also our wonderful Lt. Col. has put out an order that every man in the Regiment will have his haircut so that no hair on the head shall be longer than 1 inch. Uniformity, you know. Must have all the soldiers look alike. Also the overseas hat will be worn slightly tipped to the right and a little forward. No other way will be becoming, according to the West Point ideas. Hell. — Heard today that the venereal rate in this Division is higher than any other Division over here. Something like 1200 men of the 28,000 are afflicted. Heard that if the rate increases our chances of going home in April will be pretty slim. Don't believe any of this rot.[45]

Mar. 7, 1919   Drill and snap. That's all we've been doing this week. Sure will be glad when Pershing gets here and leaves. — Haven't heard any more about the school, but expect to tomorrow. — Mooney leaves for the States tonight. He's in a pretty bad way. Hate to see him go. We got in the Army about the same time; were

---

45. The AEF's concern with the rate of venereal disease among the troops in the Rainbow Division was serious. In early March, with outbreaks of venereal disease on the increase, the AEF threatened to retain soldiers in Europe until they were treated, regardless of their unit's scheduled return to America. See Cooke, *Rainbow Division*, 223; Freidel, *Over There*, 231; Smythe, *Pershing*, 250–51. A portion of Kniptash's diary entry of March 6, 1919, was published in Ferrell, *Diary of Elmer Sherwood*, 180n3.

transferred from A Battery about the same day, and buddied through the whole war together. It's best for him though, because he'd die if he staid [*sic*] over here. — Had our Review this morning and passed O.K. Repeat the performance tomorrow morn.

Mar. 8, 1919   Saturday and me on Regimental Guard. Just means 24 hours of fatigue and on Saturday and Sunday too. The only two days of the week we are given a chance to catch our breath. My luck. Caught the third relief after having taken part in one of the sloppiest guard mounts the Regiment has ever had. It was the first time I've been on Regt'l Guard since I've been in the Army, but I got through nicely, everything considered. Got two hours sleep this evening, and that was executed on a table. We get relieved at 4:00 P.M. tomorrow. Thank goodness.

Mar. 9, 1919   Sunday and still at it. Sitting around waiting for our West Point leader to show up. Must turn out the guard for him, you know. The Company is out playing ball and otherwise enjoying themselves, and here I am tied down to this guardhouse till 4 P.M. If it rained soup, I'd be holding a fork. — The buglers just blew. Pay day so the Regiment gets paid this afternoon. That helps some. Haven't heard a word about the school, so I guess all of our requests were cancelled. Again, my luck did not fail me. — Got paid this afternoon and was relieved from guard by 5 P.M. Hit the feathers at 6:30 P.M. Lack of sleep the night before. I'm not the old rounder I used to be. If I stayed up till 10 :00 o'clock, I think I've done something devilish.

Mar. 10, 1919   Had another practice review this morning, and then I was handed a pass to Neuenahr. A day off to do just as I damn please. — Went over to the "Y" and hung around all morning. Had dinner there. Bought some souvenirs for V + B. Had supper at the "Y" and danced a few with [Lloyd] Skinner. Saw the show afterwards. French performers. Best all around show I've seen since I've been over here. That finished the day, and I go to bed with tomorrow's Review to haunt me. Wonder if Pershing ever will come. The fellow that wrote "The End of the Perfect Day" never served in this man's Army, I'll bet. They ain't no perfect days for a soldier.

Mar. 11, 1919   Passed in review again this morning. In the afternoon three of us got to see a basketball game at Andernach. It was between the 42$^{\underline{nd}}$ Div. and the 4$^{\underline{th}}$ Army Corps. We won 28 to 25, and it was anybody's game up till the last minute. Sure was snappy. — Latest "snow" says the whole Division will be out of Germany by April 10. Says the 165$^{\underline{th}}$ Infantry, who were stationed at Remagen, will be the first to leave, and this Regiment will follow right on their heels. This town is to be made an Army recreation center, and that's the reason we come second. Hasn't been decided yet whether we go by rail or by river. We leave from Remagen and go to Antwerp, Belgium. Then it's home boys home. "Snow" seems to be official. I saw the delousing machine on its way up to Remagen. Hasn't been decided yet as to whether we take our equipment along with us or not. Sure hope we leave it here. Understand our Lt. Col. is trying to get rid of the boys' rifles and side arms for them. Hope he succeeds. Things sure look bright for the States by May 1. — Haven't heard any more about the school, so I suppose our requests died at Div. H.Q. Don't care much now since we've lost all this time.

See where [Secretary of War Newton] Baker turned loose a gang of conscientious objectors that were being held at Ft. Leavenworth. Gave each one 400 dollars and a suit of civilian clothes and a dishonorable discharge. That's Baker for you: always doing something wrong. Paying those dudes 400 dollars for refusing to fight. That's got me whipped. Suppose he thinks that dishonorable discharges will cause them to blush with shame. What's a man with that stamp care whether his discharge papers are honorable or dishonorable! I can picture the whole bunch of them laughing up their sleeves. They sure slipped one over on Uncle Sam.

Mar. 12, 1919   Didn't have to Pass in Review this morning. Must be something wrong. Understand we do it every morning from now on. Commencing tomorrow morning. — Albert and [Kenneth J.] Brown returned to the company this morning. Both fatter than hogs and tickled to death to get back. Had a talk with Chaplain Nash today. First time since November 11. He said it's pretty official that we'd be pulling out of here by the first of April, and that we'd sail from Antwerp. Said Black Jack will review us next Sunday. The Chaplain's "snow" is pretty reliable, I've found. Nineteen more days. Oh boy.

Mar. 13, 1919   Corporal of the guard tonight. Caught it last Sunday too. Sure getting my share. Passed in Review again this morning. Part of the schedule now. — Heard today that we turn in all motor equipment next week. Don't believe this. They said the same thing about the horses, and we've still got some on our hands. Everybody says that the first elements of the Division move out April 1st, and the whole division will be out on the ocean by April 10. Guess we'll get back just in time to boost the Liberty Loan Drive that starts April 20. Always some job waiting for this Division. — [Dean] Dooley was made a corporal today. Sure had it coming to him if anybody did. — Heard that Pershing is in Coblenz now, and is using his spare time inspecting hospitals. It seems that the Review will be held at Krepp, 9 kil. from here, and we hike there and hike back. One man says that 28,000 men shall hike there and pass in Review before him, and that 28,000 <u>have</u> to obey. That's Army for you. I just want someone to snap me out an order to do something when I get back. I'll tell them to go to hell so quick his head'll swim.

Mar. 15, 1919   Another Saturday spent away from home. Had our final Regiment Review this morning. We're all set for Jack tomorrow. We've sure done our share of snapping. A review every morning this week, and an inspection every afternoon. I've worn my helmet more in the last week than the whole time I was at the front. We all have to pass O.K. — All kinds of "snow" floating around. Today the boys were hanging crepes. Said a telegram came down to Div. H.Q. saying that our going home time had been delayed, and that Antwerp could not be used as a port. We would have to wait our chance at some French port. I don't believe this atall [*sic*]. Also "snow" says turn in all our motor equipment next week. — All passes that are due after Mar. 24 have been cancelled. That's better than the telegram "snow," I say. Also I read in the paper yesterday that the first elements of our Division will be moving on April 1st. "Snow" don't tease me now. I <u>know</u> we're going home.

Mar. 16, 1919   Well the job is done, and we'll now kneel and give thanks. Sunday morn, and we got up at 6:00 A.M. Hiked up to a big field, a little piece out of Remagen, and got there at 11:00 A.M. found out that the Review would start at 1:00 P.M. Nothing to do but stand around and wait for his Majesty. He showed up at 1:40. Only 40 minutes late. Pretty good for a man of his rank. He started the inspection immediately. There was something like 30,000 men on that field. Never knew there was so many soldiers in the world. No wonder we won the war. Jack must have walked 15 kil. to inspect that gang. After the inspection, he pinned medals on the different men and officers that were recommended for them. Sgt. [Ray H.] Murphy of A Battery got one.[46] Was mighty glad to see him get it, as the whole world knows he earned it. He kept on firing his piece when a whole box of powder charges were burning around him. Then the whole Division passed in Review. It's quite some sight to see 30,000 men marching at one time. There wasn't a hitch at any time. Then Pershing made a speech to us. We high-balled home in trucks. Got home at 6:00 P.M. That made 12 solid hours of standing on our feet. I was sure a tired soldier when I got back. Found my bed all made up with fresh, clean sheets. Also two letters from home waiting for me. That relieved the situation considerably. — Hear once more that we turn in that remaining 37 head of horses tomorrow. Sure hope it's straight stuff this time. — Am sure glad Pershing is thru with us now. It will give some of our West Point leaders a little rest. Sure had them worried. Hope I never have to take part in another review so long as I live. It's O.K. if you're on the sidelines looking on, but it's Hell on the actors. Reveille is one ½ hour later tomorrow. It's due us. — Sheets for me.

Mar. 17, 1919   It's Saint Patrick's Day, and I baked 'em most of the morning. At 1:00 this afternoon we took the horses to Ahrweiler to have them branded. We stood in the rain from 1:00 to 4:00 waiting our turn, and it never came. We were wet to the skin when they finally told us that we'd have to wait till tomorrow. So we trotted 'em back. Another example of Army efficiency. Lord, I'll be glad when I get out of it all! — Wrote Mumsey and Maude a letter this evening. — Today at noon this Div. was relieved from the A of O. And we are now in a little army of our own called the Army of Reserve. It's one step nearer home. — Some interesting

46. Ray Murphy received the Distinguished Service Cross for his action in battle. See Ray H. Murphy, Roll No. 20, "Mize, James—Myers, Edward V.," WWI SR.

statistics were published in the Stars and Stripes concerning casualties. It showed that the National Guard did their share of the fighting. The N.G. had 5,000 more men killed than the Regulars, and 15,000 more than the National Army. Concerning the Artillery branch of the service, there were only two other Regiments that had more men killed than the 150th did.[47] The big gun Regiments sure got off lucky, if that is true because we only had 36 men killed outright. Not sorry that I joined the organization I did.

Mar. 18, 1919   Took the horses down again to be branded. After standing around in the rain for four hours our turn finally came. Returned them to the picket line, and they are still on our hands. Hope I wake up some morning and find them all dead. — Bad "snow" out today, but I don't believe it. Says we can't use Antwerp as a port because there is no place there to turn in our equipment. Have to take our turn thru Le Mans and a base port in France. Boys say that means six months more in this God-forsaken country. The salvage officer called up and said that all orders for turning in any equipment this week have been cancelled. Don't believe this hurts our going home time a bit. Slipped in the theatre this evening and saw another French show. It was good, but not as good as the last one. — Sheets.

Mar. 19, 1919   Corporal of the Guard tonight. Half the company got shot in the arm today for Typhoid. They are relieved from duty for 24 hours. Their arms are very sore and swollen. The other half of us get ours day after tomorrow. Good "snow" came out today. Captain Hofmann told several of the boys that the first elements of the Division would sail from Brest on April 12. — Also heard that the Div. Q.M. had orders to pack up today. Morale's way up.

---

47. Elmer Sherwood records the casualties suffered by the 150th Field Artillery in World War I up to February 1, 1919; see *Rainbow Hoosier*, 192–94, 210–11. Sherwood categorizes the casualties thus: killed in action (20), died of wounds received in action (10), accidentally killed (3), died of disease (13). Orel Dean and John Peterson were reported as killed in action on July 28, 1918, and October 9, 1918, respectively. Sherwood, *Rainbow Hoosier*, 192. After the war, the Rainbow Veterans Association of Marion County (Indiana) recorded a total of 60 deaths. See *In Memory of the 150th*, 8.

Mar. 20, 1919   Baked 'em all morning. Baseball game, stables, and a bath this afternoon. Sit around and twiddled our thumbs all evening. If they don't get me out of this country pretty soon, I'll go nuts. Monotony's getting me down. — New York Herald gave our Review a big write up. See in the Stars and Stripes where jobs paying $250 a month and a 500 franc bonus were offered a Regiment of Engineers in the S.O.S [service of supply]. Jobs said you'd have to sign a contract for 6 mos. to stay over here and work on roads, villages, etc. There were 2700 men in the Regiment, and only 18 signed up. I guess there's others that want to get home too. — "Snow" is remaining at par. The boys who took that shot in the arm yesterday are pretty sick today. Can't move their left arm at all. I get mine tomorrow. That gets me out of Saturday morning inspection anyway, and that's worth the price. — "Mother" fried me an egg tonight. First I've had since the day we left for the front. It's against the rules for German people to put out any food, but what's a few rules amount to? — Had a nice little chat with Colonel Bob today. He was out for a walk. Said he was feeling O.K., but he couldn't get his breath just right. Said it corked him to climb a flight of stairs. Will be glad when he gets back to the Regiment. He's not the best Col. in the world, but he's a better man than Lt. Col. [Clement E.] Heth.[48]

He at least knows what we had to put up with on the front, and that's something that S.O.B. slave driver doesn't. By the way, our two West Point majors are leaving us. Transferred to the Regulars. Been terrible if I've forgotten to mention that happy event

---

48. Colonel Tyndall was seriously ill with pneumonia and remained hospitalized in Bad Neuenahr for most of February and March 1919. In his diary, he recorded: "Learn that I have been very sick. Much weight loss." Tyndall diary, February 20, RHTC. On March 4 he sent a letter to his wife noting he had been making progress and considered himself recovered. "The doctor gave me a thorough examination this morning and says that I am in fine condition but it will be four or five days before my lung is completely cleared and of course during that time I must stick to my room, although this does not mean anything as I have fully recovered." Robert H. Tyndall to Dean Tyndall, March 4, 1919, Correspondence, March 1919, Box 2, Folder 10, RHTC. Tyndall's diary entries for March 5, 6, 13, 15, and 18 show that he remained in a weakened condition. On the day that Kniptash recorded his conversation with the colonel, Tyndall noted that he had taken a boat ride down the Rhine to Cologne. Tyndall diary, March 20, RHTC.

in this book. Wish we could get rid of the old silver leaf. — So ends another day. I'm going to bed. Not because I am sleepy but just because it's the only thing left to do. Gay life! And Mumsey got up in the middle of the night to write me a letter telling me not to re-enlist. Bless her old heart. She doesn't know the Army like I do, or she wouldn't have gone to all the trouble.

Mar. 21, 1919   Got shot in the arm today. My arm's sore as a boil, but otherwise I feel O.K. Suppose I'll spend a miserable night tonight. — We spent the entire day in turning in surplus material. It's no longer "snow" about leaving. Sure hope so this time. They have even sent an order down telling where different Regiments in the Division will be mustered out. Our camp is in Ohio. Looks like the States by April 30.

Mar. 22, 1919   Been turning in my stuff all day today. Finally got rid of our wireless equipment. Start turning in rolling stock Monday. When we climb on board the ship, we won't have any more than the Lord allows. "Stars and Stripes" say[s] we follow the 26th Div. home, and will sail about the middle of April. Now that we know for sure that we're going home, the boys act very quiet. Curious. Orders say that we'll be mustered out at Camp Sherman, Ohio. There will be no parades in the U.S. Sure makes me feel good. I hate parades and all this hero stuff. Get me home, and I'll be hero enough with the folks and Maude. My arm's as sore today, and I can't move it. Have got a fever too. Suppose I'll be O.K. tomorrow.

Mar. 23, 1919   Sunday and the whole day to ourselves. Had reveille at 7:00, and [Walter] Ringo detailed four men to take care of the ten remaining horses. Our next formation will be retreat at 4:45 P.M. Don't know how I'm going to kill time. I'm up on my letters, and it's too cold and wet outside to walk around. My arm is much better, and still hurts so I can't play baseball. Suppose I'll sit around the stove with the rest of the boys and fight the war all over again. My pictures got lost in the shuffle, so the folks will just have to do without. Understand Capt. Eddie is acting major of the 2nd Bn., and Lieutenant [Floyd W.] Sense is our acting captain. Hope Eddie makes good. The remaining ten horses we turned in, and there was no retreat. Just baked 'em all day. Best Sunday I've ever spent over here. Nothing but drill tomorrow, I suppose.

Mar. 24, 1919   Snowed and rained all day, so drill was called off. Learning how to roll packs now. Thot [*sic*] I graduated from that class, but I guess not. Caught motor part guard this afternoon. It's a 24-hour guard, and it gives you the follow[ing] afternoon off. Softest guard of them all. The rest of the Co. caught Regimental Guard. Soft for yours truly. — The whole gang is acting nuts tonight. We've had a parade, a hooch dance: they've called for all the actors to be dolled up in toilet paper, a church meeting, and are now holding a horse sale. [James F.] "Duck" Hardy is the horse, and they are bidding on him. Hate to see this bunch when they get on that boat. Hell will sure break lose. "Duck" just sold for 1500 marks. "Talkie" is the auctioneer. Acting pretty goofy for a bunch of silver men.

Mar. 25, 1919   Rained all day, so no drill. Baked 'em all day. Pretty nice now. See where the 89th Div. football team has won its way to the finals. Doesn't surprise me. I saw them play at Coblenz. I think they'll win the A.E.F. championship.

Mar. 26, 1919   Another day nearer home. Learned how to make packs "encore" today. Baseball this afternoon. Best war we ever fought. — The Division's bakery has closed down, and we now eat hard tack in the place of bread. Quite a come down. — The saxophone sextet got back last night from a month's tour around different camps. They're big league players, and are going to try for Keith's when they get back.

Mar. 27, 1919   The squads right and a road march this morning. Baseball this afternoon. Party at the skipper's tonight. Broke up at 12:00. Fair time.

Mar. 28   Snow and rain all day. Damnedest weather I ever did see. Cold and warm by spells. Sun one minute, snow and rain the next. Sure hope the weatherman snaps out of it, and we start to move.

Mar. 29   Inspection with full packs this morning. The Y woman came down just before the inspection and asked Captain Eddie to line up some music for her. Said she was throwing a dance for the 150th. Kind of a grand finale for the miserable failure they were to us. Eddie passed the buck to me, and I lined up the sex-tet. The only reason I helped her out was because she was buck-ing Old Man Boison. It was because of him that our Y was such a farce. He was King, and one couldn't do a thing. — Night — The dance was a success as far as it goes. There were 50 fellows for every girl, but everybody had a good time, I think. Skinner and I danced most of them. Can't go these women. — The Division starts moving next week. It just doesn't seem possible. Can't bring myself around to believe it. Just a few more days in this God-forsaken country. Oh Boy.

Mar. 30, 1919   Sunday and baked 'em all day. Got restless after dinner, and Skinner and I walked around town. Had the blues pretty bad. Monotony gets me going. Played solitaire this evening. Such is Sunday in the A. of O.

Mar. 31, 1919   We got 'em. Had 'em all day. Can't shake 'em. Damn Blues.

April 1, 1919   Had a parade this morning. Gen. Gatley pinned a ribbon on our standard, and then we Passed in Review before him. Col. Bob then made a speech. He talked to us once before at St. Nazaire in 1917. Made a fairly good speech this time. Told us what a Hell of a good regiment we were, etc., etc. He's trying pretty hard to get back on speaking terms with the boys. Not much of a job after a month under that Heth. He's a welcomed visitor, believe me. He said during his speech that the Regiment had taken part in eleven different battles; two of them were major operations, and nine were minor. It's quite a record, and one that few Regiments can boast. — There's an indescribable restlessness springing up among the American soldiers and the German people now. When we first came here they treated us like Kings, and we couldn't understand it. We were too glad to leave the cave man life and get back to civilization to try to dope out their friendliness. I savvy it now. It's their damn propaganda again. They had hopes that Wilson would make things easy for them at the peace table, and treated us accordingly. Now that Wilson is sitting on them as hard as the rest they are getting ugly. They are poor losers in the first place, and then to lose their final bet is too much for them. They're forgetting who came out on the short end of this war, and are trying to order us around. See where they killed an American soldier in Coblenz. They better watch their step and not carry things too far. I've lost patience with them, and I venture to say I'm not the only one. Damn Dutch square-heads. I loathe every last one of them. Everything they do is underhanded and sneaking. Dirtiest fighters in the world, and they have lost none of their habits since they've gotten back into civil life. Lord, how I hate this race. I don't want any Kaiser lover in the States to get sassy with me. Might lose my temper and get mad. Germany will never be the same again, I'm afraid. Too many Americans have seen her the way she really is. Sure be glad when we leave here. Am sick of it all.

CHAPTER 5

"This Guerre Is Sure Finis,"

April 2–May 9, 1919

It would be difficult to imagine a more beautiful picture than that of the marching thousands of soldiers down Washington Street from Military Park, where the Rainbow Regiment received its first greetings from the home folk.

From *Indianapolis Star*, May 8, 1919

After Vernon Kniptash received the news that the 150th Artillery was scheduled to leave Germany for France and then depart for the United States, he spent a few anxious weeks in Germany before beginning his final preparations for the end of his adventure in Europe. The imminent departure from Germany and the upcoming conclusion to his military service brought forth mixed emotions. While he was anxious to return to Indianapolis, rejoin his family and friends, resume life as a civilian, and put the regimentation of the military behind him, he regretted that his adventure in Europe was drawing to a close. "Sure hate it that I'm leaving this country," Kniptash confided to his diary on April 8, 1919.

Kniptash moved out of Coblenz on April 8, 1919, aboard a "40 and 8." His destination was the French seaport town of Brest, where the troops were scheduled to board a transport ship for the return voyage to America. The train ride from Coblenz to Brest lasted the better part of four days (April 8–12) and was a physically bruising episode. The troops found little time for sleep as they rode in the cramped, uncomfortable boxcar. The ride also took the men back through areas of war-torn France where the troops saw, once again, the destruction and desolation that the war had inflicted upon the French countryside.

Once the troops arrived at Brest, they spent the next five days (April 12–17) preparing to depart. Days were spent in the dull

194

monotony of military life as the troops waited, with considerable expectation, for the time when they were to break camp and head for the ships. Kniptash and his fellow Hoosiers learned that their time for leaving France was scheduled for April 18, 1919.

On the appointed day, more than ten thousand troops began boarding the USS *Leviathan,* a German transatlantic cruise liner seized by the Americans as a wartime measure. The *Leviathan,* which was one of the largest ships in the world, had been named the *Vaterland* (*Fatherland*) before the war. Reputed to be the second-largest ship in the world at the time, the *Vaterland* was launched in 1914 at Hamburg and became one of the prime vessels of the Hamburg-America line. The ship spanned 958 feet from stem to stern, was 160 feet wide, had fourteen decks, displaced eight thousand tons of water, and traveled at a speed of twenty-three knots. When the Americans tried to seize the ship in 1917, the *Vaterland*'s German crew attempted to destroy all of its blueprints and operating procedures while sabotaging some of its critical equipment. Between December 15, 1917, and November 1918, the *Leviathan* carried more than one hundred thousand American troops to France. On Kniptash's return voyage to the United States, the ship carried 11,505 people, including soldiers and ship's company.[1]

Unlike Kniptash's crossing to France in October 1917, aboard the *Lincoln,* the return trip to America was uneventful and smooth sailing all the way. Kniptash entertained himself on the voyage by writing entries in his diary, watching the boxing matches and band performances aboard the ship, and generally taking in the sea breezes. On April 25, 1919, the *Leviathan* landed in New York. Kniptash had returned home safely.

April 2, 1919   [William A.] Morris told me some good news today. He read our morning orders. They came down today. This Regiment leaves a week from today: April 9th. We hike to Sinsig [Sinzig], and then board the train at 11:20 P.M. The train leaves at 12:30 A.M. Our packs will be hauled to Sinsig. It will take 60 hours to get to Brest. Last boat in our convoy has to leave France

1. As mentioned earlier, Kniptash had first seen the *Leviathan* when he left the United States for France in October 1917. See also Farwell, *Over There,* 81; James, *Years of MacArthur,* 1:256, 259.

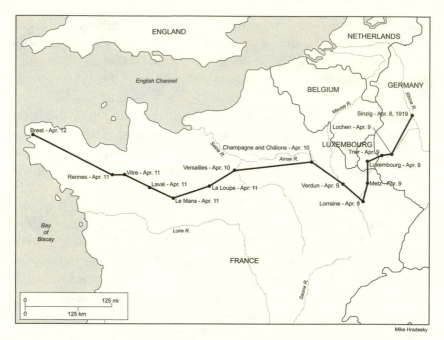

Map 2. Going Home, April 8–12, 1919. This map shows the route that Kniptash took when he left Germany for France, and then the return voyage to the United States. Map by Michael Hradesky.

by 7:00 A.M. April 17. That means we won't spend much time in that mudhole. The P.O. will not accept any more mail after 10:00 A.M. tomorrow. Div. P.O. is going to Brest Friday to collect our incoming mail and have it ready for us when we arrive. Lord, but how this next week is going to drag. Just seven more days in this God forsaken country, and only 15 more days on this side. Lord, I hope I'm home by May 1st.

April 3, 1919   Had our final field and physical exam today. All ready to highball now. Took in a show this evening. Same one [we] saw at Coblenz but it has sure improved a lot. — Hear that the 89th Div. won the A.E.F. football championship. I knew they'd turn the trick.

April 4, 1919   Took a road hike this morning, and we climbed that ungodly hill just out of town. Had me sweating blood when I reached the top. Sure was panilla coming down. H.Q. Co. beat "B" battery in a baseball game this afternoon. Snappy playing. — Only four more days of this country. Just can't realize it.

April 5, 1919   H.Q. Co. beat A Battery this afternoon 6 to 5. Pretty game. — Col. Bob is on another leave and will meet us at Brest. The slave driver is in charge again. — H.Q. Co. had a farewell this evening. Good feed!

April 6, 1919   Our last Sunday in Germany. Answered two calls today: reveille and retreat. Heard the best piano player I ever listened to before in my life this evening. He's from the 89th Division and plays everything from Grand Opera to Blues. Sure was a wonder. Just naturally had me cold-cocked. Couldn't say a word. Sat for 3 solid hours listening to him. Could have gone another three without a whimper. He's got 'em. We do all the necessary odds and ends tomorrow, and then move Tuesday. OH boy. The three papers, and the Stars and Stripes wrote up the 42nd to who tied the pup today. Never did get so much notoriety. Guess we're in for a big time when we get back, but I hope and pray we don't parade.[2] Guess there's no way out of it, though. People must see the soldiers. Poor, old soldiers.

2. The Rainbow troops in the Army of Occupation had voted against marching in a parade in New York City when they returned to the United States. Manchester, *American Caesar*, 113.

April 7, 1919   Everything's ready for the move tomorrow. All we
    have to do is roll our packs and police up around the billets, and
    we're gone from here. We start hiking at 1:30 P.M. Our packs will
    go on ahead via truck, and our bed sacks will be filled with straw
    waiting for us. Taps will be at 10:00 P.M. and everybody will have
    to be in at that time. The train pulls out the next morning at
    2:11, then a highball toward Brest. Oh boy! — Played the officers
    two games of baseball today, and we broke even. We'll play the
    rubber at Brest or in the States. Sheets.

April 8, 1919   Made packs and policed up and all ready to move
    by 10:00. Had dinner and started hiking at 1:30. "Mother" cried
    like a baby. Lots of the women folks were crying. Can't use their
    tears. Reached Sinsig at 4:00 P.M., and got on the train at 5:00.
    There are 44 men on this boxcar besides two boxes and a dog.
    Just how we're going to sleep, I don't know. It looks like 72 hours
    without a wink to me. The K of C just gave each man 10 donuts
    and four packages of cigarettes. Another boost for the Y.M.C.A.
    Already for the whistle to blow. Sure hate it that I'm leaving this
    country.

x---------x

April 9, 1919   Stood, or rather laid a hitch of guard from 8 to 11
    last night. There was no room to walk. Every inch of floor space
    was taken. Sleeping like a flock of hogs. Managed to get in some
    good licks from 11:00 P.M. on. — Woke up this morning while
    passing thru Cochen. At 9:30 A.M. we stopped at <u>Trier,</u> and had
    a meal. Stopped for an hour in this town. It's one of the oldest in
    Germany. Built by the Romans, I believe. However, we won't hold
    that against it. We've been travelling down the Moselle Valley all
    this time. Beautiful country. The 89th Division is quartered
    around here. We've passed thru five tunnels so far, longest one
    being six kilometers in length. Sure is hilly country, we've made
    fairly good time so far. — Well, we've passed through Luxem-
    bourg, and are now in Lorraine. In a country that has been Ger-
    many since 1870. Tried to talk to a French soldier and couldn't
    make the grade. Have forgotten what little French I did know.
    Finally gave up my end of the conversation, and took his picture.
    Sure is curious business to change over from the "Haben Sie" to
    "Avez-vous" in two minutes time. The girls are no longer

Frauleins, they are Mademoiselles. Sure is curious. Clear over my head, like a tent. The train has stopped now, and I can write in peace. The way that writing looks is the way we sleep at night. These Frogs are walking guard with their helmets.[3] They better move on. Pass through Metz at 3:30 P.M. It's pretty strongly fortified: a high, thick wall around the biggest portion, and a 30-ft. moat around all. It won't be long now before we'll be going over the old battlegrounds: trenches, barb-wire, etc. once again. The country now sure makes me feel at home: dug outs, bomb holes, shell holes, prison camps, ruined villages, and all the rest. It's going to take some time to straighten up that mess. — We pass thru Verdun at night, tough luck. I wanted to see that town. The boys are now making their beds and everything is noise and confusion. It's just about as easy for 45 men to sleep in this car as it is for a number 10 foot to cram into a size 6 shoe. The way we sleep tonight will cause "Shanty" and I to bump heads again. Some business.

X-----X

April 10, 1919   Woke up this morning in Vietry. Francais. Familiar country, as I hit this town quite a few times while the war was on. There's a battery of big guns sitting on the track next to us. About 12 babies: SI cans. — We're due in Brest at 7:30 tomorrow night. We're behind schedule time. — Just passed thru the Champagne region. Grave after grave. We're about 30 kil. from Chalons and ought to be there by noon. This Champagne district is awfully desolate looking. No trees to speak of. Just a big, flat plain. Hasn't changed any since July, 1918. Passed through Versailles late this eve.[4] Once before did I hit this town, and that was the day we went to Chateau-Thierry.

April 11, 1919   Woke up this morning in La Loupe. Had breakfast, washed and shaved and feel like a new man. We're way

---

3. The word "Frog" was occasionally used in reference to a French soldier or a Frenchman. See Farwell, *Over There*, 302.

4. The peace conference at Versailles was in its later stages at this point, with intense discussions going on between the representatives of the Allied countries over the powers of the proposed League of Nations. See Godfrey Hodgson, *Woodrow Wilson's Right Hand: The Life of Colonel Edward M. House* (New Haven and London: Yale University Press, 2006), 212–14.

behind time, so we'll probably spend another night on the train. — Just passed thru Le Mans. It's a big town and has billeted as high as 6 American Divisions at a time. We are going to pass thru Laval and Rennes before the trip is over. Have been in both towns before. Paid Rennes a visit while we were in training at Coetquidan. Am brain tired but never happier in my life. We're home-ward bound, and nothing can go wrong. — Have passed thru Laval, and are now in Vitre. Just a little piece to Rennes. We get into Brest tomorrow morning about 10 o'clock. We've made time today, but can't catch up with the schedule.

April 12, 1919   Got up this morning at 5:30. Raining like Hell. Made packs and cleaned up the boxcar. Hit Brest at 7:15. It rained here 322 days last year, and I suppose this year will go even better. The Bay of Biscay sure looks good. Several big boats out from shore. — Had breakfast at an enormous mess hall, and then hiked 6 kil. to our camp. We're living in tents and fighting a regular Camp Mills war again. Am sure glad that joy ride from Coblenz to Brest is over with. That was a nightmare from start to finish. Brest is the most miserable looking camp I've ever seen. Mud. Mud. Mud. Hear that every outfit has to furnish a detail every day for engineering work. Old St. Nazaire stuff. Well, we're leaving here about next Wednesday, so I guess I can stand it. Saw a bunch of casuals climbing on board the North Star. They were a happy bunch. A fellow has to watch his step pretty closely around here. An argument with a M.P. means a short stay in France. I'm going to keep my mouth shut from now on. — Mail is being passed and "soupie" just blew. So I must need to answer the call. — They've got a wonderful system to everything around here. That mess hall was a marvel. I bet they could feed a Division in a half hour's time. The whole camp is very well planned, and everything is fairly convenient. I received letters from Mumsey, Maude, V + B, Babe, and Danny. All of them were afraid to write for fear the letters would never reach me on this side. The box I sent finally got there. Everybody pleased, as I guess I didn't do so bad after all. Mrs. Vonnegut wrote me a wonderful letter, and I'm going to save it. Let me know that my old job was waiting for me when I got back. — Danny says the doctor just got thru taking the final piece of "whizbang" out of him. He's waiting for

his discharge papers now. — The boys all say that the Indiana
Legislature voted down that $60 bonus bill for returned, overseas
soldiers. The boys are pretty sore. Not that the $60 made any dif-
ference, but because of Indiana's poor spirit toward her soldiers.
She's the only state in the Union that hasn't come across. I'm
afraid the 150th will refuse to parade for them now. I don't want
the parade whether or no. I'm sick of parades. All this Hurrah
stuff. — Took a bath, and the system I had to go through slowed
me. Everything done by the count. They figure to the second just
how long it will take. So many men to go thru. It worked down to
a fine point. Awful nasty about it, though. They've sure got where
they want you, and don't hesitate a second in telling you so. —
Alabama couldn't stand their line and told them so. The whole
Regiment is on fatigue consequently. Here's one head that's
going to obey all orders, and never say a word. I've got this close
to home, and I don't want to be slowed now. — Hear that the
Leviathan is on deck now and that the 67th F.A. Brigade will use
it. Sounds good to me.

April 13, 1919   Sunday at Brest. Rained early this morning but the
sun came out later, and has stayed out. See where Baker, Pershing, and [Field Marshal Henri] Petain are going to be at this
camp tomorrow. Suppose we'll be in on the ceremony again.
Always our luck. Wish we'd load before they got here. — Had a
lot of luck and managed to get a new blouse. Couldn't get an
overcoat, however. Needed it worse than a blouse, too. It'll be a
crime to go home in this one. — Alabama loads on the Carolina
tomorrow.[5] Had their final inspection today. "Snow" says we
[take] Leviathan home, and I sure hope we do. We ought to load
Tuesday. Sure will be hard to take. I'm tired of Brest already. Its
one redeeming feature is its closeness to the boats. Otherwise
she's "par bon." — Had a surprise this afternoon. Bobby Wesler
came in to see me. He's stationed here in Brest with the Engineer
Regt. Pick and shovel work in this rainy town. Says he thinks he'll

5. The artillery units were the last of the Rainbow troops to leave Germany.
Consequently, several of the other units within the 42nd Division left for the
United States ahead of Kniptash and his fellow artillerymen. See Cooke, *Rainbow
Division*, 237.

be sailing home 6 months from now. He has my sympathy. He's looking good, and the Army isn't old stuff to him yet. I can remember when I was that way. He'll get his belly full in time. He was drafted.

April 14, 1919   The usual rain again today. The biggest part of the Company is on Engineering detail, and I drew lucky and get to bake 'em. Sure is a tough day to work, and I feel for them. The Captain tells us that we board the boat Wednesday. The boys are out working again this afternoon, and again I sit around the stove and bake 'em. First good luck I've had in a long time. — Duke, Talkie, Cope and the rest of 'em landed their commissions today. All 2nd Looes [lieutenants]. They get to go home with the Division. — A big Rainbow came out while we were standing Retreat, and I knew something was going to happen. It has never failed us. Every time the Division started a big drive, a Rainbow was sure to stretch itself across the sky. When we took our first step in our hike to the Rhine, we were greeted by a Rainbow, and tonight Lt. [Joseph T.] O'Neal told us that we have our final inspection tomorrow morning at 10:00 o'clock, and get on board the Leviathan in the afternoon. It dropped anchor at 12:00 this noon, and Baker climbed off. They fired a salute, and he was met by Pershing. They marched down a gauntlet of two miles of soldiers. Hope we don't get to see him. He means nothing to my young life.

April 15, 1919   Pay day this morning, and paid in good old greenbacks. "Snow" out now that we don't embark until tomorrow. Have our final inspection today, however. Also "snow" says that we don't go home on the Leviathan but on the Pastoria. — A, B, and C batteries have been down at the dock all day waiting for a chance to load. The Leviathan is several miles out at sea. She can't dock at Brest because she draws too much water. The sea is so rough today that the small boats that take us from the dock out to Leviathan can't make the grade. We should have been on board last night too. If this weather holds up, chances are we will never make it. The 77th Division is coming into camp too. They sail right after us, and we should be out of here. The first elements of our Division have been out to sea for 3 days now. We'll be strung out all over that old puddle. Lord, I hope we make it tomorrow. We've had all our inspections and everything's ready. Just our luck.

April 16, 1919   Had another medical inspection this morning. Rolled our packs and are ready for our orders to move. Hear that the batteries had to sleep at the docks last night, and they loaded early this morning. The boat is due to leave tomorrow, so we'll have to load some this afternoon. This suspense is awful. H.Q. Co. and F Battery are the last of the Division to get on the boat. If we don't get on pretty soon, I'll start biting my nails. Nothing doing in the way of moving. The 1$^{\underline{st}}$ Bn. of the 77$^{\underline{th}}$ Div. moves out at 7:00 A.M. tomorrow. Hate to see those birds beat us to it. Haven't heard when we leave. Am worried.

x-----x

April 17, 1919   The order came down last night. We leave at 11:30 today, and board the boat at 1:30. It's the Leviathan, too. Brigade H.Q. moved out at 6:45 A.M., so it's on the boat by this time. — We played the officers a game of ball yest. and beat them 15 to 10. It was a rubber game too, since each side won one at Neuenahr. They were good losers. — All the fellows that received their commissions in this camp will not get to go home with the Division. They go to a casual camp and get home the best way that they can. They are singing the Blues. — Had dinner at 10:30, and we're already [sic] to move. It's a perfect day for a change, so we won't get a ducking away. France is treating us pretty nice for our last day. Doesn't cause me much pain to leave here, however. I'm mighty glad I came over here when I did, but I'm mighty glad I'm leaving when I am. It's all been an experience I'll never forget. — Hiked to Brest and got on the lighter at 2:30 P.M. Pulled out immediately and steamed over to Leviathan. Boarded her at 4:00 P.M. She's an enormous ship, and is just about [at] carrying capacity now.[6] She has to leave by tomorrow. [Arthur] Marquette missed the boat. It was the only bad luck the company had. Sure hope he made it anyhow. His service record

6. Kniptash was obviously pleased to be on board the *Leviathan* for the transatlantic journey home. The *Leviathan* carried more than ten thousand men on the trip. It had carried as many as fourteen thousand at one time. See Cooke, *Rainbow Division*, 238; Sherwood, *Rainbow Hoosier*, 186; Ferrell, *Diary of Elmer Sherwood*, 160–61.

was left behind so that he could get it when he did show up. He'll go nuts if he does lose out. Sure was a homesick kid. — There must be 50 million men on this boat. Supper was started at 4 o'clock, and at 8:30 they were still at it. I had mine at 8:00. When I left the mess hall and started back for my bunk I got completely turned around and spent the next hour walking from one deck to another. The guides didn't know anymore about the boat than I did, and they always gave me a bum steer. I found myself in the engine room once, and finally ended up in the mess hall again. Finally met someone that I knew and hit my bunk at 9:15. I must have walked clear across the ocean and back. — Two meals a day will be served on the boat. One at 8:00 A.M. and the other at 4:00 P.M. If the confusion continues as bad as it was tonight, we'll do nothing but stand in the mess line. — Marquette showed up, and all's O.K. — Took my last peep at France tonight. Brest was lit up like a million dollars, and it was a beautiful sight. Can't compare with New York, however. Am all in, but never happier in my life. We're home-ward bound for sure, and barring accident ought to be there by April 24.

April 18, 1919   Slept like a log last night and had breakfast at 9:00. We're supposed to pull out this afternoon. The confusion has cleared up, and things are running pretty smoothly now. There's fellows from several different Divisions on board. Most of them are wounded men. Men with legs off, blinded, and 75 cases of shell shock. They're in a bad way. — Well, we're on our way. Just finished our supper and heard the engines start up. Choked the meal down and hustled on deck. At 5:30 P.M., the boat got into motion, and at 7:00 P.M. there was no more France. Nothing but water now. The boys did not cheer. They are all happy, but they regret to leave France just a little bit. Just 18 months ago today we left New York harbor. Coincidence. Quite a little difference between the two take-offs. The other one left me with an empty feeling in the pit of my stomach while this one . . . well . . . I don't know just how it does make me feel. I don't feel like yelling and raising Hell, and yet I'm not a bit sorry I'm leaving France. Curious. I didn't get sick on the other trip. Wonder if I will on this one? Don't see why I should. This boat won't ride near as rough as the Lincoln did. We'll see.

April 19, 1919   Slept like a log again last night. The ventilation is perfect. This is sure some boat. Had breakfast, and then went up and listened to a band concert. Then went thru a cootie inspection. This damn Army just can't do without inspections. — Watched the shell shocked boys for awhile. They are caged in on all sides. At times they act perfectly sane, and then again they're hog wild. One of them thinks he owns a white horse, and he spends the biggest part of the day grooming him. Another ties and unties knots in a rope for hours at a time. The worst case of them all is the one that walks back and forth with his head sunk on his chest and his hands clasped in front of him. He never says a word and never gets off his path. It's a shame to see these big huskies in such a condition. It would be far better to lose an arm or a leg. They say that they will be alright in two to three years. I sincerely hope so. — The ship is just naturally leaving this place. Doing its best, and that's 24 knots an hour (27 miles). It makes the Lincoln look like a tub. Haven't had any inkling of seasickness yet. I've seen only one boy sick as yet. The sea is like glass, and you'd never know it was moving. Don't imagine choppy waves would have much effect on this baby. — Had supper at 4 o'clock and laid around on deck till bedtime. Sure was a wonderful day. Tomorrow is Easter Sunday, and all's I got in the way of new clothes is a shirt that fits me around the neck.

x---------x

April 20, 1919   Easter Sunday. Had a very good breakfast. Oatmeal, hard-boiled eggs, apples, coffee and bread and butter. They say we've got some dinner in store for us. — [Rocco Adams] just got thru knocking Hell out of the best man this boat has. The sailor was game but wasn't in Rocko's class. The bout was called at the end of the 2nd round. Nobody's sea-sick yet. This boat rides the waves beautifully. Hardly any motion to speak of. She hasn't slackened her speed a bit. We must be 1100 miles out by now. For dinner we had turkey, mashed potatoes, asparagus, pie, cake, bread, butter, and coffee. Some meal. Baked 'em on the deck all afternoon listening to the different bands. The chaplain of this boat gave us a talk on demobilization this evening. Said we'll be sent to one of four camps around New York. We'll have to go thru a delousing plant, and maybe we will get new clothes. The men that have gone before us didn't, but Baker told this Chaplain last Sunday while on the way to Brest that he'd send a telegram from Brest ordering new clothes for every man to wear home. We get a 24 hour pass to New York too. That sounds good. We will stay in the East for about a week, and then go to our mustering-out camps. This Chaplain asked the boys whether they wanted to parade or not. And everybody yelled "No!" at the top of their lungs. He said there was a rumor out there that we would parade in Washington D. C. but didn't know whether there was anything to it or not. Said everybody he talked to was against parading of any kind. All want to get home.

April 21, 1919   Another 12 hour sleep. Never slept better in my life. This salt air is wonderful. — Have passed up three ships in the last two days. They left from Brest two days before we did. We went by 'em them like a pay car passes a tramp. This boat is right out there when it comes to speed and class. Sure drew lucky when we got her. — Boxing bouts and concerts off and on all day. Having a hard time to make the day pass. Don't worry me any. I'm perfectly happy. Every turn of that old engine is getting us nearer to the New World, and I want to say it will be some New World after living for 18 months in the Old. — Saw a couple of sailors dancing that new "shimee." She's a dandy, but I don't think it would go very big at a high brow affair. I'll sure give it a try, though. Try anything once.

April 22, 1919   Thirteen hours sleep last night. Honestly, I don't know how I'm going to get used to this 1 and 2 A.M. stuff. The day was uneventful. Outside of the fact that we're just one day nearer home, nothing else happened. Boxing bouts and concerts. I'm not finding this trip a bit monotonous, however. Always something turning up to kill time. — Except for a few rare cases, there has been no sea-sickness on board ship. I never felt better in my life. My physical condition is 100% better than it was when I got in this man's Army. If staying out to wee hours in the morn hurts it, I'm going to drop this rounder business and get in my regular sleep. — The wind blew up tonight, and the sea has got its bowels in an uproar. Doesn't seem to bother old man Leviathan a bit, however. She just rides as smoothly as ever.

April 23, 1919   Another 500 miles nearer home. Staid [*sic*] up on deck most of the day. We've had perfect weather so far. Have been taking snaps of the boat, and they all ought to turn out O.K. The sailor Jazz Band entertained us this morning. Fifteen piece brass. The Sousa band was split up into little parties like this one, and sent to the different transports. It's got 'em. — See where Lt. [Aloys] Knaff is in the hospital with appendicitis. Everybody in A battery wishes him the worst luck in the world. He's a slave driver, and A battery hates him. — Got windy and nasty out, and everybody came down. — We were 900 miles from New York at noon today. We will get there Friday noon but won't get off the boat till Saturday. — See where we've got a new General at the head of our Division. Reed [is] his name, but I don't know much about him. He won't hold his command very long because in a few weeks the Rainbow Division will be wearing long pants.[7]

April 24, 1919   We got out of the Gulf Stream last night, and the weather is snappy. Strong wind, and choppy sea. — Another cootie inspection this morn. Must give these medics something to do. — We don't have any more abandon ship drills, thank the Lord. That usually broke up the afternoon's baking. — We are 469 miles from New York this noon.

x---------x

April 25, 1919   Sea is awfully heavy this morning. Waves bigger than a horse. Raw and cold, too. We're about 50 miles from New York right now. The sailors have been working for the past two days stringing lights all over the boat. Big doings, I guess. We ought to get our first peep of the U.S.A. sometime this morning. — Saw land at 1:30 P.M. Big hill. Then we saw land on both sides. Sandy Hook on one side and Long Island on the other. The boys were silent. No one cheered or yelled. I expected it to be this way. It affects everybody this way. Had dinner and then went on deck again. Our pilot joined us and is now taking us up the harbor. Saw the Woolworth building but haven't seen Miss Liberty

7. The reference here is to Maj. Gen. George W. Read (not *Reed*, as Kniptash recorded). See W.m. Herschel, "150th Field Artillery at Camp Merritt, *Indianapolis News*, April 26, 1919, 1, 21.

yet. I'm just filled with awe at everything. It's the day I've been waiting eighteen months for. — Hear that Mrs. [Dean] Tyndal is in New York waiting for Bob. — Lafe [Lafayette] Page got a radio gram from his sister in New York. — I think we go to Camp Merritt, but I'm not sure. — Well, it's all over and I'll try to write it off the best I can. Tugs from the different States came out to greet respective Regiments. Indiana had two tugs, and we're well represented on a third. The boys finally cut loose, and the din was awful. Miss Liberty loomed into sight, and that coupled with those tug boats full of Hoosiers was too much for the boys. I'll frankly say that big tears came to my eyes, and I wasn't ashamed because everybody else was affected the same. Then somebody let out a blood-curdling yell, and that acted like a cork out of a bottle for all. Everybody went wild, dancing, sparring, yelling, and kissing. Lord knows what not. A bunch of raving maniacs. I feel as hysterical as a damned old woman. The tugs followed us till we were ready to turn into our pier, and then they had to leave. We were all chased down below after that, and we are now waiting for the ship to dock. It was a wonderful welcome, and one I'll never forget as long as I live.[8] — It's pitiful how much this country is leading the one we just left. The harbor was alive with boats of all descriptions. That old New York skyline makes Brest's skyline look like a row of huts. I don't believe I was ever quite as happy as I am at this minute. Hope to have my feet on good old USA soil by 8:00 o'clock tonight. — Finally bumped into dock, and troops began unloading immediately. H.Q. Co. got off at 7:30, and marched thru a series of dock sheds. That's as far as we got. Had to wait on the ferry till 10:30. M.P.s with their silver service stripes are thicker than fleas around here. All wear campaign hats. They try to act tough but can't get away with it. It takes a better man than a silver stripe to handle a Rainbow boy. — The boys are raising Hell around here waiting for the ferry to show up. Four of them just passed me following a Salvation Army lassie on a truck going at top speed. She kept yelling for them to stop, but

8. For an account of the entrance of the *Leviathan* into New York Harbor on April 25, see Everett C. Watkins, "Leviathan Puts In at Hoboken with Rainbow," *Indianapolis Star*, April 26, 1919, 1.

they kept it up. Everybody's acting like a ten-year-old kid. There's supposed to be absolutely no smoking in this building, but the place is thick with smoke. The old policeman on duty at first tried to stop it and finally gave up. — Red Cross women have been passing out chocolate and apple pie at regular intervals. Some treatment. We finally ferried across the North River and got on the train. It's now 11:00, and we've got a train ride and a hike ahead of us yet. — That train rode like a ship. Hiked to this camp, but as yet I don't know just in what part of the U.S. we're located. The camp is very clean if a fellow can judge a camp at 1:30 in the morning. Saw several Rainbow boys going thru the de-lousing plant. They were issued new clothes too. I'm dead tired but happy. Oh boy! — Latest "snow" has it that we stay here three days, and then leave for Camp Taylor. We stop at Indpls en route and have a parade in the morning and a reception in the afternoon. Then we climb on the train again and proceed to Taylor where we will be mustered out. I don't like the idea of meeting the folks, and then leaving again. However, that's not my wherefore.

April 26, 1919   Got to bed at 2:00 this morn. And was up and washed and shaved by 7:00. Just couldn't sleep. Just like the kid that laid awake all night waiting for Santa Claus to come the next morning. This camp is a wonder. Went down to the W.U. [Western Union] and sent Mumsey a telegram. Then went down to the Post Exchange and made a hog of myself on pie, ice cream, and chocolate. Everything a man could ask for and all he wanted of it. It's wonderful after what we had to put up with over there. To get a couple of packages of cigs, a fellow had to stand in line for an hour. Here you just bust up to the counter and order away. — Funny thing happened in the W.U. office. A doughboy edged his way into the crowd and yelled, "Where in hell are those blondes?" Several honest-to-God girls standing around too. He forgot that they weren't French and German girls. He sure felt like a nickel when he did come to. Everybody seems to be in a daze. Just can't realize that they have finally landed. Two weeks ago we were bumping down the track in a boxcar from Neuenahr to Brest. Now we're here in New Jersey. Things have taken place so swiftly that the boys are at sea. The 77th Div. has landed too, and New York is handing them a big welcome. The papers say that New York's "own" advanced 71½ kil. against the Bosche. A damn lie, but if they can get away with it, O.K. I haven't seen a 77th man yet that won't take off his hat to us. We kidded them to death about their famous "Lost Battalion."[9] That was a joke. It was a disgrace rather than an honor. Hell, anybody could get lost at the front. The big idea was to keep from getting lost. "A" and "B" batteries have been de-loused, and I hear that they get passes to New York this afternoon. We catch it sometime this morn. — See where the 165th went big in New York. The old fighting 69th and the people went wild. Father [Francis] Duffy is singing their praises up to the skies.[10] A damn good bunch of two-fisted fighters. They are at Camp Mills now. — It seems funny to me that everybody speaks English. I caught myself hesitating when I went to talk to a civilian on the street. Forgot for a second what language to speak. The folks that have never got across don't understand all this, I know, but 18 months over there causes it. — Got de-loused or rather went thru the motions and got issued a new blouse and a new overcoat. — Went down to Merritt Hall and wrote Mumsey and Maude a letter. Came back and found a letter from Peggy and Louie waiting for me. Louie's was dated the 23rd, and was not posted to overseas. It's the first letter I've received over here. Says they are building a big arch near the cir-

9. The "Lost Battalion" refers to a force of 560 Americans who engaged the Germans in a furious battle during the first week of October 1918. The unit was surrounded by the Germans after losing about 60 percent of its force. American artillery then unleashed a barrage of fire that carried into the trapped Americans' positions instead of those of the Germans. Finally, after two days of fighting, the Germans withdrew from the area and the American High Command listed the troops as lost in battle. Following the German withdrawal, the American survivors moved out of their positions and returned to the U.S. lines to the shock and amazement of their fellow soldiers. See Coffman, *War to End All Wars*, 323–24; Farwell, *Over There*, 311–13; Freidel, *Over There*, 171–75; Gilbert, *First World War*, 470. The best recent studies of this episode are Ferrell, *Five Days in October*, and Gaff, *Blood in the Argonne*.

10. Father Francis P. Duffy was the chaplain for the 165th Infantry (N.Y.) unit. Duffy followed the Rainbows into battle throughout their time in France and also accompanied the troops into Germany for the occupation. After the war, the Rainbow Veterans Association named Duffy as their honorary chaplain. After the war, Duffy published a memoir of his experience, *Father Duffy's Story* (1919).

cle, and we are in for a big reception all around. — Can't understand why I can't get a letter from Mumsey and Maude. They surely wrote me. Maybe they'll show up later. — I'm still walking around on air. Everything is impossible, and I don't care. I see where Italy has dropped out of the League of Nations. I don't give a damn now what she drops out of. I'm too busy learning how it's done in America to try to find out why she's quitting the Big Four cold. — Put my name in for a pass to New York tomorrow. Think I'll get it too. I'm anxious to see the big city again. Had an ice cream soda tonight. The first one in eighteen months. — But why keep repeating "the first time in 18 months." Everything that has taken place so far has been that way.

x---------x

April 27, 1919   Been off my feet today. Our passes to New York didn't come down, and I'm glad they didn't. Haven't eaten a bite all day, so I'll be O.K. in the morn. Perked up about bedtime and went for a long walk around camp. Feel fine now. Must have made a hog of myself on pie and ice cream, etc.

April 28, 1919   Received a telegram from the folks last night. Wanted to know if I was broke. They know me pretty well, I guess. However, I happen to be flush this time. — The reason our passes didn't come down yesterday is because the segregation lists are being made out, and no passes will be issued to nobody until they are in. All the replacements that come to the Division will be segregated here and sent to the camps nearest the place he enlisted. Half of our Regiment is new materiel. When they leave I doubt if there will be 900 originals left. Understand E Battery will have only 82 men. The lists were finished yesterday, so we'll probably get to go to the big city today. — Received a letter from Mumsey and Maude this morning, so everything's settin' pretty. They wrote about as crazy a letter as I did, talking about a million things at once. They expect us there Thursday, but I don't see how we're going to make it. — We are still waiting for our passes to come down. They are checking the casuals off at the H.Q. now, and when that's done I suppose we'll get 'em. — From Mumsey's letter I take it that we're in for a big reception when we finally do land there. Guess we go to Sherman instead of Taylor. All our Ohio casuals are staying with us. Suppose we'll go clear to Indpls and then come way back to Ohio again but we just must parade it seems. — Our passes came down at 3:00 o'clock, but we made fast time to New York. Bummed around the streets most of the time. Took in Ziegfeld's Midnight Follies and got out of there at 2:00. It was rotten. Bert Williams wasn't even up to snuff.[11] I'm sitting in the ferry station now waiting for the boat to take me to the Jersey side. It's 3:30 A.M., and I'm dog-tired. — The ferry showed up at 4:00 A.M. and I get up at 5:00. Some cut up.

April 29, 1919   Got up at 9:00. Only 4 hours sleep. Sure feel tacky. Hung around waiting for I don't know what and took in the show at the Liberty Theatre this evening. Hear a drill schedule starts tomorrow. Close-order drill and such. Lord, I hope we get out of this place! I'm through soldiering. Latest "snow" has it that we'll get to Indpls next Sunday and have that day and night with our folks. Then we parade Monday morning and then go to Camp Sherman. We'll be mustered out of the service by May 5. Another week of duty. Guess I can stand it.

April 30, 1919   Had another chance to see New York and took it. Went to Keith's in the afternoon and 44th St. Theatre at night. Both shows were excellent. Got lost in the subway, and it took me two hours to get squared around. Never was quite so far gone. Thought for awhile that I had got a good start to China. Got in bed at 2:00 A.M. . . . think that's my last trip to the big city. Nothing there for me anymore.

May 1, 1919   Got up in time for dinner. If the boys hadn't started a rough house, I'd have slept all day, I guess. Got a letter from Mumsey, Maude, and Mrs. Mueller today.[12] The boss said my job's waiting for me. Lord but they're white people. I'm lucky.

---

11. Ziegfeld Follies was one of the major musical shows then appearing on Broadway. For two studies of the Ziegfeld enterprise, see Higham, *Ziegfeld*, and Ziegfeld and Ziegfeld, *Ziegfeld Touch*. Bert Williams, an African American comedian and entertainer, was one of Ziegfeld's leading performers; see Charters, *Nobody*.

12. The Mrs. Mueller referred to was the wife of Otto Mueller, an engineer who became a partner in the firm of Vonnegut and Bohn in 1919. The new firm was entitled Vonnegut, Bohn, and Mueller. See Bodenhamer and Barrows, *Encyclopedia of Indianapolis*, 1389.

Answered the three letters and did some washing. Don't think the job will meet with Mumsey's approval. They look gray. — Bad day outside. Rain and cold.

May 2, 1919   Took in New York again. Don and I went to a dance and had a fair time. Met Jake Wellman there. He's looking good but still [indecipherable]. He sure fought a hard war. He's trying to get his discharge in New York, and he intends to make it his home. There's going to be a big parade here tomorrow, so I think I'll just have to see it.

May 3, 1919   N.Y. bound once more. Took a peek at the parade and then had dinner at the Strand. Reviews and things. Left there at 9:00 and shimmied over to Rector's. Oh daddy, that Jazz. Got in bed at 5:00 A.M. It was my last fling, and I flung hard.

May 4, 1919   Jake Wellman paid me a visit and woke me up at 9:00 A.M. Like to kill me to get out of bed, but I had to show him around. We leave tomorrow noon. It's so hot today, it's melting the street. Sure dread that hike to the train.

May 5, 1919   Made packs and policed up quarters, and started hiking at 1:00. Sweat blood before we reached the train. And she's not a boxcar either. A pullman and a darb. Got underway at 2:00 sharp, and at 8:00 this evening we passed thru Utica. Have been following the Hudson, and she's every bit as beautiful as the Rhine. Palasaides [sic]. We're due in Buffalo late tonight. — Am corporal of the guard until tomorrow noon. I always manage to draw something.

May 6, 1919   Woke up in Cleveland. We sure highballed last night. We had a parade at Bluffton [Ohio] and ended up with a meal at the Red Cross. The people went wild. Hear that Bob [Tyndall] is going to drag us out at every town. — Paraded again at Lima. It's a big town, and I guess every soul was out to look us over. I never did see such a crazy mob. We must have walked two miles, and the street was lined up on both sides the entire distance. If they treat us this way in Ohio Town, we're sure in for something when we hit Hoosierdom. — Paraded in Portland, our first Indiana town. It sure feels good to mix with the Hoosier folks again. — Passed thru Muncie and paraded in Elwood. The crowd went wild. It's terribly hot, and I won't weigh fifty pounds when I hit the big town. All these welcomes are from the heart, and a fellow can't mistake the sincerity of them. Simple country folks, and they usually mean what they say. — Pulled into Tipton at 10:00 and were extended the glad hand. Several of the boys had their folks come up to meet them. Hope I don't break down the way they did. Guess a fellow just can't help it, though. Made our beds, and piled in.

x----------x

May 7, 1919   Sprinkling this morning. Bet it pours down during the parade. It's always our luck. I don't mind it as much myself, but I hate to have the folks disappointed. The city has gone to as much trouble to make the welcome a big one, and I hate to see the rain spoil everything. Maybe it will clear up by noon. — Passed thru Cicero and Noblesville, and at 9:00 bells we hit the outskirts of Indpls. The welcome was beautiful. Finally pulled in town and got off. Marched to Military Park and were dismissed. I don't care to talk about meeting the folks and Maude. I guess I was too deeply moved to even talk then. That was the happiest minute of my life, and I'll never forget it. Even Dad had tears in his eyes, and that kid brother of mine—Lordy, what a husky. Then there was Bertha and her mother. Uncle Doc, Louie, Ott, John and everybody. It was too much. Ate and then had a good long talk. Time passed too quickly. I came very near missing the parade. Then the parade started at exactly 12:30. From then on, I don't remember a thing. People yelling and flags waving. Beautifully decorated sheets. Children singing. Flowers thrown at us. Bands playing. Everything beyond words. I was ready to bust. A wonderful welcome from start to finish.[13] Met the folks again just before the train pulled out and got together once more. Almost missed the train. Got on the way at 3:00, and we are now highballing towards Camp Taylor. — Reached Taylor at 3:00, and after a very short hike we reached our quarters. Was feeling too good to go to bed. I took in a dance at the Y.M.C.A. and trotted the Kentucky girls around the floor. Broke up at 11:00, and I hit the hay. This has been the biggest day in my life,

13. An account of the welcoming parade for the 150th Field Artillery may be found in Robert G. Tucker, "Cheering, Singing Thousands Greet Marchers amid Band Music and Waving of Flags," *Indianapolis Star*, May 8, 1919, 1.

I believe. I can't remember anything clearly, and I don't want to. Lordy, but I'm happy.

x----------x

May 8, 1919   Have been taking physical exams and signing my name to a million papers. Signing my discharge papers too. Took great care to see that I spelled it right, and made each letter distinct. It's the most important thing that I've ever signed, and I didn't want anything to be wrong. The discharge is dated May 9th. That's tomorrow, so I guess my time as a soldier can be counted in minutes now. Lordy, how I'm longing for that little red Chevron. I think H.Q., Supply, and Battery A get out tomorrow. Hope to be in Indianapolis by 7:00 P.M. — I've thought about that welcome all day today. It was the biggest whole-hearted bunch of people I ever hope to see. It sure was a tough job marching at attention when you wanted to break ranks and yell and dance and cheer back at the crowds. I didn't feel anymore like a hero than Lux did. They sure made a lot of fuss over a gang of common soldiers. The boys are deeply touched by it all, because none of us expected it to be as grand. I'll never forget the feeling that came over me when we passed under the Victory Arch. I came very near breaking down there. That white sand and roses thrown by women on pedestals and then the immense Red Cross on the Monument steps. I swallowed that mean little lump a hundred times on that block. Impressive and it affected me much more than anything else that happened in the parade. Indiana folks are wonderful. — Hung around the Y. Didn't care to go to Louisville. Stood retreat tonight. Guess it's my last one. Tomorrow night at this time I ought to be home and out of this man's Army for good. Today has passed like 3 years. I'm just crazy to get back. Two hours with the folks and Maude after almost two years absence. Enough to drive a man loco. Hear we get mustered out at 8:30 in the morning, but no one can get on the train until all are ready. They hold our discharge to the last minute. I'm out for blood if they do that. Some "snow" out about a special train to take us back. Hell with specials. Give me the old popper, and I'll get back a whole lot faster than they can get me. I want to get home.

May 9, 1919   OUT! Lined up at 9:00, and after going thru some more red tape we finally drew our pay bonus and discharge papers. Then the paper was taken away from us, and we took a streetcar to Louisville. Here the lieutenant in charge handed us our papers, and we gave him our last salute. I'm now a free man and can't realize it. Don't suppose I'll wake up till I actually get my civvies on. This train pulls into Indianapolis at 6:20 tonight, and from then on it's going to take a war with Mars to make me leave again. Indpls has changed so much since I've been away. It will take me the rest of my life to learn it all over again. I'm thru travelling. Sure have had my share.

And now this is my last entry with the diary. I was bound to write of my experiences from the time I got in the Army till I got out. I started April 26, 1917, and ended on May 9, 1919. It's enough of this girlish business, and right now is a good time to tack on "Finis."

Epilogue

KNIPTASH WAS THRILLED TO BE BACK IN AMERICA, AND simply setting foot on American soil was sufficient reward for him. Others viewed the lack of an enthusiastic public reception for the Rainbow Division by the citizens of New York as a different matter, however. As Martin Gilbert has written: "When the converted German liner *Leviathan* docked in New York on 25 April 1919, General [Douglas] MacArthur, who had commanded the Rainbow Division in the last weeks of the war, was surprised to be met at the gang plank not by a mass of dignitaries full of praise and ceremonial, but by a young boy who asked him who the men were. 'We are the famous 42nd,'" MacArthur replied. The boy then asked if they had been in France. "Amid a silence that hurt," MacArthur later wrote, "with no one not even children, to see us, we marched off the dock, to be scattered to the four winds—a sad, gloomy end of the Rainbow."[1]

Vernon Kniptash did not experience the feeling of disappointment described by MacArthur, or at least his diary reveals no such emotion. In fact, Kniptash took advantage of the two weeks that he spent at Camp Merritt, New Jersey, from April 25 to May 5, 1919, to make several trips to New York City. He attended the theatre, did some shopping for family and friends, and enjoyed the opportunity for more sightseeing. The stay of duty in New Jersey was a pleasant interlude for Kniptash between the long voyage back from Europe and his final train ride to Indiana.

1. Quoted in Gilbert, *First World War*, 512. See also James, *Years of MacArthur*, 1:259; Manchester, *American Caesar*, 113.

217

On May 5 Kniptash boarded a train in New York that was bound for the Midwest and eventually for Indiana. Interestingly, Kniptash did not know the name of the camp in the Midwest where he was headed and where he was to receive his honorable discharge from military service. He suspected that he and his fellow members of the 150th Field Artillery regiment would be assigned to either Camp Sherman in Ohio or Camp Taylor in Kentucky.

The train carried Kniptash through upstate New York, northwestern Pennsylvania, and Ohio before reaching Indiana on May 6. The troops marched in two parades in Bluffton and Lima, Ohio, on May 5 and then in Portland, Indiana, early on May 6. The train then made its way across central Indiana before stopping in Noblesville, just north of Indianapolis later that day. The troops then waited for their grand entry into Indianapolis, scheduled for the next day.

The welcome home celebration for the returning troops was an unprecedented event in the history of Indianapolis. A crowd that numbered in the hundreds of thousands turned out for the parade and celebration which began at 12:30 in the city center. Included among the celebrants in Indianapolis were sixty thousand people, from the various regions of the state, who rode into the city aboard especially reserved trains in order to participate in the festivities. Indiana governor James P. Goodrich and Indianapolis mayor Charles W. Jewett presided over the ceremony. Commenting on the honor given to the servicemen who marched in the parade, Governor Goodrich observed: "It has been a great and a notable day— a splendid tribute of the citizens of the state to her soldiers and sailors and a fitting termination to Indiana's part in the war."[2]

The highlight of the ceremony occurred when the returning troops paraded around the southeast segment of the Circle, after passing through the newly constructed Victory Arch. En route, the troops were greeted with much singing, shouting, and even the throwing of flowers by the spectators. Many soldiers picked up the flowers and attached them to their cartridge belts as they made their way along the parade route.

The 150th Field Artillery unit did not lead the procession although the Rainbows were clearly the people's choice in Indi-

2. Tucker, "Cheering, Singing Thousands," *Indianapolis Star*, May 8, 1919.

anapolis. The spectators anxiously awaited the sight of Indiana's most celebrated unit. As recorded in the *Indianapolis Star*: "A pandemonium of cheers and shouts broke loose as the 150th Field Artillery broke into view. This is Indiana's own regiment—a part of the immortal Rainbow Division—nearly every man in it's from Indiana. They have been in France, where they have fought all up and down the line, and they have been in Germany, with the Army of Occupation—and now, all of a sudden, they are in these foreign lands no longer but back home—dented tin hats, knapsacks, and all!"[3]

Following the parade, Kniptash spent some brief moments with his family and friends at Military Park, three blocks west of the route. The reunion with the family was obviously emotional for Kniptash, and he had a difficult time conveying his feelings in his diary entry of that day. Regardless, Kniptash and his fellow soldiers reboarded their train and departed for Louisville, Kentucky, and Camp Zachary Taylor. Kniptash spent the next day, May 8, tending to the duties leading to his honorable discharge. On May 9 he signed all the necessary papers, saluted his commanding officer for the last time, and boarded a street car in Louisville that took him to the train station and the train that was to take him back to Indianapolis. After slightly more than two years, Vernon Kniptash was once again a civilian—but with a difference. He was now a civilian who had seen the worst of the Great War and survived it. As the soldiers said frequently in Germany, for Kniptash, the *guerre* was indeed *finis*, and "*finis*" was the last word entered in his diary.

After his return to Indianapolis in 1919, he rejoined the firm to continue his career. In 1920 Kniptash married Maude Wolfe, and the couple's only son, William, was born in 1922.

During the 1920s, Vernon Kniptash acquired additional responsibilities with V + B, rising to the position of architectural superintendent. He represented the firm on numerous construction projects. He also began a period of study under the tutelage of George Fink, a consulting civil engineer whose firm, Fink, Roberts, and Petrie, was one of Indianapolis's leading structural engineering firms. Kniptash had a long-held desire to obtain licensing and certification as a structural engineer, and by the end of the decade,

3. Ibid.

with Fink's assistance, he passed the necessary examinations and received his license.

Kniptash's successful career with V + B and his newfound status as a licensed structural engineer received a jolt when the Depression struck Indianapolis. In the mid-1930s, Kniptash lost his job with Vonnegut and Bohn when the market for new construction collapsed. To support his family, Kniptash worked as a laborer for a general contractor named Les Colvin. Colvin managed to acquire numerous contracts for building projects with Indianapolis-based Eli Lilly and Company, the pharmaceutical company. Then, at the end of the decade, Kniptash returned to engineering work, taking a job with the U.S. Army Corps of Engineers which was then involved in a major project at the Indiana Dunes State Park in the northern part of the state.

In 1942 Kniptash accepted an offer to join the Carl M. Geupel Construction Company in Indianapolis as a consulting engineer. Employment with Carl M. Geupel meant not only a return to professional engineering for Kniptash but also employment stability, especially since the company was rapidly becoming one of Indiana's major construction management firms. Misfortune also struck Kniptash at this time, however. Maude Kniptash died in 1944, several months after her son's departure as a naval reserve officer during World War II. Like his father, Bill Kniptash became a military veteran; he returned to Indianapolis in 1946 and began a successful business career.

Vernon Kniptash's personal life took a turn for the better toward the end of World War II. He remarried, his second wife being Margaret Kellenbach, known as "Kelly," an English teacher at Manual High School. Their marriage lasted until Vernon's death in 1987 at the age of ninety. Vernon Kniptash had worked for the Carl M. Geupel Company until 1967, when he retired. During his retirement years, Kniptash remained active with his family and as an amateur artist.

APPENDIX

Roster

Battery "A," 150th Field Artillery, 67th Brigade, 42nd (Rainbow) Division (Formerly First Indiana Field Artillery) This unofficial roster listing is based on the poster included as fig. 9. Used with permission of C. Thomas Bryan.

Captain: Sidney S. Miller, Commanding Battery
First Lieutenant: Thomas E. Hibben
First Lieutenant: Clarence E. Trotter
Second Lieutenant: Victor M. Hasselman
Second Lieutenant: Aloys Knaff
First Sergeant: Charles D. Clift
Supply Sergeant: John M. Skidmore
Stable Sergeant: Amos A. Turner
Mess Sergeant: Guy F. Chilcote

Sergeants
Wright, Alonzo D.
Hastings, Frank T.
Young, William T.
Morgan, Wilbur B.
Rosson, Richard M.
Moore, Karl F.
Hastings, Gipson W.
Gillespie, Bryant W.
Hain, Lee A.
Budd, Harry F.
Kurtz, William R.

Chief Mechanic
Harbison, Berry G.

Cooks
Bozell, Glenn
Henkle, Donald S.
McLaughlin, Paul E.
Scott, Paul J.
Thomasson, John W.

Corporals
Lumpkin, Chester
Ellis, John C.

221

York, Cecil L.
Miller, Gordon E.
Hays, Donald G.
Harter, George A.
Farley, Warren
Keller, William H.
Maxwell, Howard H.
Knauss, Ralph O.
Bosson, John U.
Prather, Jonas F.
Young, Byron C.
Berry, Cleston G.
Tinney, Chester J.
Morrison, John D.
Ayres, Myron E.
Coleman, Leslie H.
Lesh, Perry W.
Miles, James A.
Shine, William J.
Bruning, William H.
Straub, Elmer F.
Hicks, Robert L.
Atkinson, Russell
Stroube, Esthel O.
Jordan, Fred W.
Bassett, Edwin H.
Leech, Garland D.

Mechanics
Proctor, James, W.
Roberts, Harold K.
Tompkins, Belmont
Crosby, Russell I.
Welch, Thomas J.

Saddler
Armstrong, Herman R.

Buglers
Green, Edwin H.
Cavanah, Orville S.
Tomlinson, Stuart

Horseshoers
Cain, Lee
Green, Norvin E.
Smith, Leslie
Wessen, Arthur H.

Privates 1st Class
Aurine, George A.
Baker, Ellis J.
Berauer, Wilbur
Biddle, Leo A..
Bryan, Norman
Callon, Gail B
Clift, Clarence E.
Coridan, Eugene I.
Dean, Orel
Dietz, Henry F.
Ensign, Gwin G.
Evans, Walter M.
Farley, James R.
Felt, Truman T.
Fox, James V.
George, Rogers H.
Goodwin, Fred
Hilligoss, Clifford
Hoover, Charles J.
Hosea, Roy E.
Huber, Ed
Johannes, Ervin M.
Johnston, Vernon T.
Kelly, Robert E.
Kniptash, Vernon
Koehler, Walter

Lamkin, Russel H.
Lyster, James P.
Magruder, Edward S.
Markey, Harry L.
Miller, Louis B.
Moon, Leroy D.
Mooney, Edward P.
Moorman, Carl H.
Moulden, Claude
Murphy, Ray
Overhiser, Harry M.
Pitsenberger, Earl
Potter, Farrel E.
Prunk, Horace W.
Redmond, Walter I.
Robinson, Rush I.
Rushton, Leslie C.
Saltmarsh, John M.
Sanders, Howard J.
Sheets, Edgar B.
Shortridge, N. H.
Taylor, Clyde C.
Tescher, George M.
Thompson, David A.
Tyner, Otis L.
Vincent, Charles E.
Von Burg, Arthur J.
Walters, Paul L.
Wheeler, Henry T.
Wright, Chester
Wright, Howard D.

Privates
Airhart, Paul T.
Alexander, Mervill
Arensmen, Charles F.
Ashley, Ira D.
Allen, Paul H.

Barcus, Earl R.
Barney, James R.
Beck, Arba E.
Black, Lewis W.
Bloom, Clinton
Brandt, Lawrence
Brickel, Harry A.
Brunner, Albert R.
Buck, Lillo
Budd, Alger E.
Burns, Charley
Carbiener, Earl G.
Caseber, Robert A.
Clapp, Werrill G.
Colestock, R. L.
Connell, Latham W.
Cooke, Vaughn
Coons, Hobart
Cooper, James W.
Coridan, Edwin F.
Daniels, Charles T.
Dill, Egleashaeo H.
Douglas, William O.
Drake, Orville E.
Feld, Oscar I.
Fisher, Jim
Gaddis, Trevor
Gordon, Ralph E.
Gould, Edwin L.
Green, John W.
Gregory, Paul
Hall, William P.
Harrington, Arthur
Harrison, Major P.
Haspel, Fred E.
Hayes, Robert E.
Hill, W. Prescott
Hillman, George W.

Hudson, John F.
Innis, Frank B.
Irvin, James
Jones, Scott W.
Kunkler, Lawrence E.
Lackland, Earnest W.
Lane, Perry C.
Laycock, Walter W.
Loomis, Emerson K.
Lowe, Forest
Lynch, Arthur M.
Lynch, Fleming
McDaniel, Charles A.
McKay, Robert L.
Mayo, George
Meadows, Lester
Meenach, Leroy
Merrell, Lewis E.
Mitchell, Chester S.
Mitchell, James E.
Morrison, Elmer R.
Moulton, Hugh
Mulholland, John E.
Mullikin, Paul W.
Neidic, Ralph
Nichols, Rowland W.
Phillips, Robert C.
Randall, Strange G.
Reif, Fred W.
Robinette, Orville G.
Rogers, Lee G.
Ross, Earl
Rule, Earl
Schmidt, Ernest W.
Schmitt, Justin G.
Schwennesen, Charles M.
Secrist, George B.

Shinn, Oakley E.
Shockley, Earl
Simms, Joseph L.
Simms, Kenneth
Small, Gilbert L.
Stiles, Fred M.
Steeckley, Gustave A.
Stoner, Oliver
Strickland, Ray R.
Strode, David B.
Sturdevant, Harry A.
Syrus, Edgar
Thomas, Leroy R.
Traub, John M.
Truax, Joseph J.
Turner, Fred W.
Veach, James I.
Weaver, Samuel
Wells, Ralph M.
Wente, Urban J.
Whelan, Bernard A.
Whitesel, Fount H.
Wylie, David G.

Bibliography

Manuscripts and Archives

Army Service Experience Questionnaire(s). World War I Research Project. Department of the Army. U.S. Army Military History Institute, Carlisle Barracks, Pennsylvania.

Indiana State Archives. Commission on Public Records. Adjutant General, World War I Service Records.

National Archives, College Park, Maryland. Record Group 120, Records of the American Expeditionary Forces (World War I), Organization Records, 42nd Division, 150th Field Art'y Regiment, Box 38, 39.

Robert H. Tyndall Collection. Indiana Historical Society, Indianapolis.

Books and Articles

American Battle Monuments Commission. *42nd Division: Summary of Operations in the World War.* Washington, D.C.: Government Printing Office, 1944.

Baker, Horace L., edited with an introduction by Robert H. Ferrell. *Argonne Days in World War I.* Columbia: University of Missouri Press, 2007.

Barry, John M. *The Great Influenza.* New York: Viking, 2004.

Bodenhamer, David G., and Robert G. Barrows, eds. *The Encyclopedia of Indianapolis.* Bloomington: Indiana University Press, 1994.

Browne, George. *An American Soldier in World War I.* Edited by David L. Sneed. Lincoln: University of Nebraska Press, 2006.

Bruce, Robert B. *A Fraternity of Arms: America and France in the Great War.* Lawrence: University Press of Kansas, 2003.

Charters, Ann. *Nobody: The Story of Bert Williams.* New York: Macmillan, 1970.

Clark, George B., ed. *His Time in Hell: A Texas Marine in France. The World War I Memoir of Warren R. Jackson.* Noveto, Calif.: Presidio, 2001.

Coffman, Edward M. *The War to End All Wars: The American Military Experience in World War I.* New York: Oxford University Press, 1968.

Cooke, James J. *The Rainbow Division in the Great War, 1917–1919.* Westport, Conn.: Praeger, 1994.

Dickson, Paul. *War Slang: American Fighting Words and Phrases from the Civil War to the Gulf War.* New York: Pocket Books, 1994.

Duffy, Francis P. *Father Duffy's Story.* New York: George Doran, 1919.

Eisenhower, Dwight D. *At Ease: Stories I Tell to Friends.* Garden City, N.Y.: Doubleday, 1967.

Eisenhower, John S. D. *Yanks: The Epic Story of the American Army in World War I.* New York: Free Press, 2001.

Farrow, Edward S. *Dictionary of Military Terms.* New York: Thomas Crowell Publishers, 1918.

Farwell, Byron. *Over There: The United States in the Great War, 1917–1918.* New York: W. W. Norton, 1999.

Ferrell, Robert H. *America's Deadliest Battle: Meuse-Argonne, 1918.* Lawrence: University Press of Kansas, 2007.

———. *Five Days in October: The Lost Battalion of World War I.* Columbia: University of Missouri Press, 2005.

———. "'Oatmeal and Coffee': Memoirs of a Hoosier Soldier in World War I." *Indiana Magazine of History* 47, no. 1 (March 2001): 31–76.

———, ed. *A Soldier in World War I: The Diary of Elmer Sherwood.* Indianapolis: Indiana Historical Society, 2004.

———. *Woodrow Wilson and World War I.* New York: Harper and Row, 1985.

Fleming, Thomas A. *The Illusion of Victory: America in World War I.* New York: Basic Books, 2004.

Fraser, Edward, comp., and John Gibbons. *Soldier and Sailor Words and Phrases.* London: George Routledge and Sons, 1925.

Freidel, Frank. *Over There: The Story of America's First Great Overseas Crusade.* New York: McGraw-Hill, 1990.

Gaff, Alan D. *Blood in the Argonne: The "Lost Battalion" of World War I.* Norman: University of Oklahoma Press, 2005.

Geelhoed, E. Bruce. "Rainbow Soldier: Vernon Kniptash and World War I." *Traces of Indiana and Midwestern History* 18, no. 2 (May 2006): 16–25.

Gilbert, Martin. *The First World War: A Complete History.* New York: Henry Holt, 1994.

Gregory, Ross. *The Origins of American Intervention in the First World War.* New York: W. W. Norton, 1971.

Higham, Charles. *Ziegfeld.* Chicago: Henry Regnery Co., 1972.

Hodgson, Godfrey. *Woodrow Wilson's Right Hand: The Life of Colonel Edward M. House.* New Haven: Yale University Press, 2006.

Horne, Alistair. *The Price of Glory.* London: Macmillan, 1962.

James, D. Clayton. *The Years of MacArthur, Volume 1: 1880–1941.* Boston: Houghton Mifflin, 1970.

Keegan, John. *The First World War.* New York: Alfred A. Knopf, 1999.

Langille, Leslie. *Men of the Rainbow.* Chicago: O'Sullivan Co., 1933.

Manchester, William. *American Caesar: MacArthur, 1880–1964.* Boston: Little, Brown, 1978.

Marshall, George C., with foreword and notes by J. Lawton Collins. *Memoirs of My Services in the Great War, 1917–1919.* Boston: Houghton Mifflin, 1976.

Persico, Joseph E. *Eleventh Month, Eleventh Day, Eleventh Hour: Armistice Day, 1918; World War I and Its Violent Climax.* New York: Random House, 2004.

Rainbow Veterans Association of Marion County. *In Memory of the 150th Field Artillery.* Indianapolis: Rainbow Veterans Association of Marion County, 1927.

Reilly, Henry F. *Americans All: The Rainbow at War.* Columbus, Ohio: F. S. Heer Printing Co., 1936.

Sherwood, Elmer. *Diary of a Rainbow Veteran.* Terre Haute, Ind.: Moore-Langen, 1929.

———. *Rainbow Hoosier.* Indianapolis: Printing Arts Co., 1925.

Slotkin, Richard. *Lost Battalions: The Great War and the Crisis of American Nationality.* New York: Henry Holt, 2005.

Smythe, Donald. *Pershing: General of the Armies.* Bloomington: Indiana University Press, 1986.

Spring, Harry H. *An Engineer's Diary of the Great War.* Edited by Terry Bareither. West Lafayette, Ind.: Purdue University Press, 2002.

Strachan, Hew. *The First World War.* New York: Viking, 2004.

Straub, Elmer Frank. *A Sergeant's Diary in the World War.* Indianapolis: Indiana Historical Bureau, 1923.

Thompson, Hugh S. *Trench Knives and Mustard Gas: With the 42nd Division in France.* Edited with an introduction by Robert H. Ferrell. College Station: Texas A&M University Press, 2004.

Tompkins, Raymond S.. *The Story of the Rainbow Division.* New York: Boni and Liveright, 1919.

Tuchman, Barbara W. *The Zimmermann Telegram.* New York: Viking, 1958.

Vandiver, Frank E. *Black Jack: The Life and Times of John J. Pershing,* vol. 2. College Station: Texas A&M University Press, 1977.

Wright, William M. *Meuse-Argonne Diary.* Edited with an introduction by Robert H. Ferrell. Columbia: University of Missouri Press, 2004.

Ziegfeld, Richard, and Paulette Ziegfeld. *The Ziegfeld Touch: The Life and Times of Florenz Ziegfeld.* New York: Harry N. Abrams, 1993.

Index

229